The Singer's Rachmaninoff

Edited, with Introductions
and Translations
by
Natalia Challis

PELION PRESS
An Imprint of The Rosen Publishing Group, Inc.
New York

Published in 1989 by Pelion Press
29 East 21st Street, New York City, New York 10010

First Edition

Rachmaninoff, Sergei, 1873–1943.
The singer's Rachmaninoff.

Includes original Russian texts, with pronunciations in the International Phonetic Alphabet, and English translations.
Bibliography: p. 252
Includes indexes.
1. Songs—Texts. 2. Rachmaninoff, Sergei, 1873–1943—Songs. I. Challis, Natalia. II. Title.
ML54.6.R18552 1989 784.305 89-28979
ISBN 0-8239-0672-8

Manufactured in the United States of America

Contents

Preface

Dedicated to Nicolai Gedda

What is music?
It is a calm moonlit night,
It is the rustle of verdant leaves,
It is the distant vesper bell,
It is that which is borne only of the heart and goes only to the heart,
It is love!
Its sister is poetry, its mother—sadness!

Sergei Rachmaninoff
December, 1932.

Настоящий мой скромный труд посвящается Николаю Гедда

Что такое музыка?
Это тихая лунная ночь,
Это шелест живых листьев,
Это отдаленный вечерний звон,
Это то, что родится только от сердца и идет только к сердцу,
Это любовь!
Сестра музыки это поэзия, а мать ее—грусть!

Сергей Рахманинов
Декабрь, 1932

Chapter I

Russian Pronunciation and Diction

"And my soul dreams of sounds and sounds,
Of words full of music"
(from a poem set to music by Rachmaninoff in 1890, no opus number).

Rachmaninoff was very sensitive to the musicality of Russian words, and in his songs he sought to reveal the inherent musical nature of poetry. Judging from his works, the sound quality both of words and music played an equally important role in his aesthetic concept. For a singer a well-prepared text is thus essential to achieve the proper realization of the composer's style.

Native performers of Russian art songs follow the refined and formal diction known as the Moscow and Leningrad norms of orthoepics. This diction is distinguished from that of everyday speech by its clearer formation of vowels, its lesser reduction of unstressed vowel sounds, and its sharper enunciation of consonants. These distinctions have been incorporated into the transcription of the song texts of this edition. The introductory guidelines that follow are intended to assist the performer in reproducing the pronunciation of the International Phonetic Alphabet symbols accurately.* Once the singer is familiar with the original text, practice on diction and pronunciation, preferably in consultation with a specialist in Russian, should enhance the quality of the artist's presentation.

Russian speech articulation

The Russian language is characterized by:

- relaxed articulation;

* It should be of great help to the singer to memorize the Russian (Cyrillic) alphabet, which will make the task of reproducing the sounds of Russian much easier and more enjoyable.

- uneven distribution of muscular energy in speech, with alternating stressed and unstressed syllables;
- longer duration and greater precision in the stressed than unstressed syllables; and
- smooth transition from consonant to vowel.

Russian vocalism is closely related to the rhythmic and melodic aspect of Russian speech. The musical quality of Russian speech, observable in the rise and fall of the voice level, is not dependent on word stress, but on rhythmic articulation and grammatical composition.

Stress

As mentioned above, the accented or stressed syllable is articulated with greater precision and force than the unaccented one. The Russian accent or stress is free, as it is in English, not fixed as in a number of other languages. It does not fall on the same syllable in every word, and it can move from one syllable to another in the same word, depending on its declension or conjugation.

Vowels and Consonants

Russian vowels and consonants may undergo a change because of their linguistic environment. This change can be effected by stress, adjacent sounds, or, for consonants, word-final position.

Russian uses a comparatively simple system of vowels and a complex system of consonants. The articulation of vowels is distinct, clear, and energetic when the vowel is in a stressed position. When the vowel is not stressed it becomes reduced, that is, articulated less forcefully.

Most Russian consonants are classified in pairs, which are contrasted by their nonpalatalization and palatalization (hardness and softness) and by their being unvoiced or voiced (use of vocal chords in their formation).

Classification and pronunciation guidelines for Russian letters should help the singer to realize their musical quality. Information specific to the pronunciation of Rachmaninoff's songs is also included.

Russian Alphabet		**International Phonetic Alphabet***	
The modern Russian alphabet comprises 33 letters:			
А	а	ɑ	a, ə when unstressed
Б	б	b	
В	в	v	
Г	г	g	
Д	д	d	
Е	е	je or e	e, i when unstressed
Ё	ё	jo	
Ж	ж	ʒ	
З	з	z	
И	и	i	
Й	й	ĭ	
К	к	k	
Л	л	l	
М	м	m	
Н	н	n	
О	о	o	a, ə when unstressed
П	п	p	
Р	р	r	
С	с	s	
Т	т	t	
У	у	u	
Ф	ф	f	
Х	х	x	
Ц	ц	ts	
Ч	ч	ʧ	
Ш	ш	ʃ	
Щ	щ	ʃtʃ	usually pronounced ʃʃ
Ъ	ъ	ъ	hard sign, mute
Ы	ы	ɨ	
Ь	ь	̦	a subscript ̦ is used to indicate a soft sign
Э	э	ɛ	ɛ, i when unstressed
Ю	ю	ju	
Я	я	ja	i when unstressed

Some editions (usually reprints) of Rachmaninoff's songs are published in the old orthography, which was used before 1917.

* English equivalents of the IPA symbols are given in the Pronunciation Examples.

These editions contain the following letters:

Russian letters	**IPA symbol**
I i	i
Ѣ ѣ	je or e
Ѳ ѳ	f

I. Vowel sounds:

Classification

Front vowel	Central vowel	Back vowel	Articulating part of tongue / Height of tongue in mouth
и i	ы ɨ	у u	Closed vowel
э ɛ	ə	о o	Half-open vowel
	а ɑ	a	Open vowel

A vowel sound depends on the position of the tongue and is classified as:

1. a front vowel — if the front of the tongue is raised toward the front of the palate
2. a central vowel — if the center of the tongue is raised toward the center of the palate
3. a back vowel — if the back of the tongue is raised toward the back of the palate

Vowels are divided into open, half-open, and closed vowels, according to the height of the tongue:

1. in an open vowel — the tongue is low and spread flat in the mouth.
2. in a half-open vowel — the tongue is raised very slightly.
3. in a closed vowel — the tongue is raised very high.

The vowels у u and о o are labialized; that is, in forming them the lips are rounded.

Pronunciation examples

Russian vowels in a stressed position should be articulated clearly and distinctly. In the following examples stress is denoted by an added accent mark.

Vowel in stressed position	IPA symbol	Example in Russian	Example in IPA trans.
1. Front, closed, unrounded.			
и	/i/ as in see*	**и́ва** (willow)	'iva
		моли́тва (prayer)	ma'ļitva
After the consonants **ж, ш, ц** ʒ, ʃ, ts /i/ is pronounced as a central closed vowel ɨ:			
		чи́жик (siskin)	'ʧiʒɨk
		тишина́ (stillness)	ţiʃɨ'nɑ
		ци́кл (cycle)	'tsɨkl
2. Central, closed, unrounded.			
ы	/ɨ/		

There is no sound like this in English, and although it may be learned easily by imitation, an equivalent example does not exist. Practice the sound by saying the word book, but while keeping the tongue in normal position for this word, spread the lips instead of rounding them. The central closed vowel will be very close to the Russian ɨ. This letter does not occur in an initial position.

		ты́ (you) informal	'tɨ
		бы́л (was)	'bɨl

* Please note that a consonant immediately preceding the letters **и** i and **ю** ju, **е** e/ye, **ё** jo, **я** ja is always palatalized (with the exception of a few words of non-Russian origin). Guidelines for forming these consonants are outlined in the section on unpalatalized and palatalized consonants.

Vowel in stressed position	IPA symbol	Example in Russian	Example in IPA trans.
3. Back, closed, rounded.			
у	/u/ as in moo	у́тро (morning)	'utra
		му́зыка (music)	'muzɨka
4. Front, half-open, unrounded.			
э	/ɛ/ as in pen	э́хо (echo)	'ɛxa
		поэ́т (poet)	po'ɛt
5. Back, half-open, rounded.			
о	/o/ as in saw		

Place lips in rounded position, simultaneously producing the English vowel in *saw*.* In an open final stressed position the vowel o has a brief off-glide, in the nature of a still more open o^{a} sound, which does not occur in a closed stressed position or in an initial position.

		о́н (he)	'on
		мело́дия (melody)	ᶆe'loȡija
		хорошо́ (good)	xəra'ʃo^{a}
		светло́ (light)	sᶌet'lo^{a}
6. Central, open, unrounded.			
а	/ɑ/ as in father	А́нна (Anna)	'ɑnna
		фонта́н (fountain)	fan'tɑn

* Make the vowel closer; that is, raise the tongue slightly in the direction of the cardinal vowel o, at the same time making the lips slightly more rounded than in the English o.

Unstressed vowels are articulated with less force and are said to be reduced. This reduction, common in everyday speech, is not as strong in poetic diction. (The IPA transcription of the song texts in this edition follows the poetic pronunciation.)

Vowel in unstressed position	IPA symbol	Example in Russian	Example in IPA trans.
1. Front, closed, unrounded.			
и	/i/ does not undergo a change.		
The preceding consonant is palatalized.			
		сире́нь (lilac)	şi'ţeņ
		зву́ки (sounds)	'zvuķi
2. Central, closed, unrounded.			
ы	/ɨ/ does not undergo a change in poetic diction.		
In spoken Russian and occasionally in songs, this sound becomes shorter and weaker.			
		былы́е (past)	bɨ'lɨje
		приве́ты (greetings)	pŗi'v̧etɨ
3. Back, closed, rounded.			
у	/u/ does not undergo a change		
		тума́н (mist)	tu'mɑn
		ра́дуйся (rejoice)	'rɑduĭşja
4. Front, half-open, unrounded.			
э	/ɛ/ or /i/ a slight change to a half-closed sound i occurs.		
		этю́д (etude)	i'ţjut
		эле́гия (elegy)	i'ļeģija

Vowel in unstressed position	IPA symbol	Example in Russian	Example in IPA trans.
5. Back, half-open, rounded.			
o	/a/ as in mark		
In a prestress position o is pronounced as an advanced back vowel a.			
		она́ (she)	a'nɑ
		моли́тва (prayer)	ma'l̦itva
o	/ə/ as in about		
In the second prestress position or in poststress position, it is pronounced as a central half-open vowel ə. In poetic diction, an advanced back vowel a can be used.			
		хорошó (good)	xəra'ʃo or xara'ʃo
		зóлото (gold)	'zolatə or 'zolata
6. Central, open, unrounded.			
a	/a/ as in mark		
In a prestress position it is pronounced as an advanced back vowel a, but in the second prestress position or in a poststress position it can be pronounced as a central half-open vowel ə.			
		маргари́тки (daisies)	mərga'r̦itk̦i or marga'r̦itk̦i
		краса́вица (beauty)	kra'sɑv̦itsə or kra'sɑv̦itsa

Vowel glides

In forming the letters е, ё, ю, я je/e, jo, ju, ja start with the position for pronouncing an i or a j (jod or yod), proceeding immediately to the position of the vowel. The semivowel i or j represents the gliding sound as the tongue passes from the i or j position to the vowel. Consonants immediately preceding these letters are always palatalized (softened) and the i or j glide must be very brief.

Classification

Front vowel	Central vowel	Back vowel	Articulating part of tongue / Height of tongue in mouth
	ю ju		Closed vowel
е je/e	ё jo		Half-closed Half-open vowel
я ja			Open vowel

Pronunciation examples

In a stressed position, the letters е, ё, ю, я je/e, jo, ju, ja are pronounced as described below.

Vowel in stressed position	IPA symbol	Example in Russian	Example in IPA trans.
1. Front, midway between half-open and half-closed, unrounded.			
е	/je/ as in yes	In initial position:	
		éсть (there is)	'jesţ
		after vowels:	
		в моéй (in my)	v ma'jeĭ
		after a soft sign:	
		в семьé (in a family)	f şiɱ'je
		after a hard sign:	
		объéкт (object)	abъ'jekt
е	/e/ as in get		

Vowel in stressed position	IPA symbol	Example in Russian	Example in IPA trans.
The preceding consonant is palatalized, and it is important to remember that the j glide is in the tongue position of the consonant and not in the vowel.			
		ве́ра (faith)	'ᶌera
		приве́ты (greetings)	pᶉi'ᶌetɨ
After the letters ж, ш, ц ʒ, ʃ, ts /e/ is pronounced as a front half-open ɛ:			
		уже́ (already)	u'ʒɛ
		в душе́ (in the soul)	v du'ʃɛ
		конце́рт (concert)	kan'tsɛrt
2. Central, half-closed, medium rounded.			
ё	/jo/ as in yore		
This sound occurs only in stressed syllables. It is written as ё in this volume, although Russian literary usage omits the writing of the diaeresis.			
		ёлка (fir or Christmas tree)	'jolka
		звезды (stars)	'zᶌjozdɨ
After the letters ж, ш, ч ʒ, ʃ, ʧ /jo/ is pronounced as o:			
		тяжёлый (burdensome)	ƫi'ʒolɨĭ
		шёпот (whisper)	'ʃopat
		чёрный (black)	'ʧornɨĭ
3. Central, closed, medium rounded.			
ю	/ju/ as in yule	ю́ность (youth)	'junasƫ
		вью́га (snowstorm)	'ᶌjuga

Vowel in stressed position	IPA symbol	Example in Russian	Example in IPA trans.
Palatalize the preceding consonant, keeping the glide very brief.			
		я люблю́ тебя́ (I love you)	ja ʎjub'ʎju ţi'ƀja
		лю́ди (people)	'ʎjuḑi
4. Front, midway between half-open and open, unrounded.			
я	/ja/ as in yard	я (I)	'ja
		пая́ц (clown)	pa'jats
		дитя́ (child)	ḑi'ţja

When unstressed, the letters е, ю, я e, ju, ja may change as described below. The letter ё jo does not occur in unstressed syllables.

Vowel in unstressed position	IPA symbol	Example in Russian	Example in IPA trans.
1. Front, midway between half-open and half-closed, unrounded.			
е	/e/ or /i/		
In spoken Russian, the unstressed e is usually pronounced as a front closed vowel i. In poetic diction the choice of pronouncing e or i depends upon neighboring sounds. The IPA transcription of the songs reflects the choice.			
		цвето́к (flower)	tsɣi'tok or tsɣe'tok
		ве́чер (evening)	'ɣetʃer
After the letters ж, ш, ц ʒ, ʃ, ts /e/ is pronounced as ɛ; /i/ as ɨ:			
		жела́ние (desire)	ʒɛ'laŋije

Vowel in stressed position	IPA symbol	Example in Russian	Example in IPA trans.
		шелесте́ть (to rustle)	ʃɨļes'ţeţ
		цена́ (price)	tsɛ'nɑ

2. Central, closed, medium rounded.

ю /ju/ is more relaxed than the stressed sound:

		люблю́ (I love)	ļjub'ļju
		любу́юсь (I admire)	ļju'bujuş

3. Front, midway between half-open and open, unrounded.

я /ja/

In most nonstress positions it changes slightly toward an open i, as in 'it' in English.

		язы́к (tongue, language)	i'zɨk
		тяжёлый (burdensome)	ţi'ʒolɨĭ

When in final position, я ja does not undergo a change:

		ми́лая (dear)	'ɱilaja
		бу́ря (storm)	'buŗja

Verbs ending in:

a) ться, тся are pronounced as tsa

b) лся are pronounced as lsa.

		моли́ться (to pray)	ma'ļitsa
		улыба́ется (he, she smiles)	ulɨ'bɑjetsa
		прослези́лся (he shed a tear)	prasļe'z̦ilsa

Short i, soft and hard signs

The letter й ĭ is a high, closed, front, unrounded sound, which occurs only after a vowel. It can be paired with a, e, ё, и, o, y, ы, э, ю, я ɑ, e/je, jo, i, o, u, ɨ, ɛ, ju, ja to form a diphthong. Russian diphthongs are easy to pronounce, but one should remember to make the second element high, very close, and short.

та́йна (mystery)	'tɑĭna
си́ний (blue)	'ʂiŋiĭ
по́й (sing)	'poĭ
Чайко́вский (Tchaikovsky)	'ʧɑĭ'kofsķiĭ

Some native singers pronounce the diphthong ий iĭ as əĭ after the letters к, г, х k, g, x in adjectival endings.

я́ркий (bright)	'jarkəĭ
стро́гий (strict)	'strogəĭ
ти́хий (quiet)	'ţixəĭ

In words of non-Russian origin, the letter й ĭ represents a consonantal glide j:

райо́н (region)	ra'jon
Нью Йо́рк (New York)	ŋju 'jork

The letter ь ¸ denoted by a subscript, is a soft sign, which is not pronounced. It occurs only after consonants, indicating that the consonant is soft or palatalized and pronounced with a brief i/j glide, when the center of the tongue is slightly raised toward the front of the palate:

ма́ть (mother)	'mɑţ
сча́стье (happiness)	'sʧɑsţje or 'ʃʃɑsţje

The letter ъ ъ is a hard sign, which is also not pronounced. It occurs between a consonant and a vowel, indicating that the vowel will be pronounced with an i/j glide. It is indicated with an ъ.

объя́тие (embrace)	abъ'jaʈije
отъе́зд (departure)	atъ'jest

In the old orthography editions of Rachmaninoff's songs, the hard sign ъ ъ occurs after all consonants in final position. This letter is mute.

о́нъ (he)	'on
поётъ (sings)	pa'jot

The letters i i and ѣ ѣ follow the pronunciation guidelines for i and e/je respectively.

For musical and phonetic reasons, a few words, usually in feminine form, have been kept in the old orthography originally used by Rachmaninoff; e.g., оне́ a'ŋe (they); ея́ je'ja (hers); and some adjectival feminine endings.

In general, the phonetic context that influences the sound of Russian vowels may seem complicated and difficult at first. The pronunciation of vowels and vowel glides varies depending upon neighboring sounds, but correct inflections of pronunciation will become automatic once the singer masters basic vowel articulation.

II. Consonant sounds

Classification

Bilabial	Labiodental	Dental	Palatodental	Mediopalatal	Back-palatal		
п p		т t			к k	Voiceless	Plosive
б b		д d			г g	Voiced	
	ф f	с s	ш ʃ щ ʃtʃ or ʃʃ		х x	Voiceless	Fricative
	в v	з z	ж ʒ	й ĭ		Voiced	
		ц ts	ч ʧ			Voiceless	Affricative
м m		н n				Nasal	Sonants
		л l р r				Liquid Trilled	

Russian consonants are classified according to:

1. the place of obstruction of the air stream.
2. the manner of forming the obstruction.
3. the use of vocal chords.

1. Consonants are divided according to the place of obstruction of the air stream:

bilabial п p, б b, м m	when the obstruction is formed by both lips pressed together.
labiodental ф f, в v	when the air stream passes between the lower lip and the upper teeth.
dental т t, д d, с s, з z ц ts, н n, л l, р r	formed by the tip of the tongue against the back of the upper teeth.
palatodental ш ʃ, щ ʃtʃ or ʃʃ ж ʒ, ч ʧ	the tip and center of the tongue are brought toward the upper teeth and the front of the palate.
mediopalatal й ĭ	obstruction is formed between the center of the tongue and the center palate.

back-palatal к k, г g, х x	obstruction is formed between back of tongue and back of palate.

2. Depending on the manner of forming the obstruction to the air stream, consonants are divided into:

plosive consonants п p, т t, к k б b, д d, г g	when the articulating organs are brought together. As lips or other obstructing organs (tongue, teeth, palate) are parted under pressure, the air stream comes out with plosion. Plosive consonants are pronounced swiftly and cannot be prolonged.
fricative ф f, с s, ш ʃ, х x щ ʃtʃ or ʃʃ в v, з z, ж ʒ, й ĭ	when articulating organs are brought together, leaving a narrow passage for the air stream. When the air stream moves through the passage, it produces friction against the articulating organs. Fricative consonants are pronounced long and can be drawn out.
affricative ц ts, ч ʧ	these consonants are a combination of a plosive and a fricative sound. The articulating organs are brought close together and then gradually drawn apart, with a narrow passage for the air stream.
sonant nasal м m, н n liquid л l trilled р r	in a nasal sonant the air stream is directed through the nasal cavity; in a liquid, the tip of the tongue obstructs the air stream, which then passes laterally; a trilled sonant is formed by a rapid succession of taps against the hard palate, with the air passing between the taps.

3. A consonant may be voiceless or voiced; that is, it can be articulated without or with vibration of the vocal chords. Some consonants in Russian have corresponding pairs for voiceless and voiced sounds; others do not.

Voiceless consonants

ц	ч	щ	х	к	т	с	ш	п	ф
ts	ʧ	ʃtʃ or ʃʃ	x	k	t	s	ʃ	p	f

Corresponding pairs

г	д	з	ж	б	в	л	р	м	н	й
g	d	z	ʒ	b	v	l	r	m	n	ĭ

Voiced consonants

A voiceless consonant changes into its corresponding voiced one when it immediately precedes a voiced consonant (except before **в** v, **л** l, **р** r, **м** m, **н** n; **й** ĭ can be preceded only by a vowel).

сдéлать (to do) śḑelaţ becomes źḑelaţ
с зарёю (at dawn) s za'ŗjoju becomes z͡ za'ŗjoju

but

с восхóдом (at sunrise) s vas'xodəm
трú (three) 'tŗi

A voiced consonant changes into its corresponding voiceless one when it immediately precedes a voiceless consonant, and when in final position.

улы́бка (smile) u'lɨbka becomes u'lɨpka
над сáдом (above the garden) nɑd 'sadəm becomes nɑt 'sɑdəm
дрýг (friend) 'drug becomes 'druk
любóвь (love) ļju'boy̧ becomes ļju'bof̧

Unpalatalized and palatalized consonants

It is extremely important to distinguish the pronunciation of an unpalatalized (hard) and a palatalized (soft) consonant. Most consonants form corresponding pairs.

Hard consonants should be executed in a clear, crisp manner. Soft consonants differ from the hard in the position of the tongue when pronounced. To form a soft consonant, the center of the tongue is raised toward the front of the palate and forms a slight i or j off-glide before pronouncing the next sound. This tongue movement does not occur in the formation of a hard consonant.*

Consonants are hard when followed by ы ɨ, у u, э ɛ, о o, а ɑ or a hard sign.

They are soft when followed by и i, ю ju, е e/je, ё jo, я ja or a soft sign.

ц ts, ш ʃ, ж ʒ are always hard.

ч ʧ, щ ʃʃ, й ĭ are always soft.

Unpalatalized (hard) consonants

ц	ш	ж	к	г	х	т	д	с	з	п	б	ф	в	л	р	м	н
ts	ʃ	ʒ	k	g	x	t	d	s	z	p	b	f	v	l	r	m	n

Corresponding pairs

к	г	х	т	д	с	з	п	б	ф	в	л	р	м	н	ч	щ	й
ķ	ģ	x̧	ţ	ḑ	ş	z̧	p̧	b̧	f̧	v̧	ļ	ŗ	m̧	ņ	ʧ	ʃtʃ or ʃʃ	ĭ

Palatalized (soft) consonants

Pronunciation examples

As the pronunciation of consonants in Russian depends upon a wide spectrum of linguistic factors, it would be difficult to cite an example for every variation in sound. The examples given below illustrate points of pronunciation most useful in acquiring good diction in the performance of Russian songs.

Plosive consonants

Russian plosives do not lose their plosion when followed by another plosive or affricate consonant. Voiceless plosives are not aspirated before vowels, but proceed smoothly from consonant to vowel.

* It is very important to remember that the j glide is in the tongue position of a palatalized consonant and not in the vowel.

Consonant	IPA symbol	Example in Russian	Example in IPA trans.
1. Bilabial, plosive, voiceless.			
hard п	/p/ as in poem	по́й (sing)	'poĭ
		проро́к (prophet)	pra'rok
soft	/p̡/ remember to palatalize all soft consonants!		
		пе́сня (song)	'p̡esn̡ja
		опя́ть (again)	a'p̡jat̡
2. Bilabial, plosive, voiced.			
hard б	/b/ as in book	бы́л (was)	'bɨl
		о́блако (cloud)	'oblaka
soft	/b̡/	бе́лый (white)	'b̡elɨĭ
		люби́ть (to love)	l̡ju'b̡it̡
3. Dental, plosive, voiceless.			
hard т	/t/ as in talent; the tip of tongue flattened against the back of the upper teeth should produce a drier sound than in English.		
		та́м (there)	'tɑm
		трава́ (grass)	tra'vɑ
soft	/t̡/	те́нь (shade)	't̡en̡
		пти́ца (bird)	'pt̡itsa
4. Dental, plosive, voiced.			
hard д	/d/ as in daffodil; this voiced sound should also be drier than in English.		

Consonant	IPA symbol	Example in Russian	Example in IPA trans.
		душа́ (soul)	du'ʃɑ
		дру́г (friend)	'druk
soft	/ḑ/	де́нь (day)	'ḑeņ
		оди́н (one, alone)	a'ḑin

5. Back-palatal, plosive, voiceless.

hard к	/k/ as in call	кольцо́ (ring)	kaļ'tso
		кто́ (who)	'kto
soft	/ķ/	кимва́л (cymbal)	ķim'vɑl
		ла́ски (caresses)	'lɑsķi

6. Back-palatal, plosive, voiced.

hard г	/g/ as in garland	го́ре (grief)	'goŗe
		гру́сть (sadness)	'grusţ
soft	/ģ/	гирля́нда (garland)	ģir'ļjanda
		ги́мн (hymn)	'ģimn

In the following words, the plosive /g/ changes to the fricative /x/:

		Бо́г (God)	'box
		мя́гкий (soft)	'ɱjaxķiĭ
		лёгкий (light, easy)	'ļjoxķiĭ

Consonant	IPA symbol	Example in Russian	Example in IPA trans.
The plosive /g/ changes to a fricative /v/ in:			
		сегóдня (today)	şi'vodŋja
and in all adjectival endings in ого ogo, его ego:			
		егó (him)	je'vo
		любúмого (of a loved)	ɭju'ḅimava
		сúнего (of a blue)	'şiŋeva

Fricative and affricate consonants

Consonant	IPA symbol	Example in Russian	Example in IPA trans.
1. Labiodental, fricative, voiceless.			
hard ф	/f/ as in fountain	фонтáн (fountain)	fan'tɑn
		Фрáнция (France)	'frɑntsɨja
soft	/ʃ/	фéя (fairy)	'ʃeja
		Афúны (Athens)	a'ʃinɨ
2. Labiodental, fricative, voiced.			
hard в	/v/ as in volume	вóля (will, freedom)	'voɭja
		úва (willow)	'iva
soft	/ɣ/	вéра (faith)	'ɣera
		живú (live)	ʒɨ'ɣi

Consonant	IPA symbol	Example in Russian	Example in IPA trans.

The preposition **в** /v/ (in, into) changes to a voiceless /f/ when it precedes a voiceless consonant:

		в тени́ (in the shade)	f ţe'ņi
		в саду́ (in the garden)	f sa'du

3. Dental, fricative, voiceless.

hard **с**	/s/ as in snow	**со́н** (dream)	'son
		весна́ (spring)	ỵes'nɑ
soft	/ş/	**сего́дня** (today)	şi'vodņja
		сире́нь (lilac)	şi'ŗeņ

The word **сча́стье** (happiness) can be pronounced as 'sʧɑsţje or 'ʃʃɑsţje.

4. Dental, fricative, voiced.

hard **з**	/z/ as in zone	**заря́** (dawn)	za'ŗja
		зво́н (ringing)	'zvon
soft	/z̧/	**зелёный** (green)	z̧i'ļjonɨĭ
		Гру́зия (Georgia)	'gruz̧ija

5. Palatodental, fricative, voiceless, always hard.

ш	/ʃ/ as in shawl, with tip of tongue drawn back slightly from its position for English /ʃ/, resulting in a much "darker" sound. As this letter is always hard, /e/, /jo/, /i/ following it will be pronounced as /ɛ/, /o/, /ɨ/ respectively. When a word ends in **шь**—/ʃ/ and a soft sign—/ʃ/ remains hard.

Consonant	IPA symbol	Example in Russian	Example in IPA trans.
		шу́м (noise)	'ʃum
		ше́лест (rustle)	'ʃɛᶅest
		лю́бишь (you love)	'ᶅjuᶀiʃ
		пла́чешь (you weep)	'plɑʧeʃ

6. Palatodental, fricative, voiceless, always soft.

щ /ʃʃ/ pronounced as a long, palatalized, soft /ʃʃ/. Some speakers pronounce it as a long /ʃtʃ/, with a very slight stop "t" element in the middle.

поща́да (mercy)	pa'ʃʃɑda
проща́й (farewell)	pra'ʃʃɑĭ

7. Palatodental, fricative, voiced, always hard.

ж /ʒ/ similar to the English /ʒ/ in pleasure, with tip of tongue drawn back slightly, resulting in a much "darker" sound. As this letter is always hard, /e/, /jo/, /i/ will be pronounced as /ɛ/, /o/, /ɨ/ respectively.

жа́р (fever)	'ʒɑr
жела́ние (desire)	ʒɛ'laᶇije
жёлтый (yellow)	'ʒoltɨĭ
жи́ть (to live)	'ʒɨƫ

8. Mediopalatal, fricative, voiced.

й /ĭ/ see page 13.

Consonant	IPA symbol	Example in Russian	Example in IPA trans.
9. Back-palatal, fricative, voiceless.			
hard х	/x/ as in Bach, but with very slight friction; the air passes between the tongue and the palate in a continuous stream.		
		хорошó (good)	xara'ʃo
		Христóс (Christ)	xɽis'tos
soft	/x̡/ as in human or huge	**херуви́м** (cherubim)	x̡eru'γim
		стихи́я (elements)	sʈi'x̡ija
10. Dental, affricate, voiceless, always hard.			
ц	/ts/ as in tsar; following this letter, /e/, /i/ will be pronounced /ɛ/, /ɨ/ respectively.		
		цáрь (tsar)	'tsɑɽ
		ценá (value, price)	tsɛ'nɑ
		ци́кл (cycle)	'tsɨkl
11. Palatodental, affricate, voiceless, always soft.			
ч	/ʧ/ as in church, but softer, more palatalized than the English sound.		
		чáс (hour)	'ʧas
		нóчь (night)	'noʧ

When a word ends in **чь**—/ʧ/ and a soft sign—the latter does not change the sound of /ʧ/.

In the words **что** 'ʃto (what, that), and **чтобы** 'ʃto bɨ (so as to), the letter /ʧ/ is now sounded as /ʃ/.

Sonants

Consonant	IPA symbol	Example in Russian	Example in IPA trans.
1. Bilabial, nasal, voiced.			
hard м	/m/ as in mother	ма́ть (mother)	'maƫ
		до́м (home, house)	'dom
soft	/ɱ/	ми́лая (dear)	'ɱilaja
		сме́х (laughter)	'sɱex
2. Dental, nasal, voiced.			
hard н	/n/ as in night	но́чь (night)	'notʃ
		ра́но (early)	'rana
soft	/ɲ/	ни́ва (field)	'ɲiva
		сире́нь (lilac)	şi'ɽeɲ

3. Dental, liquid, voiced.

hard л /l/

Isolate the l in people; pronounce it with the tip of the tongue slightly further forward than in the English sound, with the back of the tongue well raised. This will result in a "dark" l. Practice this sound with the hard vowels ɨ, u, ɛ, o, a.

ла́ска (caress)	'laska
волна́ (wave)	val'na

soft /ȴ/

The sound is similar to the l in million, but pronounce only one l, and make the i/j

Consonant	IPA symbol	Example in Russian	Example in IPA trans.

glide extremely brief. Practice this sound with the soft vowels **i, ju, je, jo, ja** and the soft sign.

		ле́бедь (swan)	'ļeb̧eţ
		моли́тва (prayer)	ma'ļitva
		е́ль (fir)	'yeļ
		то́лько (only)	'toļka

4. Dental, liquid, voiced.

hard **р** /r/

Hold tongue loosely against the middle of teeth ridge; when pressure of air stream is applied, the tongue vibrates, not unlike the action of a musical reed. Or try brrrr! Practice with hard vowels, as above.

		ра́но (early)	'rɑna
		взо́р (glance)	'vzor

soft /ŗ/

The vibration of the tongue is stopped by a very brief **i/j** glide. Practice the sound with soft vowels, as above, and a soft sign.

		река́ (river)	ŗe'kɑ
		заря́ (dawn)	zɑ'ŗja
		тепе́рь (now)	ţi'p̧eŗ
		две́рь (door)	'd̦y̧eŗ

Mute consonants

There are several words in which, in a consonantal cluster, one of the consonants is mute. The words most often occurring in art songs are:

Consonant	IPA symbol	Example in Russian	Example in IPA trans.
mute т	/t/	прелéстный (charming)	pŗi'ļesnɨĭ
		стрáстный (passionate)	'strɑsnɨĭ
		счастли́вый (happy)	ʃʃas'ļivɨĭ
		рáдостный (joyful)	'rɑdasnɨĭ
In very careful diction, т /t/ can remain in the word грустный (sad) 'grustnɨĭ.			
mute д	/d/	прáздник (holiday)	'prɑzņik
		сéрдце (heart)	'şertsɛ
		звёздный (starry)	'zγjoznɨĭ
mute в	/v/	чу́вство (feeling)	'ʧustva
		чу́вствовать (to feel)	'ʧustvəvaţ
mute л	/l/	сóлнце (sun)	'sontsɛ

And now, with the masters of sound—Rachmaninoff and Pushkin—looking (or listening) over our shoulder, let us review with a song—

Points of diction that present difficulties to English speakers:

ņe 'poĭ kra'sɑγitsa
Не пой, красавица
(Do) not sing beauty

ņe 'poĭ kra'sɑɣ̧itsa pŗi
Не пой, красавица, при
(Do) not sing, beauty before
'mņe
мне
me

ņe pŗi mņe—when consonants are palatalized the i/j glide is very brief and is in the tongue position of the consonant, not in the vowel.

tɨ 'p̧eşen 'gruz̧ii
Ты песен Грузии
You songs (of) Georgia
p̧e'ʧɑļnaĭ
печальной:
sad

tɨ—practice /ɨ/
p̧e'ʧɑļnaĭ—very soft /ļ/

napam̧i'nɑjut 'mņe a'ņe
Напоминают мне оне
Remind me they

dru'guju 'ʒɨzņ i 'b̧eŗek
Другую жизнь и берег
Another life and shore
'dɑļņiĭ
дальний.
distant

'ʒɨzņ—dark /ʒ/ + /ɨ/
'dɑļņiĭ—very soft /ļ/

u'vɨ napam̧i'nɑjut 'mņe
Увы, напоминают мне
Alas remind me

tva'i ʒɛ'stoķije na'p̧evɨ
Твои жестокие напевы
Your cruel melodies

ʒɛ'stoķije—dark /ʒ/ + /ɛ/

i 'sţep i 'notʃ i 'pŗi **И степь, и ночь, и при** And steppe and night and in lu'ŋe **луне** moon (light)	'sţep—palatalize
ʧer'tɨ da'ļjokəĭ 'ḅednəĭ **Черты далёкой, бедной** Features (of) far poor 'ḑevɨ **девы!** maid	'ḑevɨ—practice /ɨ/
ja 'pŗizrak 'ṃilɨĭ raka'voĭ **Я призрак милый, роковой,** I phantom dear fateful	'pŗizrak—soft /r/ and hard /r/ in one word
ţe'ḅja u'ɣiḑef zabɨ'vɑju **Тебя увидев, забываю;** You seeing forget	ţe'ḅja—keep the glide very brief
'no 'tɨ pa'joʃ i 'pŗeda 'mnoĭ **Но ты поёшь и предо мной** But you sing and before me	tɨ—practice /ɨ/
je'vo ja 'vnoʃ vaabra'ʒɑju **Его я вновь воображаю.** It I again imagine	vaabra'ʒɑju—dark /ʒ/
ŋe 'poĭ kra'sɑɣitsa **Не пой, красавица,** (Do) not sing, beauty pŗi 'mŋe **при мне** before me	

tɨ 'p̡eş̡en 'gruz̡ii
Ты песен Грузии
You songs (of) Georgia
p̡e'ʧɑḽnaĭ
печальной:
sad

napam̡i'nɑjut 'mn̡e a'n̡e
Напоминают мне оне
Remind me they

dru'guju 'ʒɨzn̡ i 'b̡eŗek
Другую жизнь и берег
Another life and shore
'dɑḽn̡iĭ
дальний.
distant

To N. A. Satina

Words by Alexander Pushkin Music by Sergei Rachmaninoff
(Op. 4, No. 4)

Sing not, O lovely one, in my presence
Your melodies of sorrowful Georgia,
They recall in me
Another life and a distant shore.
  Alas, your cruel song
  Recalls in me
  The steppe, the night, and in the moonlight
  The features of a maiden, sad and far away!
I see you and forget
That dear and fateful vision
But you sing
And it comes to me anew.
  Sing not, O lovely one, in my presence
  Your melodies of sorrowful Georgia,
  They recall in me
  Another life and a distant shore.

Bibliography

Helpful to have on hand:
Bryzgunova, E. A. *Vvodnyi fonetiko-razgovornyi kurs russkogo iazyka* (Introductory Russian Phonetics) with tape, Russian Language Publishers, Moscow, 1982. (Available through Victor Kamkin Inc., 149 Fifth Ave., New York, N.Y. 10010.)
Jones, Daniel and Ward, Dennis *The Phonetics of Russian*, Cambridge University Press, 1969. (The authors give a detailed description of all nuances of Russian sounds.)
The Oxford-Russian English Dictionary, Oxford University Press, 1984.

Additional Bibliography

Avanesov, R. I. *Russkoe literaturnoe proiznoshenie* (Russian Literary Pronunciation), Prosveshchenie Publishers, Moscow, 1984.
Avanesov, R. I. *Fonetika sovremennogo russkogo literaturnogo iazyka* (Phonetics of Contemporary Literary Russian), Moscow University, 1956.
Bryzgunova, E. A. *Zvuki i intonatsiya russkoi rechi* (Sounds and Intonation of Russian Speech), Moscow, 1969.
Moriarty, John *Diction*, E. C. Schirmer Music Company, Boston, 1975.
Pulkina, I. M. *A Short Russian Reference Grammar*, Foreign Language Publishers, Moscow, 1960.

Chapter II

Rachmaninoff and His Time

1. Song in the Golden Age of Russia

Within an hour's drive north of New York City lies Kensico Lake and, nearby, Kensico Cemetery, the final resting place of Sergei Rachmaninoff. The quiet countryside with its streams and groves is not unlike the countryside near Moscow, beloved and celebrated by him in song.

> How peaceful ...
> Look there, in the distance
> Shines the river like a flame.
> The fields lie like a flowered carpet.
> Light clouds above us ...
> Here there are no people ...
> Here there is silence ...
> Here is only God—and I,
> Flowers—and an aging pine,
> And you, my dream!
>
> (op. 21, no. 7)

Rachmaninoff sang the beauty of vistas lit by the early sun or slumbering in the twilight, the murmur of leaves and streams, the fragrance of springtime. When his songs express anxiety or sorrow, when he speaks of time passing swiftly and of loss, his songs are reminiscent of the reconciling images of nature by another writer of song—David, whose psalms were for centuries an inseparable part of Russian life.

Russia has a *pesennaya kultura*, a culture of song, where all of life, its joys and sorrows, holy days and work days were reflected upon in song. To sing (*pet'*) expresses a vast range of feeling and emotion: the spirit of joy and thanksgiving at the most solemn point in the liturgy—"We sing Thee" (Tebe poem), or of sorrow during the final farewell when we are "sung away from this world" (*otpevanie*).

The Golden Age of Russian culture in the nineteenth century brought a generous flowering to the art of song, poetry and music. The centers of the arts were St. Petersburg and Moscow, where Rachmaninoff had lived, studied, and worked.

St. Petersburg, the capital on the shores of the Neva River, was created by the collision of two cultures, the culture of the West and of Old Russia. The city—its fast-flowing river, streams, and canals, the poignant elegance of its architectural ensembles, the long white nights in the summer and the dark winters—all challenged and inspired poets and composers.

Moscow, the "Royal Dowager" as Pushkin called it, was a contrast to the imperial splendor of St. Petersburg. It was surrounded by ancient towns, convents and monasteries, and old familial estates. The city, which grew along the slow, meandering Moscow River, was traditional and comfortable, hospitable and religious, its "forty times forty" churches ringing out daily for matins and vespers. It was Moscow that nurtured the early musical heritage of liturgical chant and folk song.

Toward the end of the eighteenth century musicians and folklorists began to collect folk songs from various areas of the country. The interest to preserve and understand this tradition grew, and Glinka was one of the first major composers in Russia to use native melodies in his work. A group of friends in St. Petersburg met to discuss both the classical and the new music, to hear and comment on their own compositions, and from these gatherings emerged "The Mighty Handful"—Balakirev, Cui, Borodin, Musorgsky, and Rimsky-Korsakov, who developed a style based on the melodies, rhythms, and harmonies of the Russian folk song. Of the five, Musorgsky tried to follow in his music the inflections of voice and language and the natural flow of words. He searched for his sounds in the poetic repetition of folk tales and ancient laments, in liturgical chants, and in the noise and bustle of the city. Later, Rachmaninoff also would listen to the songs of men working along the river or to the voices of women selling *tsvety, tsvetochki* (flowers, pretty flowers) or *klubnika sadovaya, klubnika* (strawberries from the garden, strawberries), or he would go to one of the monasteries in Moscow. As a friend recalls: "He very much loved church singing and often, even in the winter, he would get up early in the morning and go to Taganka, to the Androniev monastery, where he stood in the dark church for long hours, listening to the ancient austere chants from the octoechos sung by the monks in parallel fifth organum. This would leave him with a lasting impression."[1]

Russian composers worked to return to indigenous canonical melodies in liturgical singing and used these melodies in their own compositions, combining them with the spirit and feeling of the folk song. While drawing upon their liturgical and folk heritage, composers at that time were inspired by the technically perfect yet also creative and beautiful poetry and prose of the Golden Age. Rachmaninoff set to music works by poets of that Age—the elegiac and contemplative poems of Zhukovsky and Khomyakov, and poems of Tyutchev, whose images of nature revealed a profoundly philosophic consciousness. He selected poems by Fet, whose language Tchaikovsky considered as "flowing over" into music, and Alexei Tolstoy, a master of both literary and folk language, who was perhaps the most prolific writer of verses that inspired Russian art songs. And Pushkin. Pushkin, who loved and mastered all forms of folk idiom, its songs and tales, but who also gave credit to the beauty of the literary language, considering its fate "to be fortunate, as in the eleventh century, the ancient Greek language suddenly opened its Lexicon, the treasury of harmony, and gave us the laws of its carefully considered Grammar, its beautiful turns of phrase, its magnificent flow of words, in short, made our language its child. Although sonorous and expressive, from that time on our language developed versatility and precision."[2] Pushkin had a classic sense of form, measure, and harmony, which resulted in perfect works of art. His verses give an impression of effortless improvisation and yet never contain a superfluous note. His poetry, sometimes compared to the music of Mozart, can be described in Pushkin's own words: "Such depth! Such audacity and harmony! You, Mozart, are a god and do not know it!"[3] Pushkin's mellifluous art inspired songs and was the source for many operas by Russian composers.

When Rachmaninoff sought to speak of his own Muse, he chose Pushkin's words:

In my childhood she loved me
And handed me the flute of seven pipes;
Smiling, she listened to me,
And gently touching the soundholes of the hollow reed
With my weak fingers, I played already then
Both solemn hymns inspired by the gods
And songs of peaceful Phrygian shepherds.
From morn to evening in the groves' mute shade
I heeded diligently the secret maiden's words;
And rejoicing me with unexpected favor,
Having brushed back the curls from her sweet brow,
She herself took the panpipes from my hands.
The reed was animated by divine breath
And my heart filled with sacred enchantment.
(op. 34, no. 1)

The abundance of song and of native poetic and musical talent, together with the rich culture of the art song coming from the West, produced the classical art song in Russia, which melded the "songs of peaceful Phrygian shepherds and the solemn hymns inspired by the gods." The art song or romance in Russian absorbed certain melodic features of the lyrical folk song and the intonational qualities of epic ballads and reflected the tradition of a cappella church songs, where the musical element is inseparably linked to the words of the text. The union of music and word in the art song is not only that of theme and imagery; it is formed by the specifics of the poetic line and the process of reconception of the text, a thoughtful and masterful process in the songs of Rachmaninoff. Conversely, nineteenth-century poets, among them Fet, Polonsky, and Apukhtin, whose verses were set to music by Rachmaninoff, were much influenced by the vocal musical culture of their time.

The romance became a vital aspect of Russian musical life, both on the concert stage and at home, and an art form often commented upon by critics and music historians. One of the first musicologists in Russia, Prince Vladimir Odoevsky, discussed the aesthetics of the new genre and the process of uniting music and text; the composer and historian Alexander Serov emphasized the importance of the art song, quoting

Glinka's words that "it would be excellent if every piece, however brief, would offer something new to the development of music and the study of its art",[4] and the critic Vladimir Stasov suggested that the imagery and realism of some art songs, particularly those of Musorgsky, had the theatrical effect and the dramatic quality of an operatic scene. Rimsky-Korsakov and, later, the eminent musicologists Nikolai Findeisen and Boris Asafiev researched and discussed the processes of composition and stylistic peculiarities of the art song of the Golden Age.

2. Rachmaninoff in Moscow of the Late Nineteenth Century

Rachmaninoff came to Moscow from St. Petersburg in 1885 and entered the Moscow Conservatory to study and live with Professor Nikolai Zverev, with whom his cousin, the pianist Alexander Ziloti, had studied and at whose house Ziloti had lived. Zverev was an exceptionally dedicated teacher of piano for beginning students at the Conservatory, who stressed the importance of a complete musical education for the young men and women in his classes. His students attended most musical events of note in Moscow and were asked to analyze the performances and discuss the critical reviews. Musical impressions received by Rachmaninoff during his first years in Moscow were highlighted by concerts of the Imperial Musical Society, conducted by Max von Erdmannsdorfer and Vasily Safonov, with violinists Leopold Auer and Adolf Brodsky, the cellist Karl Davidov and the pianist Anton Rubinstein who performed the cycle of Historical Concerts. Under Zverev's guidance, the students were introduced to the best singers of the opera and concert stage—Felia Litvin, Luisa Tetrazzini, Nikolai and Medea Figner and Mattia Battistini among others. The Bolshoi Theater staged European and Russian operas. Tchaikovsky's *Eugene Onegin* was in its repertoire from 1881, and Moscow saw the premiere of his opera *Cherevichki*, based on Gogol's tale "The Night before Christmas," in 1887. A year later Musorgsky's *Boris Godunov* had its first performance on the Bolshoi stage. But Rachmaninoff's most memorable musical encounters were, in his own words, at the Zverev household, a special nook of musical Moscow of the 1880's. "On Sunday afternoons," he recalls, "our strict teacher would be completely transfigured. He held open house for many of the most talented representatives of the Moscow musical world: Tchaikovsky, Taneyev, Arensky, Safonov, Ziloti, as well as university professors, jurists and actors. Time was spent in conversation and music-making. For us boys the most delightful aspect was that Zverev did not allow any of the guests to touch the piano, except perhaps to clarify a critical comment. We were the only performers. Our improvised performances gave the greatest joy to Zverev; no matter how we played, his judgment was always the same: 'Excellent! Beautiful! Perfect!' I cannot find words to express what a stimulus it was to our self-esteem to play before the most important Moscow musicians and to hear their strict critique, and how encouraged we were by their delight."[5]

Amongst the guests, Peter Ilyich Tchaikovsky, then at the height of his fame, made a lasting impression on young Rachmaninoff, who was deeply grateful for Tchaikovsky's support and stressed that it was his influence and personality that inspired him most in his creative efforts.

He remembers Tchaikovsky at his graduation performance in 1889: "We had to play our own composition before the committee. When my turn came, Arensky told Tchaikovsky that I wrote in his class several pieces for the piano, in three-part song form, and asked him if he would like to hear them. Tchaikovsky nodded in agreement, and I sat down to play my pieces, which I knew by heart. When I finished, I noticed that Tchaikovsky was looking over the examination page and was writing something on it. Only after two weeks did Arensky tell me what was written there; perhaps he was afraid that I should become very proud, and therefore kept it silent. The committee gave me the highest grade of 5 plus, and Tchaikovsky added three pluses—one above, one below, and one to the side ... It was agreed that in the fall I should enroll in the first-year counterpoint class taught by Taneyev, and thus my fate as a composer was decided."[6]

Rachmaninoff's years at the Moscow Conservatory were especially productive, and he worked intensely on compositions for piano and for voice. He composed his first opera, *Aleko*, based on Pushkin's poem "The Gypsies," for his final graduation, and he was delighted when the opera's first performance in 1893 was very well received. That was a year of sadness also, when his teacher Zverev died in September and a month later came the sorrowful news of Tchaikovsky's death in St. Petersburg. Almost twenty-five years later Rachmaninoff reminisced in a letter to the musicologist Boris Asafiev: "I remember well how in the month of October of that same year for the last time I saw Peter Ilyich Tchaikovsky, to whom I showed my composition *The Cliff*, and who said, with the gentle, almost sad laugh that was his wont: 'Look at what Seryozha has written over the summer! A poem, and a *concerto*, and a suite, and so on ... As for me, I have written only one symphony.' This symphony was the Sixth and his last."[7]

The Elegiac Trio, dated October 25–December 15, 1893, was dedicated "To the Memory of a Great Artist." "I worked and worked hard, painstakingly, with perseverance," he wrote to a friend. "During this time all my thoughts, feelings, and energy belonged to this song. In the words of one of my songs, I was in constant torment and my soul was sorrowful. I trembled for each phrase, sometimes I would cross out absolutely everything and again I would start to think and think."[8] His song "Music," dedicated to "P. Tch.," reflects again on Tchaikovsky's art:

> And for an instant a divine image
> A flash of elusive beauty
> Glowed, like a living vision
> Above this wave of sounds, ethereal and clear,
> And was reflected, and slightly moved ...
> Perhaps it smiled,
> Perhaps it shed a tear ...
>
> (op. 34, no. 8)

With the death of Tchaikovsky, the Golden Age of Russian culture came to a close. The creative essence of that age was expressed earlier by Dostoevsky at the dedication of the Pushkin memorial in Moscow. Dostoevsky, who perhaps more than any other Russian writer spoke of the conflict of the cultures of the West and Russia, saw the two united in the universality and grace of Pushkin's art. In music, this universality is present in the work of Tchaikovsky, who brought the melodic *pesennaya kultura*, the culture of song, to the essentially Western forms of his art, and who conveyed a graceful spirit in the expressive and elegant prose of his many letters.

3. Poetics of the Silver Age

The Silver Age in Russia presented a new refinement in poetry and significant changes in the direction of music and the visual arts. Numerous artistic circles in Moscow and St. Petersburg produced a variety of work, and although some tended toward pretentiousness and artificiality, the best combined discipline with the effervescence of the new, twentieth century. Poets Anna Akhmatova and Osip Mandelshtam followed the classical vision of Pushkin, while others—Blok, Balmont, Bryusov, whose poems were set to music by Rachmaninoff—were inspired by the Symbolist movement and created works of unusual rhythms and sonorities. Rachmaninoff's family and friends collected and suggested to him poems published at the time, and from this "fund," as they called it, he selected texts with images and impressions he would reconceive and interpret in his songs.

While it was the word, in prose and poetry, that formed the poetics of the Golden Age, it was the stage and the visual arts that kindled the imagination of the Silver Age. The productions of the Imperial Theaters were resplendent and reached their apogee in the ballets created by Petipa and Tchaikovsky. Their successes were followed by presentations by private companies with the encouragement and support of wealthy families, who became patrons on a Renaissance scale and gave of time and money to achieve their artistic ideals. Savva Mamontov, a wealthy merchant, built a private theater in Moscow and commissioned scenery and costumes from the foremost artists of the day. Mamontov joined Prince and Princess Tenishev in financing the production of a periodical titled *The World of Art*, which grew from collaboration of a group of friends in St. Petersburg and became a major aesthetic influence of the Silver Age. The artist Alexander

Benois was the heart of the group, and Sergei Diaghilev was the editor and the guiding force of their endeavor.

The achievements of the *World of Art* group displayed an unusual awareness of world culture and remarkable artistic power. The finest work by Benois in Tcherepnin's *Pavillon d'Armide* and Stravinsky's *Petrushka* evoked rather than pictured the past and the world it depicted. Leon Bakst worked meticulously on his exquisite designs for the theater, where his details in production were in harmony with the spirit of the work performed—the reconstruction seemed natural yet illusory, real yet unattainable. Vasnetsov, an inspired iconographer, and Natalia Goncharova reflected ancient religious themes in their work, and the spirit and flow of music were visually perceived in Korovin's use of color and line in his lyrical settings for the stage.

During his years as conductor of Mamontov's Private Opera and as conductor for the Russian repertoire at the Bolshoi Theater, Rachmaninoff came into close contact with the artists of the Silver Age and their quest for visual and musical synthesis. Yet his own compositions for voice—his songs and operas—show little inclination toward theatrical brilliance but rather a desire to interpret the introspective elements of the poetic texts he set to music. He respected Stanislavsky's psychological insight in the plays of the Moscow Art Theater, and he valued his friendship with Chekhov who described in his work the seemingly chance circumstances in our lives that can release wistful introspection and subsequent self-awareness.

After his marriage to Natasha Satina, Rachmaninoff spent the summers at their country home of Ivanovka, where he often worked outdoors, amid the spacious and quiet fields. More than thirty of his songs were written at Ivanovka. These songs develop in poetic convoys of thought on the passage of time, loss and sorrow mellowed by peaceful images of nature.

The Vespers, which include many psalms, were the culmination of the contemplative theme in Rachmaninoff's work, where he best expressed his musical and spiritual self. The voices of the diatonic melody flow softly, the rhythmic patterns are austere and restrained, yet with such fine and detailed nuances that the songs seem to breathe, achieving a singular purity of expression.

> Bless the Lord, O my soul,
> O Lord my God, You are wondrously great,
> Vested in glory and majesty,
> Clothed in a robe of light,
> You have spread the heavens like a tent,
> You have set Your heavens over the waters,
> You take the clouds for Your chariot,
> Riding on the wings of the wind.
> (Vespers, op. 37,
> psalm 103 in the Russian Translation)

Commenting on Rachmaninoff's work, the musicologist Boris Asafiev suggested that the composer's greatest merit was in his "most singing melody," where he stubbornly asserted himself. "It was not a theoretical quest," wrote Asafiev; "Rachmaninoff's melodic line always reaches out, as a path winding through a field. It is not artificial, it is not forced. In his music we feel a flowing spirit, a naturalness of design, born of a strong but deeply disciplined emotion. In the decades following the death of Tchaikovsky, Russian composers worked on the transformation of Tchaikovsky's heritage and the riches of the Five, and this resulted in a new lyrical union of Petersburg and Moscow, a union especially noticeable in the art song, where Rachmaninoff played a major role."[9]

The Silver Age in Russia ended during the First World War and the political and social upheavals that followed. Rachmaninoff left the country in 1917, and during the twenty-five years he lived in exile he devoted his talent to interpreting music. Although he was urged by his friends to compose songs, he remained silent.

Now, on the eve of the twenty-first century, as we listen to Rachmaninoff's voice in his songs and music, an image comes to mind from Turgenev's story "The Singers":

"I recall how one evening, at the ebbing of the tide, on the smooth, sandy shore of the sea, which thundered heavily far away, I saw a large white seagull: it stood motionless, turning its silky breast to the golden radiance of the sunset, and only now and then it slowly spread out its long wings towards the familiar sea, towards the low, scarlet sun. I recalled this, as I listened to the singer. He sang, oblivious of his rival, and all of us, but it seemed uplifted by our silent, passionate response, as a spirited swimmer is borne by the waves. He sang, and in every sound of his voice, there was something of home, infinitely spacious, as if a familiar steppe opened before us, reaching out into the endless distance."

Chapter III

Rachmaninoff and the Russian Poetic Tradition

In his compositions for voice Rachmaninoff draws upon a poetic heritage that can be considered as three separate elements, each distinct yet sharing the one spiritual culture, its imagery and forms of expression.

Liturgical poetry, translated from ancient Hebrew and Byzantine texts into Church Slavonic, is set to music by Rachmaninoff in the spiritual *pesnopenya* (hymn-songs): "In prayers, the Ever-Caring Mother of God," "Heavenly King," and the "Vespers," in which the composer shows a unique affinity for the texts and musicality of Slavonic and its textural and harmonic qualities. He presents the songs in a musical language of clarity and beauty, based on early Russian liturgical chants. The contemplative mood of the "Vespers" is often heard in his secular songs, when he selects poems set at the time of twilight and uses the lyrical and exclamatory poetry of the Psalms in the songs that describe the beauty of nature around him. The musical form Rachmaninoff gives to the "Liturgy of Saint John Chrysostom" is in harmony with the measured Hellenic expression and the lucidity of thought and poetic form that express the aspirations of a community, the ecclesia, at prayer.

The second element in Rachmaninoff's poetic heritage is that of the Russian folk tradition of lyrical and humorous songs, chanted laments, and spiritual poems, with their free rhythm, sporadic end rhymes and inner rhymes, and alliterations. The elaborate metaphors built on symbols from the world of nature are understood by those familiar with this tradition—for example, the distant sky conveys to the listener the image of the aspirations of the soul, flowering or weeping trees represent the joy or sorrow of the singer, the long road ahead speaks of our journey through life. Rachmaninoff often composed his songs using traditional folk textual and musical forms, particularly the form of the ancient *protyazhnaya* (slowly sung) song, with its flowing, slowly developing melody, as he does in "Night is sorrowful," opus 26, no. 12:

> Night is sorrowful, as my dreams are ...
> Far away, in the deep and spacious steppe
> Glows a solitary light ...
> In my heart there is much sadness and much love.
> But to whom and how does one explain
> What beckons, what fills one's heart?
> The path is long, the silent steppe remote,
> Night is sorrowful, as my dreams are ..."

In this song, set to words by Ivan Bunin, the poet and the composer combine the *protyazhnaya* and the lament forms of the folk tradition to create an image of the distant journey traveled by each of us.

The third element in Rachmaninoff's work is the secular poetry of Russia, which often draws upon the liturgical and folk traditions for inspiration. A large number of texts selected by Rachmaninoff for his songs are by minor poets of the nineteenth century and do not represent a poetic school or movement. The texts quite often came from a "poetry fund" collected for Rachmaninoff by his family, and suggestions for songs were given by friends and colleagues. Rachmaninoff's selection of texts depended on the artistic images or emotional states he wished to convey, such as the love lyrics of his youth, or on images he presented in a complete cycle, such as his reflections on loneliness and death in Opus 21, on the passage of time in Opus 26, on the aspirations and the role of the artist in Opus 34, and again on his reflections on love in his last cycle of songs.

Like his contemporaries the writers Chekhov and Bunin, Rachmaninoff believed that the personal and lyrical could be seen through the objective truth of artistic images, and he often reconceived texts of little poetic significance into musical images of depth and beauty, which arose from an inner vision that he perceived in a text. He preferred composing in the quiet summer days at his country home of Ivanovka, where he merged the images of nature with his perception of the meaning and beauty of the world around him. "I compose slowly," he admitted. "For a long time, I walk surrounded by nature. My eyes encompass the reflection of light on leaves, fresh from the rain; I listen to the quiet whisper of leaves in the forest, or I observe the pale nuances of the sky on the horizon, and in my soul voices arise, all at once. Not a drop here, or a drop there, but all at once—a whole song arises."[10]

Several of the major poets of the nineteenth century to whom Rachmaninoff returned for songs texts have a similarity of poetic concept and expression: Feodor Tyutchev endowed his vision of nature with a metaphysical dimension and wrote love lyrics of sorrow and loss; Afanasy Fet, a poet with a deeply musical poetic utterance, spoke of fleeting images and nuances of feeling and came close to the Symbolist school in Russia at the end of the century; and Alexei Tolstoy, who used liturgical and folk elements in his work, is well represented in Rachmaninoff's songs and the cantata *Saint Panteleimon, who heals*.

Rachmaninoff knew Pushkin's poetry well; in addition to four songs on poetic inspiration, he composed two monologues based on Pushkin texts and wrote two operas—*Aleko* from the poem "The Gypsies" and *The Covetous Knight* from a tragedy by the same title. The expressiveness and suppleness of Pushkin's language undoubtedly influenced the development of Rachmaninoff's musical language, and the poet's gift of simplicity, his pastel-like lightness and transparency of design, are often reflected in Rachmaninoff's work. We can truly say that Rachmaninoff's poetic school is the whole of the Russian poetic heritage—its liturgical, folk, and secular tradition.

When he left Russia in 1917 Rachmaninoff ceased to compose songs, and, although he was encouraged to write music to Russian and English poetry, he remained silent. "Having left Russia," he wrote, "I lost my desire to compose. Having lost my native land, I lost myself. An exile, who is deprived of his musical roots, traditions and native soil, has no other consolation but an inviolable silence of undisturbed reminiscences."[11]

Sing not, O lovely one, in my presence
Your melodies of sorrowful Georgia,
They recall in me
Another life and a distant shore.

Alas, your cruel song
Recalls in me
The steppe, the night, and in the moonlight
The features of a maiden, sad and far away!

I see you and forget
That dear and fateful vision,
But you sing
And it comes to me anew.

Sing not, O lovely one, in my presence
Your melodies of sorrowful Georgia,
They recall in me
Another life and a distant shore.

(op. 4, no. 4)

Chapter IV

Songs

I. Songs of Opus 4

1. **О, нет, молю, не уходи (O, no, I beg you, do not leave)**
2. **Утро (Morning)**
3. **В молчаньи ночи тайной (In the silence of the secret night)**
4. **Не пой, красавица (Sing not, O lovely one)**
5. **Уж ты, нива моя (Oh, my field)**
6. **Давно-ль, мой друг (It wasn't long ago, my friend)**

Rachmaninoff's first songs were written during the years 1890–1893, when he was not yet twenty years old. Although the songs have a strong affinity with the Russian classical romance of that period, we hear the composer's own voice in his musical reconception of poetic texts, in his sensitive attention to the expressivity of words, the breadth and eloquence of vocal melody, and the rich pianistic texture—all essentially equal in conveying to the listener the composer's musical idea.

The song "In the silence of the secret night" was written by Rachmaninoff earlier than the first two songs of Opus 4. He wrote it in 1890 at Ivanovka, where he spent the summer with the Satin and Skalon families, and he completed it in October. The song is dedicated to Vera, the youngest of the Skalon sisters. Set to a romantic text by Afanasy Fet, it recreates the silence of a secret night of dreams and memories. The quiet, contemplative mood surges to a sudden burst of passion, as Rachmaninoff adds an emotional contrast in the music, not evident in the text. Twice he repeats the lines "With your cherished name, awaken the darkness of the night," and he concludes the song with the first line of the poem, "O, long will I, in the silence of the secret night, with your cherished name awaken the darkness of the night." The passionate memory subsides in the coda, which reechoes the introduction now only as a reminiscence of the past. In a brief song-romance, Rachmaninoff recreates an emotional, personal drama.

The second song, "Morning," was composed in 1891 and dedicated to Yuri Sakhnovsky, a classmate at the Moscow Conservatory. The text by M. Yanov is of little poetic significance, but Rachmaninoff achieves an almost visual effect of the approaching dawn by means of a "pastoral" tonality in the piano accompaniment. The vocal part, declamatory and restrained at first, grows stronger and reaches a wider diapason. The poetic image of the song, delineated in the harmonic development, is that of a gradually lightening sunrise that envelops the sky.

The first song of Opus 4, "O, no, I beg you, do not leave," was written in 1892. It was composed for Anna Lodyzhenskaya, a friend in Moscow, to whom Rachmaninoff later dedicated his First Symphony. In this song the composer changes Dmitri Merezhkovsky's passive and timid plea to a bitter protest at the impending separation from his beloved. The final words "O, be with me and do not leave" are repeated twice by Rachmaninoff, while the triplets in the accompaniment accentuate the turbulent, anxious pathos of the song.

Pushkin's magnificent poem "Sing not, O lovely one" was set to music by more than twenty composers, among them Glinka, Balakirev, Rimsky-Korsakov, and Lyadov. Rachmaninoff dedicated this song, written in 1893, to his cousin and future wife Natasha Satina. The song's theme is an expressive, slowly descending melody, reminiscent of a melancholy Georgian song. The music rises in a crescendo to a brief dramatic climax, then returns to the same melody.

The composer reflects the poet's text perfectly. Upon hearing a song, both poet and composer recall "Another life and a distant shore ... and a maiden far away ..." The longed-for vision may be that of a lost love, the artist's muse, or spiritual yearning (the melisma on the word "one"—they (the melodies) is reminiscent not only of an eastern influence, but also of melismatic passages in Russian liturgical music). In the process of expressing their yearning in word or music, Pushkin and Rachmaninoff resolve their torment and the poem and the song return to a serene, contemplative mood. This resolution, romantic as it may seem at first glance, is very much part of Pushkin's and Rachmaninoff's spiritual tradition: "Such an experience seems to belong to the soul which loves what is beautiful. Hope always draws the soul from the beauty which is seen to what is beyond, always kindles the desire for the distant through what is constantly perceived. Therefore, the ardent lover of beauty, although receiving what is always visible as an image of what he desires, yet longs to be filled with the very peace of the archetype."[1]

When Rachmaninoff rested at the Lysikov country estate Lebedin during the summer of 1893, he composed the fifth song of the cycle, "Oh, my field," dedicated to Mme. E. Lysikova. The poem by Tolstoy is in the manner of a Russian folk lament, where the vision of the field that cannot be harvested is a metaphor for a love that cannot be subdued or forgotten. The vocal part is rich in Russian folk intonations and progresses in intensity from sadness to deep sorrow. The piano accompaniment surrounds the lament with an arpeggiated texture, which evokes a picture of a field of grass blown by the wind.

The last song of the cycle, "It wasn't long ago, my friend," was also written in 1893, to the words of Count Arseny Golenischev-Kutuzov and dedicated to the Countess. The elegiac mood is changed in the finale by the young composer, when his song bursts out in delight at the words "And songs are pouring from my heart, inspired by you," repeated again "from my heart, inspired by you!"

The songs of Opus 4 are love songs, passionately expressed in music, but in which the ebullience of youth engenders a serious and deeply felt emotion. Rachmaninoff's songs "In the silence of the secret night" and "Sing not, O lovely one" are masterpieces of the Russian vocal repertoire.

1

'o 'n̡et ma'l̡ju n̡e uxa'd̡i

О, нет, молю, не уходи!

O, no (I) beg (do) not leave

Date of composition: ***1892.***
Date of publication: ***1893.***
Publisher: ***A. Gutheil, Moscow.***
Dedicated to Anna A. Lodyzhenskaya.
Source: ***Dmitri Merezhkovsky.***

'o 'n̡et ma'l̡u n̡e uxa'd̡i
О, нет, молю, не уходи!
O, no (I) beg (do) not leave

fs̡ja 'bol̡ n̡i't͡ʃto p̡e'r̡et raz'lukaĭ
Вся боль ничто перед разлукой,
All pain naught before parting

ja 's̡l̡iʃkəm 'ʃtʃɑs̡l̡if 'ɛtaĭ 'mukaĭ
Я слишком счастлив этой мукой,
I (am) too happy (with) this torment

s̡il̡'n̡eĭ p̡r̡i'ʒm̡i m̡e'n̡ja g͡ gru'd̡i
Сильней прижми меня к груди,
Stronger hold me to breast

ska'ʒɨ l̡jub'l̡ju
Скажи "люблю".
Say (I) love.

p̡r̡i'ʃol ja v'nof̡
Пришёл я вновь,
Came I again

О, нет, молю, не уходи!
Вся боль ничто перед разлукой,
Я слишком счастлив этой мукой
Сильней прижми меня к груди,
Скажи "люблю".
Пришёл я вновь,
Больной, измученный и бледный.
Смотри, какой я слабый, бедный,
Как мне нужна твоя любовь …
Мучений новых впереди я жду,
Как ласк, как поцелуя,
И об одном молю, тоскуя:
О, будь со мной, не уходи!
О, будь со мной, не уходи!

baļ'noĭ iz'muʧennɨĭ i 'bļednɨĭ
Больной, измученный и бледный.
Ill tormented and pale

sma'ţri ka'koĭ ja 'slɑbɨĭ 'b̦ednɨĭ
Смотри, какой я слабый, бедный,
See how I (am) weak poor

kak 'mņe nuʒ'nɑ tva'ja ļju'boţ
Как мне нужна твоя любовь …
How (to) me (is) needed your love …

mu'ʧeņiĭ 'novɨx fp̦eŗe'd̦i ja 'ʒdu
Мучений новых впереди я жду,
Torments new ahead I await

kak 'lɑsk kak patsɛ'luja
Как ласк, как поцелуя,
As caresses as kiss

i əb ad'nom ma'ļju tas'kuja
И об одном молю, тоскуя:
And about one (I) beg in anguish

'o 'buţ sa 'mnoĭ ņe 'uxad̦i
О, будь со мной, не уходи!
O be with me not leave

'o 'buţ sa 'mnoĭ ņe 'uxad̦i
О, будь со мной, не уходи!
O be with me not leave

O, no, I beg you, do not leave!
All pain is naught compared to parting,
I'm so enraptured by this torment,
Please hold me closer to your heart
And say "I love you."
I came again,
Tormented, ill and pale.
See how I am weak and sad
And how I need your love …
New torments I await before me
Like kisses and caresses,
I only ask of you in anguish—
O, be with me and do not leave!
O, be with me and do not leave!

2
'utra
Утро
Morning

Date of composition: ***1981.***
Date of publication: ***1893.***
Publisher: ***A. Gutheil, Moscow.***
Dedicated to Yuri S. Sakhnovsky.
Source: ***M. L. Yanov.***

ļub'ļju ţe'b̧ja ʃɛp'nula 'dņju za'ŗja
"Люблю тебя!" Шепнула дню заря
(I) love you Whispered (to) day dawn

i 'ņeba apxva'ţif zar'ḑelaş at
И, небо обхватив, зарделась от
And sky clasping blushed from
pŗiz'naņja
признанья,
confession

i 'sontsa 'lutʃ pŗi'rodu aza'ŗja
И солнца луч, природу озаря,
And sun's ray nature lighting

s u'lɨpkəĭ pasɨ'lɑl jeĭ 'ʒgutʃije
С улыбкой посылал ей жгучие
With smile sent her ardent
lab'zɑņja
лобзанья.
kisses

"Люблю тебя!" Шепнула дню заря
И, небо обхватив, зарделась от признанья,
И солнца луч, природу озаря,
С улыбкой посылал ей жгучие лобзанья.
А день, как бы ещё не доверяя
Осуществлению своих заветных грёз,
Спускался на землю, с улыбкой утирая
Блестевшие вокруг ряды алмазных слёз …

ɑ 'ḑeņ kak bɨ je'ʃʃo ņe dayeˈŗjaja
А день, как бы ещё не доверяя
And day as if still not believing

asuʃʃestˈvļeņiju svaˈix zaˈyetnɨx ˈgŗjos
Осуществлению своих заветных грёз,
Realization (of) its cherished dreams

spusˈkɑlşa ˈnɑ z̧emļju s uˈlɨpkəĭ uţiˈrɑja
Спускался на землю, с улыбкой утирая
Descended to earth with smile wiping

bļeˈsţefʃɨje vaˈkruk ŗjaˈdɨ alˈmɑznɨx
Блестевшие вокруг ряды алмазных
Shining around rows (of) brilliant
sˈļjos
слёз …
tears …

"I love you" to the coming Day
whispered Dawn
Enveloping the sky, and blushed
from her confession;
A ray of sun, caressing nature,
Smiled and sent forth its burning
kisses.
And Day, as if not yet believing
The realization of his cherished
dreams,
Descended upon earth, gently
wiping
The sparkling rows of starry
tears …

3
v malˈʧɑņji ˈnoʧi ˈtɑĭnaĭ
В молчаньи ночи тайной
In silence (of) night secret

Date of composition: ***1890.***
Date of publication: ***1893.***
Publisher: ***A. Gutheil, Moscow.***
Dedicated to Vera D. Skalon.
Source: ***Afanasy Fet.***

ˈo ˈdolga ˈbudu ˈja v malˈʧɑņji ˈnoʧi
О, долго буду я, в молчаньи ночи
O long will I in silence (of) night
ˈtɑĭnaĭ
тайной,
secret

ka'vɑrnɨĭ 'ļeţet 'tvoĭ u'lɨpku 'vzor 'vzor
Коварный лепет твой, улыбку, взор, взор
Beguiling whisper your smile gaze gaze
slu'ʧɑĭnɨĭ
случайный,
random

ţers'tɑm pas'luʃnuju va'los va'los
Перстам послушную волос, волос
(To) fingers obedient (of) hair, (of) hair
tva'ix gus'tuju p'ŗjaḑ
твоих густую прядь
your thick lock

iz 'mɨsļeĭ izga'ņjaţ i 'snova
Из мыслей изгонять, и снова
From thoughts banish and again
pŗizɨ'vɑţ
призывать;
call

ʃɛp'tɑţ i paprav'ļjaţ bɨ'lɨje vɨra'ʒɛņija
Шептать и поправлять былые выражения
Whisper and correct past expressions

ŗe'ʧeĭ ma'ix s ta'boĭ is'polņennɨx
Речей моих с тобой, исполненных
(Of) words my with you filled
smu'ʃʃeņija
смущения,
(with) embarrassment

i v aţja'ņeņii naţeŗi'kor u'mu
И в опьянении, наперекор уму,
And in intoxication contrary (to) reason

О, долго буду я, в молчаньи ночи тайной,
Коварный лепет твой, улыбку, взор, взор случайный,
Перстам послушную волос, волос твоих густую прядь
Из мыслей изгонять, и снова призывать;
Шептать и поправлять былые выражения
Речей моих с тобой, исполненных смущения,
И в опьянении, наперекор уму,
Заветным именем будить ночную тьму,
Заветным именем будить ночную тьму.
О, долго буду я, в молчаньи ночи тайной,
Заветным именем будить ночную тьму.

i 'sţep̧ i 'notʃ i pŗi
И степь, и ночь, и при
And steppe and night and in the
lu'ņe
луне
moon(light)

ʧer'tɨ da'ļjokəĭ 'ђednəĭ ḑevɨ
Черты далёкой, бедной девы!
Features (of) far poor maid

ja 'pŗizrak 'ṃilɨĭ raka'voĭ
Я призрак милый, роковой,
I phantom dear fateful

ţe'ђja u'ɣiḑef zabɨ'vɑju
Тебя увидев, забываю;
You seeing forget

no tɨ pa'joʃ i 'pŗeda m'noĭ
Но ты поёшь и, предо мной
But you sing and before me

je'vo ja 'v'noʃ vaabra'ʒɑju
Его я вновь воображаю.
It I again imagine

ņe 'poĭ krɑ'sɑɣi'tsɑ pŗi 'mņe
Не пой, красавица, при мне
(Do) not sing, beauty before me

tɨ 'p̧eşen 'gruẓii p̧e'ʧɑļnaĭ
Ты песен Грузии печальной:
You songs (of) Georgia sad

Sing not, O lovely one, in my presence
Your melodies of sorrowful Georgia,
They recall in me
Another life and a distant shore.
Alas, your cruel song
Recalls in me
The steppe, the night, and in the moonlight
The features of a maiden, sad and far away!
I see you and forget
That dear and fateful vision
But you sing
And it comes to me anew.
Sing not, O lovely one, in my presence
Your melodies of sorrowful Georgia,
They recall in me
Another life and a distant shore.

napaɱiˈnɑjut ˈmɲe aˈɲe
Напоминают мне оне
Remind me they

druˈɡuju ˈʒɨzɲ i ɓeɽek ˈdɑʎɲiĭ
Другую жизнь и берег дальний.
Another life and shore distant.

5
uʒ ˈtɨ ˈɲiva maˈja
Уж ты, нива моя!
Oh you field my

Date of composition: ***1893.***
Date of publication: ***1893.***
Publisher: ***A. Gutheil, Moscow.***
Dedicated to E. N. Lysikova.
Source: ***Alexei Tolstoy.***

uʒ ˈtɨ ˈɲiva maˈja ˈɲivuʃka
Уж ты, нива моя, нивушка,
Oh you field my (little, dear) field

ɲi skaˈʂiʈ ʈiˈɓja s ˈmɑxu jeˈɗinava
Не скосить тебя с маху единого,
Not mow you with sweep one

ɲi sɣjaˈzɑʈ ʈiˈɓja ˈfʂju va jeˈɗinɨĭ ˈsnop
Не связать тебя всю во единый сноп!
Not tie you all into one sheaf

uʒ ˈvɨ ˈdumɨ maˈji ˈdumuʃʞi
Уж вы, думы мои, думушки,
Oh you thoughts my (little, sad) thoughts

Уж ты, нива моя, нивушка,
Не скосить тебя с маху единого,
Не связать тебя всю во единый сноп!
  Уж вы, думы мои, думушки,
  Не стряхнуть вас разом с плеч долой,
  Одной речью то вас не высказать!
По тебе ль, нива, ветер разгуливал,
Гнул колосья твои до земли,
Зрелы зёрна все размётывал!
  Широко вы, думы, порассыпались,
  Куда пала какая думушка,
  Там всходила люта печаль трава,
  Вырастало горе горючее.
  А! А!

ŋ̧i stʈjax'nuʈ vas 'razəm s 'pʈetʃ
Не стряхнуть вас разом с плеч
Not shake you at once off shoulders
da'loĭ
долой,
away

ad'noĭ 'ɽetʃju ta 'vas ŋ̧i 'vɨskazɑʈ
Одной речью то вас не высказать!
(With) alone speech — you not express

pa ʈi'ƀe ʈ 'ŋ̧iva 'ɣeʈir raz'guʈival
По тебе ль, нива, ветер разгуливал,
Upon you — field wind played

'gnul ka'loşja tva'i da ʐem'ʈi
Гнул колосья твои до земли,
Bent stalks your to earth

z'ɽelɨ 'ʐjornɑ 'fşe raz'ɱjotɨval
Зрелы зёрна все размётывал!
Ripe grain all threw around

ʃɨra'ko vɨ 'dumɨ paras'sɨpɑʈiş
Широко вы, думы, порассыпались,
Widely you thoughts scattered

kuɗa 'pɑla ka'kaja 'dumuʃka
Куда пала какая думушка,
Where fell which thought

tam fsxa'ɖila 'ʈjuta p̧i'ʧɑʈ tra'vɑ
Там всходила люта печаль трава,
There rose cruel sorrow grass

vɨra'stɑla 'goɽe ga'ɽjuʧeje ɑ ɑ
Вырастало горе горючее. А! А!
Grew grief grievous Ah Ah

Oh, my field, my beloved field,
I cannot harvest you in one full sweep,
I cannot tie you into a single sheaf …
Oh, my thoughts, my sad thoughts,
I cannot cast you off my shoulders,
I can't express you in words alone!
Was it not over you, my field, that the wind blew ardently,
Bent your grasses to the very earth,
Blew the ripened seeds all around …
How widely you have scattered,
Oh, my thoughts,
Where a sad thought fell
There grew the cruel grass of sorrow,
Bitter grief appeared. Ah! Ah!

6

dav'no ļ moi 'druk

Давно-ль, мой друг

Long — my friend

Date of composition: ***1893.***
Date of publication: ***1893.***
Publisher: ***A. Gutheil, Moscow.***
Dedicated to Olga A. Golenischeva-Kutuzova.
Source: ***Arseny Golenischev-Kutuzov.***

dav'no ļ 'moĭ 'druk 'tvoĭ 'vzor p̧e'ʧɑļnɨĭ
Давно ль, мой друг, твой взор печальный
Long — my friend your gaze sad

'ja v rassta'vɑņja 'smutnɨĭ 'm̧ik la'ɣil
Я в расставанья смутный миг ловил.
I in parting dim moment caught

'ʃtop 'luʧ je'vo pra'ʃʃɑļnɨĭ
Чтоб луч его прощальный
So that ray its farewell

na'dolga v 'duʃu 'm̧ņe pra'ņik
Надолго в душу мне проник.
Long into soul (to) me enter

dav'no ļ bluʒ'dɑja aḑi'noka
Давно ль, блуждая одиноко,
Long — wandering alone

f tal'p̧e ţes'ņjaʃʃeĭ i ʧu'ʒoĭ
В толпе теснящей и чужой
In crowd oppressive and alien

Давно ль, мой друг, твой взор печальный
Я в расставанья смутный миг ловил.
Чтоб луч его прощальный
Надолго в душу мне проник.
Давно ль, блуждая одиноко,
В толпе теснящей и чужой
К тебе, желанной и далёкой
Я мчался грустною мечтой.
Желанья гасли … Сердце ныло …
Стояло время … Ум молчал …
Давно ль затишье это было?
Но вихрь свиданья набежал …
Мы вместе вновь, и дни несутся,
Как в море волн летучих строй,
И мысль кипит, и песни льются
Из сердца полного тобой!
Из сердца полного тобой!

k ţe'b̦e ʒe'lɑnnaĭ i dɑ'ļjokaĭ
К тебе, желанной и далёкой
To you desired and far away

ja 'mʧɑlsa 'grustnaju m̦eʧ'toĭ
Я мчался грустною мечтой.
I rushed (with) sad dream

ʒɛ'lɑņja 'gɑsļi 'şertsɛ 'nɨla
Желанья гасли ... Сердце ныло ...
Desires dying out Heart ached

sta'jala 'v̦rem̦ja 'um mal'ʧɑl
Стояло время ... Ум молчал ...
Stood time Mind silent

dav'no ļ za'ţiʃje 'ɛta 'bɨla
Давно ль затишье это было?
Long — stillness this was

'no 'v̦ixŗ sv̦i'dɑņja nab̦e'ʒɑl
Но вихрь свиданья набежал ...
But whirlwind (of) meeting came

mɨ 'vm̦esţe v'noʃ i dņi ņe'sutsa
Мы вместе вновь, и дни несутся,
We together again and days rush

kak v 'moŗe 'voln ļe'tuʧix st'roĭ
Как в море волн летучих строй,
As in sea (of) waves flying row

i 'mɨsļ ķi'p̦it i 'p̦esņi 'ļjutsa
И мысль кипит, и песни льются
And thought (is) ebullient and songs pour

It wasn't long ago, my friend,
when your saddened gaze
I sought in parting's anxious moments,
So that its farewell ray
Long in my soul would dwell.
It wasn't long ago, when wandering alone
In an oppressive and an alien crowd,
To you, longed for and distant,
I hurried in my melancholy dreams ...
Desires were dying ... My heart was heavy ...
Time stood ... And thoughts were silent ...
Not long ago this stillness reigned,
Then came the whirlwind of our meeting ...
We are again together, days rush by
As in the sea the rows of flying waves,
My thoughts are flowing and songs are pouring
From my heart, inspired by you!
From my heart, inspired by you!

is	'şertsa	'polnavə	ta'boĭ
Из	**сердца**	**полного**	**тобой!**
From	heart	full	(of) you

is	'şertsa	'polnavə	ta'boĭ
Из	**сердца**	**полного**	**тобой!**
From	heart	full	(of) you

II. Songs of Opus 8

1. **Речная лилея (Water lily)**
2. **Дитя, как цветок ты прекрасна (My child, your beauty is that of a flower)**
3. **Дума (*Duma* [Thoughts, Reflection])**
4. **Полюбила я на печаль свою (I fell in love, to my sorrow)**
5. **Сон (A dream)**
6. **Молитва (Prayer)**

The personal and emotional involvement in Rachmaninoff's first cycle of songs is set aside when the composer presents in music poems by Alexei Plescheyev. The songs were written at the time of the poet's death in 1893.

Rachmaninoff selects three poems by Plescheyev—"Water lily," "My child, your beauty is that of a flower," "A dream" (translations from Heine)—and writes elegant musical miniatures, similar to miniatures by Cui. In these songs, dedicated to his friends Adolf Yaroshevsky, Michael Slonov, and Natalia Skalon, the composer keeps the clarity of the original poetic structure and at the same time vividly states the descriptive and psychological moments in the texts.

Duma (translated from Shevchenko) is in the form of an operatic monologue and was composed for Leonid Yakovlev, a singer at the Maryinsky Theater in St. Petersburg. A *duma* is a traditional poetic or musical reflection, here a reflection on the passage of time and the artist's lack of inspiration when he lives without experiencing life's joys or sorrows. The reflection-monologue has a musical similarity to the work of Musorgsky, as the intonation of the vocal part follows the intonation of the spoken word.

"I fell in love, to my sorrow" (also from Shevchenko) is dedicated to Maria Olferieva. It is in the manner of a folk lament, and Rachmaninoff writes a beautiful melody to the simple and laconic words of the text. The song follows authentic Russian folk lament intonations of a woman who cries out in her lonely and bitter fate. As folk laments are usually unaccompanied, Rachmaninoff keeps this tradition, with the piano barely accentuating the melody of the song.

The last song of Opus 8, "Prayer" (from Goethe), is a

monologue written for Maria Deisha-Sionitskaya, a well-known singer at the Bolshoi Theater in Moscow, who sang the role of Zemphira in the first production of Rachmaninoff's opera *Aleko* in 1893. Although the translation is of little literary value, and despite the poem's sentimentality, Rachmaninoff outlines with compassion the emotional state of a woman at prayer, who seeks forgiveness.

In this cycle, Rachmaninoff shows a discerning talent in giving musical form to a variety of literary texts—a few lines of poetry, traditional folk intonations, or operatic monologues. In reviewing *Aleko* the critic S. Kruglikov suggested that "Rachmaninoff is a talented man, with good training and excellent taste. He can become a good composer of opera, because he feels the stage and already has a good understanding of writing for voice, and has the fortunate gift of melody."[2]

1
ɽetʃ'nɑja ʎi'ʎeja
Речная лилея
River lily

Date of composition: ***1893.***
Date of publication: ***1894.***
Publisher: ***A. Gutheil, Moscow.***
Dedicated to Adolf A. Yaroshevsky.
Source: ***Alexei Plescheyev*** **(translation from Heine).**

ɽetʃ'nɑja ʎi'ʎeja ga'lofku pad'ɲjafʃɨ nɑ 'ɲeba
Речная лилея, головку поднявши на небо
River lily head lifting to sky
gʎja'ɖit
глядит;
looks

ɑ 'ɱeşjats vl̡jub'l̡jonnɨĭ lu'ʧɑɱi
А месяц влюблённый лучами
And crescent moon enamored (with) rays
u'nɨla je'jo şeŗeb'ŗit
уныло её серебрит …
dolefully her silvers

i 'vot a'nɑ 'snova pa'ȵikla stɨd'l̡iva k
И вот она снова поникла стыдливо, к
And here she again drooped shyly to
lɑ'zurnɨm va'dɑm
лазурным водам;
azure waters

'no 'ɱeşjats fşjo 'bl̡ednɨĭ i
Но месяц всё бледный и
But crescent moon still pale and
'tomnɨĭ kɑk 'pŗizrɑk şi'jaet i 'tɑm
томный как призрак, сияет и там …
languishing like apparition shines too there

Речная лилея, головку
поднявши на небо глядит;
А месяц влюблённый лучами
уныло её серебрит …
И вот она снова поникла
стыдливо, к лазурным водам;
Но месяц всё бледный и
томный как призрак, сияет и
там …

A water lily, opening her petals,
looks at the sky,
The amorous moon sadly touches
her with its silvery rays,
And when she turns shyly toward
the blue waters
The moon's pale and languid
reflection caresses her there …

2

ɖi'tja kak tsye'tok tɨ pŗe'krɑsna
Дитя! как цветок ты прекрасна
Child as flower you (are) beautiful

Date of composition: ***1893*.**
Date of publication: ***1894*.**
Publisher: ***A. Gutheil, Moscow*.**
Dedicated to Michael A. Slonov.
Source: ***Alexei Plescheyev*** **(translation from Heine).**

ɖi'ţja kak tsye'tok tɨ pŗe'krɑsna
Дитя! как цветок ты прекрасна,
Child as flower you (are) beautiful

syet'lɑ i ʧis'tɑ i ɱi'lɑ
Светла, и чиста, и мила.
Radiant and pure and sweet

smat'ŗju nɑ ţi'ḅja i ļju'bujuş
Смотрю на тебя и любуюсь,
(I) look at you and admire

i 'snova du'ʃɑ azɨ'lɑ
И снова душа ожила …
And again soul came to life

a'xotna͡ p ţi'ḅe nɑ ga'lofku
Охотно б тебе на головку
Willingly — (to) you on (small) head

ja 'ruķi sva'i vazla'ʒɨl
Я руки свои возложил;
I hands my lay upon

pra'şja 'ʃtobɨ 'box ţe'ḅja 'yeʧna
Прося чтобы Бог тебя вечно
Asking for God you eternally

pŗe'krɑsnaĭ i 'ʧistaĭ xrɑ'ŋil
Прекрасной и чистой хранил.
Beautiful and pure preserve

Дитя! как цветок ты прекрасна,
Светла, и чиста, и мила.
Смотрю на тебя и любуюсь,
И снова душа ожила …
Охотно б тебе на головку
Я руки свои возложил;
Прося чтобы Бог тебя вечно
Прекрасной и чистой хранил.

My child, your beauty is that of a flower—
Radiant, pure and sweet.
I look at you and admire you
And my soul comes to life again.
I would gladly place my hands
Upon your head,
Asking God to keep you
Eternally fair and pure.

3
'duma
Дума
Duma (thoughts, reflection)

Date of composition: *1893*.
Date of publication: *1894*.
Publisher: *A. Gutheil, Moscow*.
Dedicated to Leonid G. Yakovlev.
Source: *Alexei Plescheyev* (translation from Shevchenko).

pra'xoḑjat	'dņi	pra'xoḑjat	'notʃi
Проходят	**дни …**	**проходят**	**ночи;**
Pass	days	pass	nights

pra'ʃlo	i	'ļeta
Прошло	**и**	**лето;**
(Is) past	too	summer

ʃɛļes'ţit	'ļist	paʒɛl'ţefʃɨĭ
Шелестит	**лист**	**пожелтевший;**
Rustles	leaf	yellowed

'gɑsnut	'otʃi
Гаснут	**очи;**
Grow dim	eyes

zas'nuļi	'dumɨ
Заснули	**думы;**
Fell asleep	thoughts

'şertsɛ	'sp̧it
Сердце	**спит.**
Heart	(is) asleep

Проходят дни … проходят ночи;
Прошло и лето;
Шелестит лист пожелтевший;
Гаснут очи;
Заснули думы;
Сердце спит.

Заснуло всё …
Не знаю я живёшь ли ты, душа моя.
Бесстрастно я гляжу на свет,
И нету слёз, и смеху нет!
И доля где моя?
Судьбою знать не дано мне никакой …
Но если я благой не стою,
Зачем не выпало хоть злой?

Не дай, о Боже! как во сне блуждать …
Остынуть сердцем мне.
Гнилой колодой на пути
лежать меня не попусти,

zas'nula 'fşjo
Заснуло всё …
Fell asleep everything

n̦e 'znɑju 'ja zɨ'ɣjoʃ l̦i 'tɨ du'ʃɑ
Не знаю я живёшь ли ты, душа
(Do) not know I, live if you soul
ma'ja
моя.
my

b̦es'strɑstna ja gl̦ja'ʒu nɑ 'sɣet
Бесстрастно я гляжу на свет,
Passionless(ly) I look at world

i 'n̦etu 'sl̦joz i 'sm̦exu 'n̦et
И нету слёз, и смеху нет!
And no tears and laughter (there is) not

i 'dol̦ja 'gd̦e ma'ja
И доля где моя?
And lot where (is) my

sud̦'boju 'znɑț n̦e da'no mn̦e n̦ika'koĭ
Судьбою знать не дано мне никакой …
(By) fate seems not given (to) me any

'no 'jesl̦i ja bla'goi n̦i s'toju
Но если я благой не стою,
But if I (of) good (one) not worthy

za'ʧem n̦i 'vɨpala 'xoț 'zloĭ
Зачем не выпало хоть злой?
Why not befell at least evil (one)

Но дай мне жить, Творец,
О, дай мне сердцем, сердцем жить!
Чтоб я хвалил Твой мир чудесный,
Чтоб мог я ближнего любить!

Страшна неволя!
Тяжко в ней!

Days pass … nights pass …
The summer is gone;
The yellowed leaf is rustling;
The eyes' fire is fading;
Thoughts have eased into slumber;
The heart is asleep.

Everything is sleeping …
I know not whether you, dear soul, still live.
Unmoved, I glance out at the world
With neither tears nor laughter!
And what is my lot?
None is given me by Fate to know …
But if I am not to merit happiness,
Then why has not an evil lot befallen me?

Let me not, O God, wander as in a dream …
Let not my heart grow cold.
Keep me from being without purpose,
A decayed log by the roadside.

ņe 'dɑĭ o 'ɓoʒɛ kak va 'sņe
Не дай, о Боже! как во сне
(Do) not give O God as in dream
ɓluʒ'dɑţ
блуждать …
to wander

as'tɨnuţ 'şertsɛm 'm̧ņe
Остынуть сердцем мне.
Grow cold (with) heart me

gņi'loĭ ka'lodaĭ nɑ pu'ţi ļi'ʒɑţ m̧i'ņja
Гнилой колодой на пути лежать меня
(As) rotten log on road to lie me
ņi papus'ţi
не попусти,
(do) not allow

'no 'dɑĭ mņe 'ʒɨţ tva'ŗets
Но дай мне жить, Творец,
But give me to live Creator

'o 'dɑĭ mņe 'şertsɛm 'şertsɛm 'ʒɨţ
О, дай мне сердцем, сердцем жить!
O give me (with) heart, (with) heart to live

'ʃtop 'ja xvɑ'ļil 'tvoĭ m̧ir ʧu'ḑesnɨĭ
Чтоб я хвалил Твой мир чудесный,
So that I praise Your world wonderful

'ʃtop 'mok ja 'ɓļiʒņeva ļju'ɓiţ
Чтоб мог я ближнего любить!
So that could I neighbor to love

But let me live, O my Creator,
Give me to live in fullness of my heart!
That I might praise Your wondrous world,
That I might love my neighbor!

My bondage is fearsome!
There is great burden in it.

stra'ʃnɑ ṉe'voḻja
Страшна неволя!
Fearsome (is) bondage

'ţjaʃka v 'ṉeĭ
Тяжко в ней!
Burdensome in it

4
paḻju'ḇila ja nɑ p̧i'ʧɑḻ sva'ju
Полюбила я на печаль свою
Fell in love I to sorrow my

Date of composition: ***1893*.**
Date of publication: ***1894*.**
Publisher: ***A. Gutheil, Moscow*.**
Dedicated to Maria V. Olferieva.
Source: ***Alexei Plescheyev*** **(translation from Shevchenko).**

paḻju'ḇila ja nɑ p̧i'ʧɑḻ sva'ju
Полюбила я на печаль свою
Fell in love I to sorrow my

şira'ţinuʃku ḇesta'lɑnnava
Сиротинушку бесталанного.
(With) orphan luckless

uʃ ta'kɑja 'doḻja mṉe 'vɨpala
Уж такая доля мне выпала.
As such lot (to) me befell

razlu'ʧiḻi nɑs 'ḻjuḑi 'şiḻnɨje
Разлучили нас люди сильные;
Separated us people powerful

Полюбила я на печаль свою
Сиротинушку бесталанного.
Уж такая доля мне выпала.
Разлучили нас люди сильные;
Увезли его, сдали в
рекруты …
И солдаткой я, одинокой я,
Знать в чужой избе и
состареюсь.
Уж такая доля мне выпала. А!

uɣez'ʎi je'vo 'zdaʎi v 'ɽekrutɨ
Увезли его, сдали в рекруты ...
Took away him gave away as soldier

i sal'datkəĭ 'ja aɖi'nokəĭ 'ja
И солдаткой я, одинокой я,
And (as) soldier's wife I, lonely I

'znaʈ f ʧu'ʒoĭ iz'ɓe i sasta'ɽejuʂ
Знать в чужой избе и состареюсь.
Seems in someone else's hut — will grow old

uʃ ta'kaja 'doʎja mɳe 'vɨpala a
Уж такая доля мне выпала. А!
As such fate (to) me befell. A!

I fell in love, to my sorrow,
With a lonely and unlucky man.
Such a fate befell me ...
Powerful men separated us,
They took him away to be a lifelong soldier ...
And a soldier's wife, all alone,
I'll grow old in a stranger's house.
Such a fate befell me ... A!

5
'son
Сон
Dream

Date of composition: ***1893.***
Date of publication: ***1894.***
Publisher: ***A. Gutheil, Moscow.***
Dedicated to Natalia D. Skalon.
Source: ***Alexei Plescheyev*** **(translation from Heine).**

i u ɱe'ŋja 'bɨl 'kraĭ rad'noĭ
И у меня был край родной;
And I had land native

pɽe'kraʂen 'on
Прекрасен он!
Beautiful it (is)

tɑm 'jeļ ka'ʧɑlaş 'nɑda 'mnoĭ
Там ель качалась надо мной …
There fir swayed over me

'no 'to bɨl 'son
Но то был сон!
But that was dream

şe'm̧ja dru'z̧eĭ ʒɨ'vɑ bɨ'lɑ
Семья друзей жива была.
Family (of) friends living was

sa 'fşex sta'ron
Со всех сторон
From all sides

zvu'ʧɑļi 'mņe ļjub'v̧i sla'vɑ
Звучали мне любви слова …
Resounded (to) me love's words

'no 'to bɨl 'son
Но то был сон!
But that was dream

И у меня был край родной;
Прекрасен он!
Там ель качалась надо мной …
Но то был сон!
Семья друзей жива была.
Со всех сторон
Звучали мне любви слова …
Но то был сон!

I, too, had a home,
A beautiful one!
There a fir tree swayed …
But it was only a dream!
A family of friends
Surrounded me
With words of love …
But it was only a dream!

6
ma'ļitva
Молитва
Prayer

Date of composition: ***1893.***
Date of publication: ***1894.***
Publisher: ***A. Gutheil, Moscow.***
Dedicated to Maria A. Deisha-Sionitskaya.
Source: ***Alexei Plescheyev*** **(translation from Goethe).**

'o 'boʒɛ 'moĭ vzg̡ļja'ņi nɑ 'g̡ŗeʃnuju
О, Боже мой! Взгляни на грешную
O God my Look upon sinful
m̡e'ņja
меня;
me

ja 'muʧuş ja baļ'nɑ du'ʃoĭ
Я мучусь, я больна душой,
I (am) tormented, I (am) suffering (with) soul

iz'rɨta 'skorb̡ju 'gruḑ ma'ja
Изрыта скорбью грудь моя.
Scarred (with) grief breast my

'o 'moĭ tva'ŗets ye'ļik 'moĭ 'g̡ŗex
О, мой Творец, велик мой грех,
O my Creator great (is) my sin

ja nɑ z̡im'ļe p̡ŗi'stupņeĭ 'fşex
Я на земле преступней всех.
I (am) on earth more sinful (than) all

ki'p̡ela v 'ņjom mla'dɑja 'krof̡
Кипела в нём младая кровь,
Boiling in him young blood

bɨ'lɑ ʧis'tɑ je'vo ļju'bof̡
Была чиста его любовь,
Was pure his love

'no 'on je'jo v gru'ḑi sva'jeĭ
Но он её в груди своей
But he it in breast his

ta'il tak 'sy̧jata at ļju'ḑeĭ
Таил так свято от людей.
Concealed so sacredly from people

О, Боже мой! Взгляни на
грешную меня;
Я мучусь, я больна душой,
Изрыта скорбью грудь моя.
О, мой Творец, велик мой
грех,
Я на земле преступней всех.
Кипела в нём младая кровь,
Была чиста его любовь,
Но он её в груди своей
Таил так свято от людей.
Я знала всё …
О, Боже мой! Прости мне
грешной и больной.
Его я муки поняла;
Улыбкой, взором лишь одним
Я б исцелить его могла,
Но я не сжалилась над ним.
Томился долго, долго он,
Печалью тяжкой удручён;
И умер, бедный наконец,
О, Боже мой, о, мой
Творец!
Тронься грешною
мольбой …
Взгляни, как я больна
душой.

ja 'znalɑ 'fşjo
Я знала всё …
I knew everything

'o 'bozɛ 'moĭ pras'ţi mņe 'gɽeʃnaĭ i
О, Боже мой! Прости мне грешной и
O God my Forgive me sinful and
baļ'noĭ
больной.
suffering

je'vo ja 'muķi paņja'lɑ
Его я муки поняла;
His I torments understood

u'lɨpkaĭ 'vzoram 'ļiʃ ad'ņim
Улыбкой, взором лишь одним
(With) smile, glance only one

ja͡p istsɛ'ļiţ je'vo mag'lɑ
Я б исцелить его могла,
I — heal him could

'no ja ņe 'sʒɑļilɑş nɑt 'ņim
Но я не сжалилась над ним.
But I not took pity upon him

ta'ɱilsa 'dolga 'dolga 'on
Томился долго, долго он,
Languished long long he

pi'ʧɑļju 'ţjaʃkaĭ udru'ʧon
Печалью тяжкой удручён;
(With) sadness heavy (was) depressed

O God, look down upon a sinner;
I suffer much; my soul is wounded,
My heart is torn by grief.
O, my Creator, my sin is great,
I have transgressed more than anyone on earth.
He was hot blooded,
His love was pure,
He kept it as a sacred trust,
Concealed it in his heart.
I knew of it …
O, my God! forgive me, a sinner and in anguish.
I understood his torments;
With a smile, a glance
I could have healed him,
But I did not pity him.
He languished for a while,
With sorrow laden,
And died, distressed.
O, my God! O, my Creator!
Hear my sinful prayer
For I am wounded in my soul.

i 'um̡er 'b̡ednɨĭ naka'n̡ets
И умер, бедный наконец,
And died poor (one) finally

'o 'boʒɛ 'moĭ 'o 'moĭ tva'r̡ets
О, Боже мой, о, мой Творец!
O God my O my Creator

'tron̡ş̡ja gr̡eʃ'noju maɫ̡'boĭ
Тронься грешною мольбой…
Be moved (by) sinful prayer

vzgl̡ja'n̡i kak ja baɫ̡'nɑ du'ʃoĭ
Взгляни, как я больна душой.
Look how I (am) suffering (with) soul

III. Songs of Opus 14

1. **Я жду тебя (I await you)**
2. **Островок (Small island)**
3. **Давно в любви (How fleeting is delight in love)**
4. **Я был у ней (I was with her)**
5. **Эти летния ночи (Summer nights)**
6. **Тебя так любят все (You are so loved by all)**
7. **Не верь мне, друг! (Do not believe me, friend)**
8. **О, не грусти (Oh, do not grieve)**
9. **Она, как полдень, хороша (She is as beautiful as midday)**
10. **В моей душе (In my soul)**
11. **Весенние воды (Spring torrents)**
12. **Пора! (It is time)**

Rachmaninoff's third cycle of songs, written in 1896 (except for the first song, written in 1894), is diverse in thematic material. The texts used by Rachmaninoff in this cycle are also of diverse poetic significance. He sets to music poems by established authors of the nineteenth century as well as texts by popular poets of the time.

"I await you," dedicated to Ludmila Skalon, is by Maria Davidova. In her poem, the protagonist is a woman, and Rachmaninoff interprets with sensitivity her feelings while waiting for her beloved. The impatience and anxiety expressed by her in song do not disturb the aura of tenderness in the piano accompaniment.

Rachmaninoff wrote "Small island" for his cousin and future sister-in-law Sophia Satina. Sophia became a cherished friend, who during Rachmaninoff's lifetime and after his death collected and catalogued his musical and literary heritage. The song "Small island" gives an impression of a musical watercolor. The restrained, declamatory vocal melody and the unhurried piano accompaniment create a mood of serene rest, and only at the words "There breezes softly blow" the measured quarter notes in the piano change to quietly "rippling" triolets of eighth notes, as if a breeze has gently touched the waters surrounding the island. In this musical portrait, Rachmaninoff captures the young girl's serene and peaceful character.

According to Tchaikovsky, Afanasy Fet was a poet whose poetry "flowed over into music." Fet was an impressionist of associations, nuances, and fleeting images, which brought him close to the symbolist poets of the 1890's. Rachmaninoff chose his poem "In the silence of the secret night" for his first song, and several times he returned to Fet's lyrics for inspiration. Fet's musical verse is beautifully defined by the composer in the song "How fleeting is delight in love," dedicated to his niece Zoya Pribytkova. It is one of the few songs in which he uses an autumnal imagery when he speaks of the passage of time. Rachmaninoff follows the poet's cadences and emphasizes the nuances of sounds in the poem, when the singer's voice "falls" on the syllables *roZY*, *grioZY* (fallen are the petals of roses, dispersed are the dreams). The mood is autumnal; love and its dreams will soon become only a reminiscence of the past.

Alexei Koltsov is known almost entirely for his stylized renditions of Russian city and folk songs, fresh and unsophisticated. In the song "I was with her" Rachmaninoff underlines the emotional steadfastness of the protagonist—the words "A faithless one I shall never be" are emphasized in both the vocal and piano parts. The song was dedicated to his conservatory friend Yuri Sakhnovsky.

"Summer nights" by Daniil Rathaus was dedicated to Mme. Maria Gutheil, the wife of Rachmaninoff's publisher, Karl Gutheil. Rathaus was a popular Russian poet of the nineteenth century, now almost forgotten but for a few poems set to music by Rachmaninoff and Tchaikovsky (op. 73). It is possible that Rachmaninoff chose the text of "Summer nights" for its almost onomatopoeic quality in expressing the languor of a summer night. The open sound *ya* is repeated throughout the poem both in internal and end rhymes. (This sound is retained in the transcription of the song in this volume; modern Russian versions use the sound *ye* in certain instances, which does not always reproduce the sounds in the original text.) The open vocal melody and the piano accompaniment, here almost a piano etude, emphasize the poetic image of a night under a spacious sky.

Two songs, "You are so loved by all" and "Do not believe me, friend," are set to texts by Count Alexei Tolstoy, a well-known literary figure of the time. The first song is a gentle elegy for voice, with musical intonations following the spoken word and the piano softly accompanying the recitative. It was dedicated to a friend, A. Ivanovsky. The text of the second song was set to music by Tchaikovsky in his vocal cycle op. 6 and by Rimsky-Korsakov in his cycle "By the Sea." Both composers interpret the poem as a gentle assurance to the beloved and capture the poetic mood of the poem with a delicate sensitivity. Rachmaninoff, on the contrary, uses Tolstoy's metaphor of the sea returning to the shore for an ecstatic culmination to his song. The mood of energy and enthusiasm is evident in the last two songs of this cycle, "Spring torrents" and "It is time." "Do not believe me, friend" is dedicated to his cousin Anna Klokacheva, née Pribytkova.

"O, do not grieve," to words by Alexei Apukhtin, was written for Nadezhda Alexandrova, a singer and sister of Anna Lodyzhenskaya. The song is reminiscent of the elegiac and lyrical romances of Tchaikovsky, with a softness of the vocal melody. The elegy is sung by a woman and is one of several of Rachmaninoff's songs that interpret a woman's gift to console and to comfort.

Elizaveta Lavrovskaya, who sang at the Maryinsky Theater, had a deep and sensuous contralto, and it was for her that Rachmaninoff wrote the songs "She is as beautiful as midday" and "In my soul," to the words of Nikolai Minsky. Both songs display the composer's growing assurance in writing for a specific voice range and timbre. The vocal melody of the first song has a slow, unchangeable rhythmic movement, presenting an image of a woman who has not suffered, and contrasted to the image of an artist whose life is "grief and struggle," just as "the weeping sea is in love with the silent shore." "In my soul love rises" gives an expressive contrast of the vocal melody and the long, developing phrase in the piano accompaniment, at first as a distant echo, gradually rising in volume, and culminating in a passionate burst at the end of the second strophe.

One of the most popular songs-romances in Russia is Rachmaninoff's "Spring Torrents," written to the words of the well-known poet Feodor Tyutchev, and dedicated to his first piano teacher, Anna Ornatskaya. The joyful vocal melody and the fast, impetuous passages in the piano accompaniment recreate the sounds of the earth's awakening, the long silence of the Northern winter broken by the sounds of melting snows and spring torrents.

The last song of op. 14, "It is time," to Semyon Nadson's words, without a dedication, expresses Rachmaninoff's hopes for the new twentieth century.

1
ja ʒ'du ţe'b̦ja
Я жду тебя!
I wait (for) you

Date of composition: ***1894.***
Date of publication: ***1896.***
Publisher: ***A. Gutheil, Moscow.***
Dedicated to Ludmila D. Skalon.
Source: ***Maria Davidova.***

ja ʒ'du ţe'b̦ja		za'kɑt	u'gɑs
Я жду тебя!		**Закат**	**угас,**
I wait (for) you		Sunset	died

i	'notʃi	'ţjomnɨje	pa'krovɨ
И	**ночи**	**тёмные**	**покровы**
And	night's	dark	covers

spus'ţitsa	'nɑ	z̦em'l̦ju	ga'tovɨ
Спуститься	**на**	**землю**	**готовы**
Come down	on	earth	(are) ready

i	s'p̦ŗjatɑţ	'nɑs
И	**спрятать**	**нас.**
And	hide	us

Я жду тебя! Закат угас,
И ночи тёмные покровы
Спуститься на землю готовы
И спрятать нас.
Я жду тебя!
Душистой мглой ночь
напоила мир уснувший,
И разлучился день минувший
навек с землёй.
Я жду! Терзаясь и любя,
Считаю каждые мгновенья,
Полна тоски и нетерпенья.
Я жду тебя!

ja ʒ'du ţe'b̧ja
Я жду тебя!
I wait (for) you

du'ʃɨstaĭ mg'loĭ 'noʧ napa'ila 'm̧ir
Душистой мглой ночь напоила мир
(With) fragrant mist night quenched world
us'nufʃɨĭ
уснувший,
asleep,

i razlu'ʧilsa 'ḑeņ m̧i'nufʃɨĭ na'ɣek
И разлучился день минувший навек
And separated day past forever
s‿z̧em'ļjoĭ
с землёй.
with earth

ja ʒ'du ţer'zɑjaş i ļju'b̧ja
Я жду! Терзаясь и любя,
I wait tormented and loving

sʧi'tɑju 'kɑʒdɨje mgno'ɣeņja
Считаю каждые мгновенья,
Counting each moment

pal'nɑ tas'ķi i ņeţer'p̧eņja
Полна тоски и нетерпенья.
Full (of) anguish and impatience

ja ʒ'du ţe'b̧ja
Я жду тебя!
I wait (for) you

I await you! The sunset has died,
And night's dark covers
Are ready to descend
And hide us.
I await you!
The night suffuses the sleeping world with fragrant mist,
And this past day has said farewell to earth.
I am waiting! Tormented and in love
I count each moment,
Full of anguish and impatience
I wait for you!

2
astra'vok
Островок
Small Island

Date of composition: ***1896.***
Date of publication: ***1896.***
Publisher: ***A. Gutheil, Moscow.***
Dedicated to Sophia A. Satina.
Source: ***Konstantin Balmont*** **(translation from Shelley).**

iz	'moŗja	'smoţŗit	astra'vok
Из	**моря**	**смотрит**	**островок,**
From	sea	looks	small island

je'vo	z̧e'ļjonɨje	u'klonɨ
Его	**зелёные**	**уклоны**
Its	green	slopes

u'krɑşil	'trɑf	gu'stɨx	v̧e'nok
Украсил	**трав**	**густых**	**венок,**
Adorned	(of) grasses	thick	wreath

f̧i'ɑlķi	ɑņe'monɨ
Фиалки,	**анемоны.**
Violets	anemones

nɑt	'ņim	sp̧ļe'tɑjutsa	ļis'tɨ
Над	**ним**	**сплетаются**	**листы,**
Over	it	(are) interlaced	leaves

va'kruk	ņe'vo	'ʧuţ	'p̧ļeʃʃut	'volnɨ
Вокруг	**него**	**чуть**	**плещут**	**волны.**
Around	it	barely	splash	waves

Из моря смотрит островок,
Его зелёные уклоны
Украсил трав густых венок,
Фиалки, анемоны.
  Над ним сплетаются листы,
  Вокруг него чуть плещут волны.
  Деревья грустны как мечты,
  Как статуи, безмолвны.
Здесь еле дышит ветерок,
Сюда гроза не долетает,
И безмятежный островок
Всё дремлет, засыпает.

There is a small island out in the sea …
Its green slopes
Are adorned by a wreath of luxuriant grasses,
  Leaves interlace over the island,
  Waves barely splash.
  Trees are as sad as daydreams
  And silent as statues.
There breezes softly blow,
Storms do not come,
And this serene, small island
Sleeps and dreams …

ḑe'ŗeɣja 'grustnɨ 'kak m̧etʃ'tɨ
Деревья грустны как мечты,
Trees sad like dreams

'kak 'stɑtui b̧ez'molvnɨ
Как статуи, безмолвны.
Like statues silent

'zḑeş 'jeļe 'dɨʃɨt ɣeţe'rok
Здесь еле дышит ветерок,
Here just breathes breeze

şju'dɑ gra'zɑ ņe daļe'tɑjet
Сюда гроза не долетает,
Here storm (does) not come

i b̧ezm̧ja'ţeʒnɨĭ astra'vok
И безмятежный островок
And serene small island

'fşjo 'dŗemļet zasɨ'pɑjet
Всё дремлет, засыпает.
Always dreams falls asleep

3
dav'no v ļjub'ɣi
Давно в любви
For a long time in love

Date of composition: ***1896.***
Date of publication: ***1896.***
Publisher: ***A. Gutheil, Moscow.***
Dedicated to Zoya A. Pribytkova.
Source: ***Afanasy Fet.***

dav'no v ļjub'yi at'radɨ 'mala
Давно в любви отрады мало:
For a long time in love delight little

ḅez 'otzɨva vz'doẋi ḅez 'radasţi
Без отзыва вздохи, без радости
Without answer sighs without joy
'sļjozɨ
слёзы;
tears

'ʃto 'bɨla 'slatka 'goŗka 'stala
Что было сладко, горько стало,
What was sweet bitter became

a'sɨpaļiş 'rozɨ ras'şejaļiş 'gŗjozɨ
Осыпались розы, рассеялись грёзы.
Fell (petals) (of) roses dispersed dreams

a'staʃ ɱe'ŋja sɱe'ʃaĭ s tal'poju
Оставь меня, смешай с толпою!
Leave me merge (me) with crowd

'no 'tɨ atyer'nulaş a 'şetujeʃ 'yidna
Но ты отвернулась, а сетуешь видно,
But you turned away but saddened it seems

i 'fşjo e'ʃʃo baļ'na tɨ 'mnoju
И всё ещё больна ты мною.
And still wounded you (by) me

'o 'kak ʒɛ mŋe 'ţjaʒka i 'kak mŋe
О, как же мне тяжко и как мне
Ah how — I am burdened and how I am
a'ḅidna
обидно!
hurt

Давно в любви отрады мало:
Без отзыва вздохи, без радости слёзы;
Что было сладко, горько стало,
Осыпались розы, рассеялись грёзы.
Оставь меня, смешай с толпою!
Но ты отвернулась, а сетуешь видно,
И всё ещё больна ты мною.
О, как же мне тяжко и как мне обидно!

How fleeting is delight in love,
Sighs without answer, tears without joy,
What was sweet has become bitter;
Rose petals fell, dreams were dispersed.
Leave me, let me meld with the crowd!
But you turned away, saddened, it seems,
Still wounded by me.
Ah, how burdened my heart, how painful!

4
ja 'bɨl u 'ņeĭ
Я был у ней
I was with her

Date of composition: ***1896.***
Date of publication: ***1896.***
Publisher: ***A. Gutheil, Moscow.***
Dedicated to Yuri S. Sakhnovsky.
Source: ***Alexei Koltsov.***

ja 'bɨl u 'ņeĭ a'na ska'zala
Я был у ней; она сказала:
I was with her she said

ļjub'ļju ţe'ḃja 'moĭ 'ṃilɨĭ 'druk
"Люблю тебя, мой милый друг!"
Love you my dear friend

'no 'ɛtu 'taĭnu at pa'druk
Но эту тайну от подруг
But this secret from (girl)friends

xra'ņiţ mņe 'stroga zaɣe'ʃʃala
Хранить мне строго завещала.
Keep (to) me strictly bequeathed

ja 'bɨl u 'ņeĭ na 'pŗeļesţ 'zlata
Я был у ней, на прелесть злата
I was with her for lure (of) gold

kļja'laş ṃe'ņja ņe praṃe'ņjaţ
Клялась меня не променять;
Swore me not to exchange

Я был у ней; она сказала:
"Люблю тебя, мой милый друг!"
Но эту тайну от подруг
Хранить мне строго завещала.
Я был у ней, на прелесть злата
Клялась меня не променять;
Ко мне лишь страстию пылать,
Меня любить, любить, как брата.
Я был у ней; я вечно буду
С её душой душою жить
Пускай она мне изменит,
Но я изменником не буду.

ka 'm̧ņe ļiʃ 'strasţiju pɨ'laţ
Ко мне лишь страстию пылать,
For me only (with) passion to burn

m̧e'ņja ļju'b̧iţ ļju'b̧iţ kak 'brata
Меня любить, любить, как брата.
Me to love to love as brother

ja 'bɨl u 'ņeĭ ja 'ɣetʃna 'budu
Я был у ней; я вечно буду
I was with her I eternally will

ş je'jo du'ʃoĭ du'ʃoju ʒɨţ
С её душой душою жить
With her soul (with my) soul to live

pus'kaĭ a'na m'ņe izm̧e'ņit
Пускай она мне изменит,
Even if she (to) me unfaithful

'no 'ja iz'm̧enņikam ņe 'budu
Но я изменником не буду.
But I traitor will not be

I was with her; she said:
"I love you, my dear friend!"
But asked to keep her secret,
To keep it as a sacred trust.
I was with her; she swore
Never to trade our love for lure of gold,
To love me with a burning passion,
To love me as a brother.
I was with her; I will eternally
Live as one with her soul,
Though she be faithless,
A faithless one I shall never be.

5
'ɛţi 'ļetņija 'notʃi
Эти летния ночи
These summer nights

Date of composition: ***1896.***
Date of publication: ***1896.***
Publisher: ***A. Gutheil, Moscow.***
Dedicated to Maria I. Gutheil.
Source: ***Daniïl Rathaus.***

'ɛţi 'ļetņija 'noʧi pŗe'krɑsnɨja
Эти летния ночи прекрасныя,
These summer nights beautiful

'jarķim 'sɣetam lu'nɨ aza'ŗjonnɨja
Ярким светом луны озарённыя,
(With) bright light (of) moon lit

para'ʒdɑjut tŗe'voģi ņe'jasnɨja
Порождают тревоги неясныя,
Give rise (to) anxieties vague

prabu'ʒdɑjut pa'rɨvɨ vļju'bļjonnɨje
Пробуждают порывы влюблённые.
Awaken gusts loving

zabɨ'vɑjetsa 'skorb̦ ņeab̦'jatnaja
Забывается скорбь необьятная,
Forgotten (is) sorrow immense

'ʃto da'rujetsa 'ʒɨzņju u'nɨlaju
Что даруется жизнью унылою,
Which is given (by) life desolate

i bla'ʒɛnstva kra'ja blaga'dɑtnɨje
И блаженства края благодатные
And (of) bliss lands full of grace

raskrɨ'vɑjutsa 'tɑĭnaju 'şilaju
Раскрываются тайною силою …
(Are) revealed (by) mysterious force

i at'krɨļi druk 'drugu ņe'vlastnɨje
И открыли друг другу невластные
And opened (to) each other powerless

Эти летния ночи прекрасныя,
Ярким светом луны озарённыя,
Порождают тревоги неясныя,
Пробуждают порывы влюблённые.
Забывается скорбь необьятная,
Что даруется жизнью унылою,
И блаженства края благодатные
Раскрываются тайною силою …
И открыли друг другу невластные
Над собою сердца мы влюблённые,
В эти летния ночи прекрасныя,
Светом ярким луны озарённыя.

Beautiful summer nights,
Resplendent in the light of the moon,
Evoke vague anxieties,
Awaken longings of love.
The immense sorrow
Of our desolate lives is forgotten,
And the graceful realms of happiness
Are revealed to us mysteriously.
We opened our hearts to each other,
Helplessly in love,
On that beautiful night in the summer,
In the light of the moon resplendent.

nat sa'boju şer'tsa mɨ vʎju'bʎjonnɨje
Над собою сердца мы влюблённые,
Over ourselves hearts we in love

v 'ɛţi 'ʎetnija 'noʧi pŗe'krɑsnɨja
В эти летния ночи прекрасныя,
In these summer nights beautiful

'sɣetam 'jarķim lu'nɨ aza'ŗjonnɨja
Светом ярким луны озарённыя.
(With) light bright (of) moon lit

6
ţe'ɓja tak 'ʎjuɓjat 'fşe
Тебя так любят все
You so loved (by) all

Date of composition: ***1896.***
Date of publication: ***1896.***
Publisher: ***A. Gutheil, Moscow.***
Dedicated to A. I. Ivanovsky
Source: ***Alexei Tolstoy.***

ţe'ɓja tak 'ʎjuɓjat 'fşe a'ɖin 'tvoĭ 'ţiχiĭ 'ɣit
Тебя так любят все; один твой тихий вид
You so loved (by) all alone your quiet appearance

'fşex 'ɖelajet da'bŗeĭ i s 'ʒɨzɲiju ɱi'ŗit
Всех делает добрей и с жизнию мирит,
All makes kinder and with life reconciles

'no 'tɨ ɡrust'nɑ f ţe'ɓe 'jesţ 'skrɨtaje mu'ʧeɲje
Но ты грустна, в тебе есть скрытое мученье,
But you are sad in you is hidden torment

v du'ʃɛ tva'jeĭ zvu'ʧit ka'koĭ ta
В душе твоей звучит какой-то
In soul your resounds some
pŗiga'vor
приговор;
condemnation

za'ʧem 'tvoĭ 'lɑskavɨĭ fşeg'dɑ tak 'robak
Зачем твой ласковый всегда так робок
Why your tender always so timid
'vzor
взор,
gaze

i 'oʧi 'grustnɨje tak 'moḽat a
И очи грустные так молят о
And eyes sad so beg for
pra'ʃʃeŋji
прощеньи,
forgiveness

kɑk 'butta 'sontsa 'sʏet i 'ʏeʃŋije tsʏe'tɨ
Как будто солнца свет и вешние цветы
As if sun's light and spring flowers

i 'ţeŋ f pal'dŋevnɨĭ 'znoĭ i 'ʃopot
И тень в полдневный зной, и шёпот
And shade in midday heat and whisper
pa du'brɑvam
по дубравам,
in woods

Тебя так любят все; один твой тихий вид
Всех делает добрей и с жизнию мирит,
Но ты грустна, в тебе есть скрытое мученье,
В душе твоей звучит какой-то приговор;
Зачем твой ласковый всегда так робок взор,
И очи грустные так молят о прощеньи,
Как будто солнца свет и вешние цветы
И тень в полдневный зной, и шёпот по дубравам,
И даже воздух тот, которым дышишь ты,
Всё кажется тебе стяжанием неправым?

You are so loved by all; your quiet look
Warms everyone and reconciles with life;
But you are sad, in you there is a hidden torment,
And in your soul you hear a condemnation;
Why is your tender gaze so timid,
Your eyes so sad and beg forgiveness,
As if the light of sun and flowers in the spring,
And shade in midday heat and whispering woods,
And even the very air you breathe
All seem to you an undeserved gift?

i	'dɑʒɛ	'vozdux	'tot	ka'torɨm	'dɨʃɨʃ
И	**даже**	**воздух**	**тот,**	**которым**	**дышишь**
And	even	air	that	which	breathe
tɨ					
ты,					
you					

'fşjo	'kɑʒɛtsa	ţe'b̦e	sţja'ʒɑņijem
Всё	**кажется**	**тебе**	**стяжанием**
All	seems	(to) you	(an) acquiring
ņe'prɑvɨm			
неправым?			
undeserved			

7
ņe 'ɣeŗ mņe 'druk
Не верь мне, друг
(Do) not believe me friend

Date of composition: ***1896.***
Date of publication: ***1896.***
Publisher: ***A. Gutheil, Moscow.***
Dedicated to Anna G. Klokacheva.
Source: ***Alexei Tolstoy.***

ņe	'ɣeŗ	mņe	'druk	kag'dɑ	v
Не	**верь**	**мне,**	**друг,**	**когда**	**в**
(Do) not	believe	me	friend	when	in
iz'bɨtķe	'goŗja				
избытке	**горя,**				
overflowing	(of) grief				

ja	gava'ŗju	'ʃto	razļju'b̦il	ţe'b̦ja
Я	**говорю**	**что**	**разлюбил**	**тебя!**
I	say	that	ceased loving	you

v at'ļiva 'ʧɑs ɲe 'ɣeɽ iz'ɱeɲe
В отлива час не верь измене
In ebb-tide hour (do) not believe faithlessness
'moɽja
моря:
(of) sea

a'no k ʐem'ļe va'roţitsa ļu'ɓja
Оно к земле воротится, любя.
It to earth returns loving

uʃ 'ja tas'kuju 'preʒɲeĭ 'strasţi
Уж я тоскую, прежней страсти
Already I anxious (of) former passion
'polnɨĭ
полный,
full

ma'ju sva'bodu v'noʃ ţe'ɓe at'dɑm
Мою свободу вновь тебе отдам
My freedom again (to) you will give

i uʒ ɓe'gut s ab'rɑtnɨm 'ʃumam
И уж бегут с обратным шумом
And already run with return sound
'volnɨ
волны
waves

izdaļe'kɑ k ļu'ɓimɨm ɓeɽe'gɑm
Издалека к любимым берегам.
From afar to beloved shores

Не верь мне, друг, когда в избытке горя,
Я говорю что разлюбил тебя!
В отлива час не верь измене моря:
Оно к земле воротится, любя.
Уж я тоскую, прежней страсти полный,
Мою свободу вновь тебе отдам
И уж бегут с обратным шумом волны
Издалека к любимым берегам.

Do not believe me, friend, when overwhelmed by grief
I say I do not love you anymore!
In ebb tide do not think the sea capricious:
It will return to earth, with love.
And even now—impatient, with former passion filled,
My freedom I will give to you again—
As waves rush back with a returning murmur
From far away to their beloved shore.

8
'o ŋ̧e grus'ţi
О, не грусти
Oh not be sad

Date of composition: ***1896.***
Date of publication: ***1896.***
Publisher: ***A. Gutheil, Moscow.***
Dedicated to Nadezhda A. Alexandrova.
Source: ***Alexei Apukhtin.***

'o ŋ̧e grus'ţi pa 'mŋ̧e ja 'tɑm
О, не грусти по мне! Я там,
Oh (do) not be sad for me I (am) there
gḑe 'ŋ̧et stra'dɑŋ̧iĭ
где нет страданий.
where no suffering

za'buţ bɨ'lɨx skar'b̧ei mu'ʧiţeļnɨe
Забудь былых скорбей мучительные
Forget (of) former grief tormenting
'snɨ
сны.
dreams

'pusţ 'budut aba 'mŋ̧e
Пусть будут обо мне
Let be about me
tva'i vaspaŋ̧i'nɑŋ̧ja
твои воспоминанья
your remembrance

v̧et'ļei 'ʧem 'p̧ervɨĭ 'ḑeŋ̧ v̧es'nɨ
Светлей, чем первый день весны.
Brighter than first day (of) spring

О, не грусти по мне!
Я там, где нет страданий.
Забудь былых скорбей
мучительные сны.
Пусть будут обо мне твои
воспоминанья
Светлей, чем первый день
весны.
О, не тоскуй по мне!
Меж нами нет разлуки,
Я так-же, как и встарь, душе
твоей близка.
Меня по-прежнему твои
волнуют муки,
Меня гнетёт твоя тоска.
Живи! ты должен жить!
И если силой чуда
Ты здесь найдёшь отраду и
покой,
То знай, что это я
Откликнулась оттуда
На зов души твоей больной.

'o ņe tas'kuĭ pa 'mņe
О, не тоскуй по мне!
Oh (do) not grieve for me

m̧eʒ 'nɑm̧i ņet raz'luķi
Меж нами нет разлуки,
Betwixt us no separation

ja 'tɑk-ʒɛ kak i 'fstɑŗ du'ʃɛ tva'jei
Я так-же, как и встарь, душе твоей
I the same as — of old (to) soul your
b̧ļis'kɑ
близка.
(am) close

m̧e'ņja pa'pŗeʒņemu tva'i val'nujut 'muķi
Меня по-прежнему твои волнуют муки,
Me as before your move torments

m̧e'ņja gņe'ţjot tva'ja tas'kɑ
Меня гнетёт твоя тоска.
Me burdens your anguish

ʒi'ɣi tɨ 'dolʒɛn ʒɨţ
Живи! ты должен жить!
Live you must live

i 'jesļi 'şilaĭ 'ʧuda
И если силой чуда
And if (by) force (of) miracle

tɨ 'zḑeş naĭ'ḑjoʃ at'rɑdu i pa'koĭ
Ты здесь найдёшь отраду и покой,
You here find comfort and peace

Oh, do not grieve for me! There is no suffering here.
Forget the dreams and torments of sorrows past,
Let your remembrances of me
Be brighter than spring's first day.
Oh, do not grieve for me!
Betwixt us there is no separation,
For as of old, I am close to your soul,
I am still moved by your torments
And feel your anguish.
Live! You must live!
And if, with heaven's intercession,
You find joy and peace,
Then you will know, that it is I
Who answered from there the cry
Of your wounded soul.

to 'znaĭ ʃto 'ɛta ja
То знай, что это я
Then know that it (is) I

at'kl̦iknulaş at'tuda
Откликнулась оттуда
Answered from there

na 'zov du'ʃi tva'jei bal̦'noĭ
На зов души твоей больной.
To call (of) soul your wounded

9

a'na kak 'polḑeņ xara'ʃa
Она, как полдень, хороша
She like midday beautiful

Date of composition: ***1896.***
Date of publication: ***1896.***
Publisher: ***A. Gutheil, Moscow.***
Dedicated to Elizaveta A. Lavrovskaya.
Source: ***Nikolai Minsky.***

Она, как полдень, хороша,
Она загадочней полночи.
У ней не плакавшие очи
И не страдавшая душа.
А мне, чья жизнь борьба и горе,
По ней томиться суждено.
О! Так вечно плачущее море
В безмолвный берег влюблено.

a'na kak 'polḑeņ xara'ʃa
Она, как полдень, хороша,
She like midday (is) beautiful

a'na za'gadaʧņeĭ pal'noʧi
Она загадочней полночи.
She more mysterious (than) midnight

u 'ņeĭ ņe 'plakafʃɨje 'oʧi
У ней не плакавшие очи
She has not wept eyes

i ɲe stra'dɑfʃaja du'ʃɑ
И не страдавшая душа.
And not suffered soul

ɑ 'mɲe ʧ'ja 'ʒɨzɲ baŗ'bɑ i
А мне, чья жизнь борьба и
And (to) me whose life struggle and
'goŗe
горе,
grief

pa 'ɲeĭ ta'ɱiţsa suʒḑe'no
По ней томиться суждено.
For her to pine is fated

'o tak 'ɣeʧna 'plɑʧuʃʃeje 'moŗe
О! Так вечно плачущее море
O thus eternally weeping sea

v b̦ez'molvnɨĭ 'b̦eŗek vļjub̦ļe'no
В безмолвный берег влюблено.
In silent shore is in love

She is as beautiful as midday,
And more mysterious than midnight.
Her eyes have not wept,
Her soul has not suffered.
And I, whose life is grief and struggle,
Am fated to yearn for her.
O! Thus the eternally weeping sea
Is in love with the silent shore.

10
v ma'jeĭ du'ʃɛ
В моей душе
In my soul

Date of composition: ***1896.***
Date of publication: ***1896.***
Publisher: ***A. Gutheil, Moscow.***
Dedicated to Elizaveta A. Lavrovskaya.
Source: ***Nikolai Minsky.***

v maˈjeĭ duˈʃɛ l̡juˈbof̡ vasˈxod̡it
В моей душе любовь восходит,
In my soul love rises

kak ˈsontsɛ v ˈblesk̡e krasaˈtɨ
Как солнце в блеске красоты,
As sun in brilliance (of) beauty

i ˈp̡esn̡i ˈstroĭnɨje raʒˈdɑjet
И песни стройные рождает,
And songs melodious gives birth (to)

kak araˈmɑtnɨje tsʏeˈtɨ
Как ароматные цветы.
As fragrant flowers

v maˈjeĭ duˈʃɛ ˈtvoĭ ˈvzor xaˈlodnɨĭ
В моей душе твой взор холодный
In my soul your gaze cold

ˈto ˈsontsɛ ˈznoĭnaje zɑˈʒok
То солнце знойное зажёг.
That sun passionate lit up

ˈɑx ˈjesl̡i͡ p ja t̡em ˈznoĭnɨm
Ах, если б я тем знойным
O if I (with) that passionate
ˈsontsɛm
солнцем
sun

zɑˈʒɛʧ ˈtvoĭ vzor xaˈlodnɨĭ mok
Зажечь твой взор холодный мог.
Light up your gaze cold could

В моей душе любовь
восходит,
Как солнце в блеске красоты,
И песни стройные рождает,
Как ароматные цветы.
В моей душе твой взор
холодный
То солнце знойное зажёг.
Ах, если б я тем знойным
солнцем
Зажечь твой взор холодный
мог.

In my soul love rises
Like the sun in its brilliant beauty,
And gives birth to melodious
songs
As the sun brings forth fragrant
flowers.
In my soul your cold gaze
Set afire this passionate sun.
O! If I could with that
passionate sun
Your cold gaze set afire!

11
y̧e'şenņije 'vodɨ
Весенние воды
Spring torrents

Date of composition: ***1896.***
Date of publication: ***1896.***
Publisher: ***A. Gutheil, Moscow.***
Dedicated to Anna D. Ornatskaya.
Source: ***Feodor Tyutchev.***

i'ʃʃo f pa'ļjax b̧e'ļejet 'sņek
Ещё в полях белеет снег,
Still in fields whitens snow

ɑ 'vodɨ uʒ y̧es'noĭ ʃu'm̧jat
А воды уж весной шумят,
And torrents already (with) spring resound

b̧e'gut i 'b̧uḑjat 'sonnɨĭ 'b̧ŗek
Бегут и будят сонный брег,
Run and awaken sleeping shore

b̧e'gut i 'b̧ļeʃʃut i gla'şjat
Бегут и блещут, и гласят,
Run and sparkle and proclaim

ą'ņi gla'şjat va 'fşe kan'tsɨ
Они гласят во все концы:
They proclaim to all ends

y̧es'nɑ i'ḑjot y̧es'nɑ i'ḑjot
"Весна идёт, весна идёт,
Spring comes spring comes

Ещё в полях белеет снег,
А воды уж весной шумят,
Бегут и будят сонный брег,
Бегут и блещут, и гласят,
Они гласят во все концы:
"Весна идёт, весна идёт,
Мы молодой весны гонцы,
Она нас выслала вперёд.
Весна идёт, весна идёт!"
И тихих, тёплых майских дней
Румяный, светлый хоровод
Толпится весело за ней.

mɨ mala'doĭ ɣes'nɨ gan'tsɨ
Мы молодой весны гонцы,
We (of) young spring messengers

a'nɑ nas 'vɨslala fp̡e'r̡jot
Она нас выслала вперёд.
She us sent ahead

ɣes'nɑ i'd̡jot ɣes'nɑ i'd̡jot
Весна идёт, весна идёт!"
Spring comes spring comes

i 't̡ix̡ix 't̡joplɨx 'mɑĭsk̡ix 'dn̡eĭ
И тихих, тёплых майских дней
And (of) gentle, warm May days

ru'm̡janɨĭ 'sɣetlɨĭ xara'vot
Румяный, светлый хоровод
Rosy bright round dance

tal'p̡itsa 'ɣeş̡ela za 'n̡eĭ
Толпится весело за ней.
Crowds joyfully behind her

In the fields snow still lies,
But torrents resound with the joy of spring,
They surge and awaken the sleeping shore,
Flowing, sparkling, proclaiming,
Proclaiming to all ends of the earth:
"Spring comes, spring comes,
We are heralds of spring,
We are sent forth to say:
Spring comes, spring comes!"
And the quiet, warm days of May
In a rosy, bright round dance,
Crowd joyfully in spring's steps.

12
pa'rɑ
Пора!
(It is) time

Date of composition: ***1896.***
Date of publication: ***1896.***
Publisher: ***A. Gutheil, Moscow.***
Source: ***Semyon Nadson.***

pa'rɑ ja'ɣiş pra'rok 'fşeĭ 'şilaju
Пора! Явись пророк! Всей силою
(It is) time Appear prophet (With) all force
ţe'ʧɑļi
печали,
(of) sorrow

'fşeĭ 'şilaju ļjub'ɣi vzɨ'vɑju ja k ţe'ƀe
Всей силою любви взываю я к тебе!
(With) all force (of) love call I to you

vzgļja'ŋi kak 'dŗjaxlɨ mɨ vzgļja'ŋi kak
Взгляни, как дряхлы мы, взгляни, как
Look how feeble we (are) look how
mɨ us'tɑļi
мы устали,
we tired

kak mɨ ƀes'pomaʃʃnɨ v mu'ʧiţeļnaĭ
Как мы беспомощны в мучительной
How we helpless in tormenting
baŗ'ƀe
борьбе!
struggle

ţe'peŗ iļ ŋikag'dɑ sa'znɑŋje
Теперь, иль никогда! Сознанье
Now or never Consciousness
uɱi'rɑjet
умирает,
is dying

Пора! Явись пророк! Всей силою печали,
Всей силою любви взываю я к тебе!
Взгляни, как дряхлы мы, взгляни, как мы устали,
Как мы беспомощны в мучительной борьбе!
Теперь, иль никогда! Сознанье умирает,
Стыд гаснет, совесть спит, ни проблеска кругом,
Одно ничтожество свой голос возвышает.

It is time! Come forth, O prophet! In sorrow
And with love I call out to you!
See how we are feeble, how we are tired,
How we are helpless in tormenting struggles.
Now or never! Thoughts are dying,
Shame dies, conscience sleeps, no ray of hope for us,
And only the unworthy raise their voice.

'stɨt 'gɑsn̦et 'soɣesț 'sp̦it n̦i
Стыд гаснет, совесть спит, ни
Shame dies conscience sleeps no
'probl̦eska kru'gom
проблеска кругом,
ray (of hope) around

ad'no n̦i'ʧtoʒɛstva 'svoĭ 'golas vaz'vɨʃɑet
Одно ничтожество свой голос возвышает.
Alone worthlessness its voice raises

IV. Songs of Opus 21

1. **Судьба (Fate)**
2. **Над свежей могилой (By a fresh grave)**
3. **Сумерки (Twilight)**
4. **Оне отвечали (They replied)**
5. **Сирень (Lilacs)**
6. **Отрывок из А. Мюссе (Fragment from A. Musset)**
7. **Здесь хорошо (How peaceful)**
8. **На смерть чижика (On the death of a siskin)**
9. **Мелодия (Melody)**
10. **Пред иконой (Before the icon)**
11. **Я не пророк (I am not a prophet)**
12. **Как мне больно (How pained I am)**

Rachmaninoff's First Symphony was performed in St. Petersburg in March 1897 and was judged a failure by such eminent critics as Vladimir Stasov and César Cui, who accused the twenty-four-year-old composer of incoherence, modernist tendencies, and musical decadence. Only the musicologist Nikolai Findeisen wrote of Rachmaninoff's desire to seek new themes and images and considered the symphony as having much that was beautiful and inspiring.[3] Rachmaninoff suffered deeply from the failure of his major work and did not return to composition for three years.

In September 1897, Rachmaninoff became conductor for Mamontov's Russian Opera, where he widened his creative and personal ties, which until then had been mostly from the academic milieu of the Moscow Conservatory. He entered the world of Russia's foremost artists, who often gathered on country estates near Moscow and held lengthy conversations "at the table" on aesthetics and philosophy, the poetics of nature and their representation in art and in music. Here he became lifelong friends with Feodor Chaliapin, whom he accompanied on the piano while the singer worked on operatic roles and for whom he composed the first song of op. 21, "Fate," suggested by the theme of destiny in Beethoven's Fifth Symphony. It is possible that Chaliapin, a consummate singer and actor, performed the ballad quite effectively, but the song, set to a melodramatic text by Apukhtin, is ponderous and full of theatrical pathos.

In the summer of 1901 Rachmaninoff stayed at Ivanovka to work on his Second Piano Concerto with Alexander Ziloti. After experiencing an artistic and personal crisis, he returned to composition with a maturity of musical expression, reworking the lyrical and epic idiom of his national melos to reflect and interpret his world view.

The other eleven songs of op. 21, written in the spring of 1902 at Ivanovka, have a thematic similarity to Tchaikovsky's last songs, in which the thoughts of loneliness and death are expressed as an inseparable part of life and are conveyed with an emotional and spiritual understanding achieved through suffering. The songs "By a fresh grave," "Fragment from A. Musset," and "How pained I am" combine a depth of dramatic expression with an economy of musical means, with each detail justified to create eloquent songs on loneliness and sorrow. "Melody," "On the death of a siskin," and "Before the icon" speak of separation and death in a contemplative, philosophic mood. In "Melody" Rachmaninoff surrounds the poet's voice (the text is by Semyon Nadson, who died at the age of twenty-five) with the sounds of nature the poet wants to hear at the hour of his death—"the flowering lilacs gently stirring and the brook's mysterious murmur"—and as the poet's song ends the melody in the piano continues singing as a reflective postlude. In Vasily Zhukovsky's whimsical poem on love and death "Death of a siskin," Rachmaninoff changes several words but keeps the cadences and purity of the poet's verse. The song has the melodiousness of romances written during Zhukovsky's lifetime, and the piano accompaniment resembles the light sounds of a clavichord. "Before the icon" is a contemplative song that reveals a warmth of feeling in a serene religious setting. The songs "They replied" and "I am not a prophet" emphasize the composer's belief that loneliness and grief can be consoled by love and work and that the poet's and singer's gift is to interpret life and "to speak to hearts through a song, waking in them the spark of God."

Into these philosophic meditations Rachmaninoff brings his miraculous gift of song in "Twilight," "Lilacs," and "How peaceful." He sets to music simple texts by little-known authors—Jean-Marie Guyot, Ekaterina Beketova, and Glafira Galina—and reconceives the brief poems as spacious and complex images of nature. In "Twilight" he is truly a "singer of nature's quiet" in the words of the musicologist and composer Boris Asafiev,[4] realizing in sound the stillness of twilight and the appearance of stars in a darkening sky. In "Lilacs" and "How peaceful" Rachmaninoff uses a Russian folk idiom to create two masterpieces of European classical music. The exquisite miniature "Lilacs" has a freshness and a subtle *dushevnost* (heartfelt sincerity) of expression that grows out of the variations on the opening intonation, characteristic of Russian folk melodies. Because of its simplicity the intonation easily adapts itself now in a joyfully "spoken" vocal part, now permeating the streaming accompaniment. In the last measures of the song, as the diapason of the intonation widens, the joyful melody is touched by a hint of sadness as the subtle, elusive quality of the song reflects the search for an elusive happiness. In the song "How peaceful" Rachmaninoff uses the melodic development of Russian *protyazhnye* (slowly sung) folk songs in which images of nature portray the spiritual and emotional state of the singer. The vocal part in Rachmaninoff's song presents the opening motif in a high register, as a wide musical "gesture" showing the beauty of nature to an unseen listener—"How peaceful ... Look there, in the distance ..." The development of the melody from the one intonation and the lack of contrasting elements give the music a feeling of tranquility and rest. After the last measures of the song, "Here is only God—and I ... and you, my dream ..." the melody lingers in the piano as if to capture or at least prolong a beautiful moment. "In these songs," writes the musicologist Vasina-Grossman, "the melody grows from an intonation which is subdued, plain, unadorned—the initial image is simple, as the impression which brought it to life. But then the melody reveals itself in its unexpected beauty, as if realizing in music all the wealth of feelings, thoughts, reminiscences, which rise in our souls from a glance at familiar scenes of nature, onto simple spring flowers."[5]

1
suḑ'ba
Судьба
Fate

Date of composition: ***1900.***
Date of publication: ***1900/1902.***
Publisher: ***A. Gutheil, Moscow.***
Dedicated to Feodor I. Chaliapin.
Source: ***Alexei Apukhtin.***

s͡ sva'jeĭ pa'xodnaju kļju'koĭ
С своей походною клюкой,
With its marching crutch

s͡ sva'im̧i 'mrɑʧnɨm̧i a'ʧɑm̧i
С своими мрачными очами
With its somber eyes

suḑ'bɑ kak 'groznɨĭ ʧasa'voĭ
Судьба, как грозный часовой,
Fate like stern sentry

paf'şjudu 'sļedujet zɑ 'nɑm̧i
Повсюду следует за нами.
Everywhere follows behind us

b̧e'doĭ ļi'tso je'jo gra'z̧it
Бедой лицо её грозит,
(With) misfortune face hers threatens

a'nɑ v͡ u'grozax paşe'ḑela
Она в угрозах поседела,
She in threats become gray

С своей походною клюкой,
С своими мрачными очами
Судьба, как грозный часовой,
Повсюду следует за нами.

Бедой лицо её грозит,
Она в угрозах поседела,
Она уж многих одолела,
И всё стучит, и всё стучит:
Стук, стук, стук …
Полно, друг,
Брось за счастием гоняться!
Стук, стук, стук …

Бедняк совсем обжился с ней:
Рука с рукой они гуляют,
Сбирают вместе хлеб с полей,
В награду вместе голодают.
День целый дождь его кропит,
По вечерам ласкает вьюга,
А ночью с горя, да с испуга
Судьба сквозь сон ему стучит:
Стук, стук, стук …
Глянька, друг,
Как другие поживают.
Стук, стук, стук …

a'nɑ uʃ 'mnoɡix ada'ɭela
Она уж многих одолела,
She already many has overcome

i 'fşjo stu'ʧit i 'fşjo
И всё стучит, и всё
And continually knocks and continually
stu'ʧit
стучит:
knocks

'stuk 'stuk 'stuk
Стук, стук, стук …
Tap tap tap

'polna 'druk
Полно, друг,
Enough friend

'broş za 'ʃʃɑsţijem ɡa'ŋjatsa
Брось за счастием гоняться!
Give up after happiness pursuing

'stuk 'stuk 'stuk
Стук, стук, стук …
Tap tap tap

ɓed'ŋjak saf'şem ab'ʒiļşa s 'ŋeĭ
Бедняк совсем обжился с ней:
Poor man quite at home with her

ru'kɑ s ru'koĭ a'ŋi ɡu'ɭjajut
Рука с рукой они гуляют,
Hand in hand they walk

Другие праздновать сошлись
Богатство, молодость и славу,
Их песни радостно неслись,
Вино сменилось им в забаву:
Давно уж пир у них шумит.
Но смолкли вдруг бледнея
гости …
Рукой дрожащею от злости,
Судьба в окошко к ним
стучит:
Стук, стук, стук …
Новый друг
К вам пришел, готовьте
место!
Стук, стук, стук …

Но есть же счастье на земле!
Однажды, полный ожиданья,
С восторгом юным на челе,
Пришёл счастливец на
свиданье.
Ещё один он. Всё молчит,
Заря за рощей потухает,
И соловей уж затихает
А сердце бьётся и стучит:
Стук, стук, стук …
Милый друг,
Ты придёшь ли на свиданье?
Стук, стук, стук …
Но вот идёт она,
И в миг любовь, тревога,
ожиданье,
Блаженство, всё слилось у них
В одно безумное лобзанье!

sb̦i'rɑjut 'vm̦esţe 'xļep s pa'ļeĭ
Сбирают вместе хлеб с полей,
Gather together bread from fields

v na'grɑdu 'vmesţe gala'dɑjut
В награду вместе голодают.
As reward together hunger

'ḑeņ 'tşɛlɨĭ 'doʃţ je'vo kra'p̦it
День целый дождь его кропит,
Day whole rain him sprinkles

pa ɣeʧe'rɑm lɑs'kɑjet ɣ'juga
По вечерам ласкает вьюга,
In evenings caresses snowstorm

ɑ 'noʧju c 'goŗja dɑ s‿is'puga
А ночью с горя, да с испуга
And (at) night from grief, and from fear

suḑ'bɑ sk'voş 'son i'mu stu'ʧit
Судьба сквозь сон ему стучит:
Fate in dream (to) him knocks

'stuk 'stuk 'stuk
Стук, стук, стук …
Tap tap tap

'gļjaņka 'druk
Глянька, друг,
Look friend

kak dru'g̦ije paʒɨ'vɑjut
Как другие поживают.
How others live

Немая ночь на них глядит,
Всё небо залито огнями.
А кто-то тихо за кустами
Клюкой докучною стучит:
Старый друг
К вам пришёл
Довольно счастья!
Стук, стук, стук …

With her walking crutch
And somber eyes
Fate, like a stern watchman,
Follows us.

Her face forebodes misfortune,
She has grown old in threats,
Prevailing over many.
And she continually knocks,
continually knocks:
Tap, tap, tap …
Enough, my friend,
Give up pursuing happiness!
Tap, tap, tap …

A poor man knows her well,
For hand in hand they walk,
They harvest fields together,
As a reward, they hunger both.
Rain soaks him in the day,
And evenings, blowing snow
caresses him,
And in his grief and fear, at night
he hears
Fate knocking in his sleep:
Tap, tap, tap …
Look, my friend,
How others live!
Tap, tap, tap …

'stuk 'stuk 'stuk
Стук, стук, стук …
Tap tap tap

dru'ģije 'praznavaţ sa'ʃļiş
Другие праздновать сошлись
Others to celebrate came together

ba'gatstva 'moladaşţ i 'slavu
Богатство, молодость и славу,
Riches youth and fame

ix 'ņesņi 'radastna ņes'ļiş
Их песни радостно неслись,
Their songs joyfully resounded

ỵi'no sm̧e'ņilaş im v za'bavu
Вино сменилось им в забаву:
Wine became (to) them a pastime

dav'no uʃ 'ņir u 'ņix ʃu'm̧it
Давно уж пир у них шумит.
For a long time already feast theirs resounds

'no 'smolkļi v'druk bļed'ņeja
Но смолкли вдруг бледнея
But (are) silent suddenly becoming pale
'gosţi
гости …
guests

ru'koĭ dra'ʒaʃʃeju at 'zlosţi
Рукой дрожащею от злости,
(With) hand trembling from fury

They celebrate their
Riches, youth and fame.
Their songs resound,
And wine flows freely.
Their feast proceeds in merriment,
But suddenly, the guests grow pale …
With a trembling hand,
Fate spitefully knocks at their window:
Tap, tap, tap …
A new friend
Came to your feast, prepare a place for her!
Tap, tap, tap …

But there is happiness on earth!
Once, full of expectation,
In youthful rapture,
A lover came to meet his beloved.
He is still alone. All is silent.
The sunset dims beyond the woods,
The nightingale grows silent,
His heart pounds and beats
Tap, tap, tap …
Dear friend,
Will you come to be with me?
Tap, tap, tap …
She is coming …
And all at once—love, anxiety, expectation,
Bliss—all flowed together
Into one mad embrace.

Mute night watches them,
The sky is filled with fiery lights,
And someone quietly, back of the bushes,
Knocks with her persistent crutch:
An old friend
Came to see you,
Enough of happiness!
Tap, tap, tap …

suḑ'bɑ v a'koʃka k 'ņim stu'ʧit
Судьба в окошко к ним стучит:
Fate on window to them knocks

'stuk 'stuk 'stuk
Стук, стук, стук …
Tap tap tap

'novɨĭ 'druk
Новый друг
New friend

k 'vɑm pŗi'ʃol gɑ'toţţe 'm̡esta
К вам пришел, готовьте место!
To you came prepare place

'stuk 'stuk 'stuk
Стук, стук, стук …
Tap tap tap

no 'jesţ ʒɛ 'ʃʃasţje nɑ z̡em'ļe
Но есть же счастье на земле!
But there is — happiness on earth

ad'nɑʒdɨ 'polnɨĭ aʒɨ'dɑņja
Однажды, полный ожиданья,
Once full (of) expectation

s va'storgam 'junɨm nɑ ʧe'ļe
С восторгом юным на челе,
With rapture youthful on brow

pŗi'ʃol ʃʃɑs'ļiyets nɑ syi'dɑņje
Пришёл счастливец на свиданье.
Came fortunate (one) to rendezvous

je'ʃʃo a'ḑin 'on 'fşjo mal'ʧit
Ещё один он. Всё молчит,
Still alone he (is) Everything silent

za'ŗja za 'roʃʃeĭ patu'xɑjet
Заря за рощей потухает,
Sunset beyond woods dimming

i sala'ɣeĭ uʒ zaţi'xɑjet
И соловей уж затихает
And nightingale already quieting (down)

ɑ 'şertsɛ 'ḇjotsa i stu'ʧit
А сердце бьётся и стучит:
And heart beats and pounds

'stuk 'stuk 'stuk
Стук, стук, стук …
Tap tap tap

'ɱiliĭ 'druk
Милый друг,
Dear friend

tɨ pŗi'ḑjoʃ ļi nɑ sɣi'dɑņje
Ты придёшь ли на свиданье?
You will come — to rendezvous

'stuk 'stuk 'stuk
Стук, стук, стук …
Tap tap tap

no 'vot i'ḑjot a'nɑ
Но вот идёт она,
But here comes she

i v 'm̧ik ļju'bof̧ ţe'voga aʒɨ'daņje
И в миг любовь, тревога, ожиданье,
And in moment love anxiety expectation

bla'ʒɛnstva 'f̧sjo sļi'loş u 'ņix
Блаженство, всё слилось у них
Bliss all merged with them

v ad'no b̧ez'umnaje lab'zaņje
В одно безумное лобзанье!
In one insane kiss

ņe'maja 'notʃ na 'ņix gļja'ḑit
Немая ночь на них глядит,
Mute night at them looks

'f̧sjo 'ņeba 'zaļita ag'ņjam̧i
Всё небо залито огнями.
All sky covered (with) lights

a 'kto-ta 'ţixa za kus'tam̧i
А кто-то тихо за кустами
And someone quietly behind bushes

kļju'koĭ da'kutʃnaju stu'tʃit
Клюкой докучною стучит:
(With) crutch persistent knocks

'starɨĭ 'druk
Старый друг
Old friend

k 'vam p̧ŗi'ʃol
К вам пришёл
To you came

da'voļna 'ʃʃɑsţja
Довольно счастья!
Enough happiness

'stuk 'stuk 'stuk
Стук, стук, стук …
Tap tap tap

2

'nɑt 'sy̡eʒɛĭ ma'ģilaĭ

Над свежей могилой.

Over new grave

Date of composition: ***1902.***
Date of publication: ***1902.***
Publisher: ***A. Gutheil, Moscow.***
Source: ***Semyon Nadson.***

ja v'noţ a'ḑin i v'noţ kru'gom
Я вновь один и вновь кругом
I again alone and again around

'fşjo 'tɑ ʒɛ 'notʃ i 'mrɑk u'nɨlɨĭ
Всё та же ночь и мрак унылый,
Still the same night and darkness gloomy

i 'ja v raz'dum̡ji raka'vom
И я в раздумьи роковом,
And I in reflection fateful

sta'ju 'nɑt 'sy̡eʒɛju ma'ģilaĭ
Стою над свежею могилой!
Stand over new grave

Я вновь один и вновь кругом
Всё та же ночь и мрак унылый,
И я в раздумьи роковом,
Стою над свежею могилой!
Чего мне ждать, к чему мне жить,
К чему бороться и трудиться:
Мне больше некого любить,
Мне больше некому молиться!

ʧe'vo 'mɲe ʒ'dɑʈ k ʧe'mu 'mɲe 'ʒɨʈ
Чего мне ждать, к чему мне жить,
What (to) me wait to what me live

k ʧe'mu ba'rotsa i tru'ɖitsa
К чему бороться и трудиться:
To what struggle and labor

'mɲe 'boʎʃɛ 'ɲekava ʎju'ɓiʈ
Мне больше некого любить,
(To) me any more no one to love

'mɲe 'boʎʃɛ 'ɲekamu ma'ʎiʈʂa
Мне больше некому молиться!
(To) me any more (to) no one to pray to

I am again alone, again
It is night; a gloomy darkness surrounds me;
Reflecting upon my fate
I stand by a fresh grave.
What can I expect, why should I live,
Why should I struggle and labor,
I have no one to love,
I have no one to adore!

3
'suɱerʞi
Сумерки
Twilight

Date of composition: ***1902.***
Date of publication: ***1902.***
Publisher: ***A. Gutheil, Moscow.***
Dedicated to Nadezhda I. Vrubel.
Source: ***Jean-Marie Guyot*** **(translated by Ivan Tkhorzhevsky).**

a'nɑ za'dumalaş a'dnɑ ɲe'ʈet ak'nom
Она задумалась. Одна перед окном
She became pensive Alone before window

skla'ɲjaş a'nɑ şi'ḑit i f 'sumraķe
Склонясь, она сидит и в сумраке
Lowering (head) she sits and in dusk
natʃ'nom
ночном
(of) night

ɱer'tsɑjet 'dolģiĭ 'vzor i f şine'ɣe
Мерцает долгий взор и в синеве
Glimmers long gaze and in blueness
b̧ez'b̧ŗeʒnaĭ
безбрежной
limitless

ţem'ɲejuʃʃix ɲe'b̧es ra'ɲjaja 'lutʃ 'svoĭ
Темнеющих небес, роняя луч свой
(Of) darkening skies letting fall ray its
'ɲeʒnɨĭ
нежный,
tender

vas'xoḑjat 'zɣjozdatʃķi b̧es'ʃumnaju tal'poĭ
Восходят звёздочки бесшумною толпой,
Arise stars (in) silent crowd

i 'kɑʒɛtsa 'ʃto 'tɑm ka'koĭ ta 'sɣetlɨĭ
И кажется, что там какой-то светлый
And seems that there some light
'roĭ
рой
swarm

Она задумалась. Одна перед окном
Склонясь, она сидит и в сумраке ночном
Мерцает долгий взор и в синеве безбрежной
Темнеющих небес, роняя луч свой нежный,
Восходят звёздочки бесшумною толпой,
И кажется, что там какой-то светлый рой
Таинственно парит и, словно восхищённый,
Трепещет над её головкою склонённой.

She sits pensively, alone by the window.
In the evening dusk
Her thoughtful look reflects
The limitless blue of darkening skies.
Stars silently rise
In a luminous cloud
Which mysteriously ascends
And dwells upon her bowed head.

ta'instyenna pa'ʀit i 'slovna
Таинственно парит и, словно
Mysteriously soars and as if
vasʀi'ʃʃonnɨĭ
восхищённый,
enraptured

tʀe'peʃʃet 'nat je'jo ga'lofkaju skla'ŋjonnaĭ
Трепещет над её головкою склонённой.
Quivers over her head bent

4
a'ŋe atye'tʃaʎi
Оне отвечали
They replied

Date of composition: ***1902.***
Date of publication: ***1902.***
Publisher: ***A. Gutheil, Moscow.***
Dedicated to Elena Kreutzer.
Source: ***Victor Hugo*** **(translation by Lev Mey).**

spra'ʂiʎi a'ŋi kak v ʎe'tutʃix tʃel'nax
Спросили они: "Как в летучих челнах
Asked they How in fleeting boats

nam 'ɓelaju 'tʃaĭkaĭ skaʎ'ʐiʈ
Нам белою чайкой скользить
(To) us (as) white seagull to glide
na val'nax
на волнах,
on waves

Спросили они: "Как в летучих челнах
Нам белою чайкой скользить на волнах,
Чтоб нас сторожа не догнали?"
"Гребите!" Оне отвечали.

ˈʃtop ˈnɑs staraˈʒɑ ɲe daˈgnɑʎi
Чтоб нас сторожа не догнали?"
So that us guards not overtake

gɾeˈbʲiʈe aˈɲe atɣeˈʧɑʎi
"Гребите!" Оне отвечали.
Row They replied

spraˈʂiʎi aˈɲi kak zaˈbɨʈ nafʂeˈgdɑ
Спросили они: "Как забыть, навсегда,
Asked they how to forget forever

ˈʃto v ˈɱiɾe juˈdoʎnam ˈjesʈ ˈbʲednasʈ
Что в мире юдольном есть бедность,
That in world sorrowful is poverty
bʲeˈdɑ
беда,
misfortune

ˈʃto ˈjesʈ v ˈɲjom graˈzɑ i pʲeˈʧɑʎi
Что есть в нём гроза и печали?"
That is in it storm and sadness

zɑˈsɲiʈe aˈɲe atɣeˈʧɑʎi
"Засните!" Оне отвечали.
Fall asleep they replied

spraˈʂiʎi aˈɲi kak kraˈsɑɣits pɾiˈvʎeʧ
Спросили они: "Как красавиц привлечь
Asked they How beauties to attract

Спросили они: "Как забыть, навсегда,
Что в мире юдольном есть бедность, беда,
Что есть в нём гроза и печали?"
"Засните!" Оне отвечали.

Спросили они: "Как красавиц привлечь
Без чары: чтоб сами на страстную речь
Оне нам в объятия пали?"
"Любите!" Оне отвечали.

They asked: How in fleeting boats
Can we glide like white seagulls on waves,
So watchmen would not overtake us?
Row! They replied.

Asked they: How can one forget, forever,
This sorrowful world's misfortunes and needs,
Its sadness and storms?
Fall asleep! They replied.

Asked they: How will beautiful girls
Love us, without an illusion—and to our passionate words,
They would be drawn into our embrace?
Love! They replied.

ḅes 'ʧɑrɨ 'ʧop 'sɑm̡i nɑ 'strɑstnuju
Без чары: чтоб сами на страстную
Without charm(s): so themselves to passionate
'ŗeʧ
речь
words

a'ņe nɑm v ab'ъjaţija 'pɑḷi
Оне нам в объятия пали?"
They (to) us into arms would fall

ḷju'ḅiţe a'ņe atɣe'ʧɑḷi
"Любите!" Оне отвечали.
Love They replied

5
şi'ŗeņ
Сирень
Lilacs

Date of composition: ***1902.***
Date of publication: ***1902.***
Publisher: ***A. Gutheil, Moscow.***
Source: ***Ekaterina Beketova.***

pa ut'ru na za'ŗe
По утру на заре,
In morning at dawn

pa ra'şistaĭ tra'ɣe
По росистой траве,
On dewy grass

ja paĭ'du 'sɣeʒɨm 'utram dɨ'ʃɑţ
Я пойду свежим утром дышать;
I will go (with) fresh morning to breathe

i v du'ʃɨstuju 'ţeņ
И в душистую тень,
And to fragrant shade

gḑe ţes'ņitsa şi'ŗeņ
Где теснится сирень,
Where cluster lilacs

ja paĭ'du sva'jo 'sţʃɑsţje iskɑţ
Я пойду своё счастье искать …
I will go my happiness to seek

v 'ʒɨzņi 'sţʃɑsţje ad'no
В жизни счастье одно
In life happiness one

'mņe nɑĭ'ţi suʒḑe'no
Мне найти суждено,
(To) me to find is fated

i 'to 'sţʃɑsţje f şi'ŗeņi ʒɨ'ɣjot
И то счастье в сирени живёт,
And that happiness in lilacs lives

nɑ ȥe'ļjonɨx ɣet'ɣjax
На зелёных ветвях,
On green branches

na du'ʃɨstɨx ķis'ţjax
На душистых кистях
On fragrant clusters

ma'jo 'b̧ednaje 'sţʃasţje tsɣe'ţjot
Моё бедное счастье цветёт …
My poor happiness blooms

По утру на заре,
По росистой траве,
Я пойду свежим утром
дышать;
И в душистую тень,
Где теснится сирень,
Я пойду своё счастье
искать …
В жизни счастье одно
Мне найти суждено,
И то счастье в сирени живёт,
На зелёных ветвях,
На душистых кистях
Моё бедное счастье цветёт …

In the morning, at dawn,
Through grass wet with dew,
I will go to breathe the fresh air.
In the fragrant shade
Where lilacs crowd
I will search for my happiness
there …
One happiness only
In my life I will find,
And it dwells in a lilac bower,
On green branches,
In fragrant clusters,
My meek happiness comes into
flower …

6

at'rɨvak iz ɑ. ɱju'ssɛ

Отрывок из А. Мюссе

Fragment from A. Musset

Date of composition: ***1902.***
Date of publication: ***1902.***
Publisher: ***A. Gutheil, Moscow.***
Dedicated to Alexandra A. Liven.
Source: ***Alfred de Musset*** **(translation by Alexei Apukhtin).**

'ʃto 'tɑk u'şiļena 'şertsɛ baļ'noje
Что так усилено сердце больное
Why so intensely heart pained

'ɓjotsa i 'proşit i 'ʒɑʒɟet pa'koja
Бьётся и просит и жаждет покоя?
Beats and asks and thirsts (for) rest

'ʧem ja vzval'novan is'pugan
Чем я взволнован, испуган
(With) what I (am) troubled frightened
v na'ʧi
в ночи?
in night

'stuknula 'dɣeɽ zasta'nɑf i za'noja
Стукнула дверь, застонав и заноя?
Rapped door groaning and moaning

'gɑsnuʃʃeĭ 'lɑmpɨ bļes'nuļi lu'ʧi
Гаснущей лампы блеснули лучи …
(Of) dimming lamp flashed rays

Что так усилено сердце больное
Бьётся и просит и жаждет покоя?
Чем я взволнован, испуган в ночи?
Стукнула дверь, застонав и заноя?
Гаснущей лампы блеснули лучи …
Боже мой! Дух мне в груди захватило!
Кто-то зовёт меня, шепчет уныло …
Кто-то вошёл … Моя келья пуста,
Нет никого. Это полночь пробило …
О, одиночество, о нищета!

'boʒɛ 'moĭ 'dux mɲe v gru'ḑi zaxva'ţila
Боже мой! Дух мне в груди захватило!
God my Breath (to) me in breast taken away

'kto-ta za'ɣjot ɱe'ɲja 'ʃɛpʧet
Кто-то зовёт меня, шепчет
Some one calls me whispers
u'nɨla
уныло …
despondently

'kto-ta va'ʃol ma'ja 'ķeļja pus'tɑ
Кто-то вошёл … Моя келья пуста,
Some one came in My room empty

'ɲet ɲika'vo 'ɛta 'polnaʧ pra'b̦ila
Нет никого. Это полночь пробило …
No anyone It midnight struck

'o aḑi'noʧestva 'o ɲiʃʃe'tɑ
О, одиночество, о нищета!
O loneliness O poverty

Why does my pained heart so intensely
Beat, begging and thirsting for peace?
Why am I troubled, frightened in the night?
A door closed, groaning and sighing?
The lamp's light flashed and died down …
Oh, my God! My spirit is faint!
Someone is calling me, whispering despondently,
Someone came in … But my room is empty,
There is no one. It was midnight that struck …
Oh, loneliness! Oh, my distress!

7
z'ḑeş xara'ʃo
Здесь хорошо
Here it is good to be

Date of composition: ***1902.***
Date of publication: ***1902.***
Publisher: ***A. Gutheil, Moscow.***
Source: ***Glafira Galina.***

z'ḑeş xara'ʃo
Здесь хорошо …
Here it is good to be

vzgļja'ņi vda'ļi
Взгляни, вдали
Look in the distance

ag'ņjom ga'ŗit ŗe'kɑ
Огнём горит река,
(As) fire burns river

tsɣet'nɨm kav'rom lu'gɑ ļeg'ļi
Цветным ковром луга легли,
(As) flowered carpet meadows lie

ḃe'ļejut abla'kɑ
Белеют облака.
Whiten clouds

'zḑeş 'ņet ļju'ḑeĭ
Здесь нет людей …
Here no people

'zḑeş ţiʃɨ'nɑ
Здесь тишина …
Here silence

'zḑeş 'toļka 'box da 'ja
Здесь только Бог да я.
Here only God and I

tsɣe'tɨ dɑ 'stɑraja sas'nɑ
Цветы, да старая сосна,
Flowers and old pine

dɑ 'tɨ ɱetʃ'ta ma'ja
Да ты, мечта моя!
And you dream my

Здесь хорошо …
Взгляни, вдали
Огнём горит река,
Цветным ковром луга легли,
Белеют облака.
Здесь нет людей …
Здесь тишина …
Здесь только Бог да я.
Цветы, да старая сосна,
Да ты, мечта моя!

How peaceful …
Look there, in the distance
Shines the river like a flame,
The fields lie like a flowered carpet,
Light clouds above us …
Here there are no people …
Here there is silence …
Here is only God—and I,
Flowers—and an aging pine,
And you, my dream!

8
na sm̧erţ 'ʧiʒɨka
На смерть чижика
On death (of) siskin

Date of composition: ***1902.***
Date of publication: ***1902.***
Publisher: ***A. Gutheil, Moscow.***
Dedicated to Olga A. Trubnikova.
Source: ***Vasily Zhukovsky.***

f 'şem 'grob̧e 'ɣernɨĭ 'ʧiʒɨk 'moĭ
В сем гробе верный чижик мой!
In this coffin faithful siskin my

p̧ŗi'rodɨ 'm̧ilaje tva'ŗeņje
Природы милое творенье,
Nature's sweet creation

iz 'm̧irnaĭ 'oblasţi z̧em'noĭ
Из мирной области земной
From peaceful province earthly

'on uļe'ţel kak snoɣi'ḑeņje
Он улетел, как сновиденье.
He flew away as dream

'on 'dļja ļjub'ɣi na 'sɣeţe 'ʒɨl
Он для любви на свете жил
He for love on earth lived

'on 'ņeʒnaĭ 'p̧eşenkaĭ p̧ŗi'ɣetnaĭ
Он нежной песенкой приветной,
He (with) tender song friendly

В сем гробе верный чижик мой!
Природы милое творенье,
Из мирной области земной
Он улетел, как сновиденье.

Он для любви на свете жил
Он нежной песенкой приветной,
За ласку нежную платил,
И подлетал к руке приветной.

Но в свете страшно и любить:
Ему был дан дружок крылатый;
Чтоб милого не пережить.
Он в гробе скрылся от утраты.

In this coffin my faithful siskin lies,
Nature's sweet creation,
From earth's peaceful province,
He flew away, as a fleeting dream.

za 'lasku 'ɲeʒnuju pla'ţil
За ласку нежную платил,
For caress tender paid

i padļe'tal k ru'ķe pri'ɣetnaĭ
И подлетал к руке приветной.
And flew up to hand friendly

'no f 'sɣeţe 'straʃna i ļju'ḅiţ
Но в свете страшно и любить:
But in world (it is) frightening even to love

je'mu bɨl 'dan dru'ʒok krɨ'latɨĭ
Ему был дан дружок крылатый;
(To) him was given friend winged

'ʃtop 'ɱilava ɲe peŗe'ʒɨţ
Чтоб милого не пережить.
So that dear (one) not to survive

'on v 'groḅe 'skrɨlsa at ut'ratɨ
Он в гробе скрылся от утраты.
He in coffin hid from loss

He lived on earth for love,
And with a tender song,
He returned our affection
By flying up to a friendly hand.

But in this world one can be afraid to love:
A winged friend was given to our siskin,
But, so as not to survive his beloved,
He died …

9
ɱe'loḑija
Мелодия
Melody

Date of composition: ***1902.***
Date of publication: ***1902.***
Publisher: ***A. Gutheil, Moscow.***
Dedicated to Natalia N. Lanting.
Source: ***Semyon Nadson.***

ja͡p u'ɱe'ɽeţ xa'ţel nɑ 'krɨļjax upa'jeŋja
Я б умереть хотел на крыльях упоенья,
I — to die wish on wings (of) ecstasy

v ļe'ŋivam palu'sŋe nɑ'ɣejannam
В ленивом полусне навеянном
In lazy somnolence evoked
ɱeʧ'toĭ
мечтой,
(by) dream

ƀeʒ 'muk ras'kajaŋja ƀes
Без мук раскаянья, без
Without torments (of) repentance without
'pɨtķi rɑzmɨʃ'ļeŋja
пытки размышленья,
torture (of) reflection

ƀeʒ mɑla'duʃnɨx 'sļjoz pra'ʃʃɑŋija
Без малодушных слёз прощания
Without fainthearted tears (of) farewell
s͡ ʑem'ļjoĭ
с землёй.
with earth

ja͡p uɱe'ɽeţ xa'ţel du'ʃɨstaju ɣes'noĭ
Я б умереть хотел душистою весной,
I — to die wish (in) fragrant spring

v zɑ'puʃʃenam sɑ'du v blagau'xɑnnɨĭ
В запущенном саду, в благоуханный
In overgrown garden on sweet scented
'ɖeŋ
день,
day

Я б умереть хотел на крыльях упоенья,
В ленивом полусне навеянном мечтой,
Без мук раскаянья, без пытки размышленья,
Без малодушных слёз прощания с землёй.
Я б умереть хотел душистою весной,
В запущенном саду, в благоуханный день,
Чтоб купы тёмных лип дремали надо мною
И колыхалася цветущая сирень.
Чтоб рядом бы ручей таинственным журчаньем
Немую тишину тревожил и будил,
И синий небосклон торжественным молчаньем
Об райской вечности мне внятно говорил …
Чтоб не молился я, не плакал умирая,
А сладко задремал, и чтобы снилось мне …
Что я плыву … плыву и что волна немая
Безвучно отдаёт меня другой волне …

'ʃtop 'kupɨ 'ţjomnɨx 'ļip dŗe'mɑļi
Чтоб купы тёмных лип дремали
So that arbors (of) dark lindens would doze
'nɑda 'mnoju
надо мною
over me

i kalɨ'xɑlaşja tsye'tuʃʃaja şi'ŗeŋ
И колыхалася цветущая сирень.
And would sway flowering lilacs

'ʃtop 'ŗjadam bɨ ru'ʧeĭ tɑ'instyennɨm
Чтоб рядом бы ручей таинственным
So that along — brook (with) mysterious
ʒur'ʧɑŋjem
журчаньем
murmur

ŋe'muju ţiʃi'nu tŗe'voʒɨl i buḑil
Немую тишину тревожил и будил,
Mute silence would disturb and waken

i 'şiŋiĭ ŋeba'sklon tar'ʒɛstyennɨm
И синий небосклон торжественным
And blue sky (with) solemn
mal'ʧɑŋjem
молчаньем
silence

ab 'rɑĭskaĭ 'yeʧnasti mŋe 'vŋjatna
Об райской вечности мне внятно
About heavenly eternity (to) me clearly
gava'ŗil
говорил …
would speak

When I die, would that it were on wings of rapture,
In quiet somnolence, evoked by daydreams,
No torments or regrets, no agonized reflections
Or fainthearted tears of farewell to earth.
If I could only die in fragrant spring,
In an old garden, on a sweet-scented day,
With leafy arbors hushed above
And flowering lilacs gently stirring …
A brook's mysterious murmur
Would waken and disturb the silence,
The sky in solemn stillness
Of paradise eternal to me would clearly speak.
And I will not pray, nor weep when dying,
But sweetly dream, and in that dream
A silent wave would carry
And gently pass me on to another wave …

'ʃtop ɲe ma'ļilsa 'ja ɲe 'plakal
Чтоб не молился я, не плакал
So that would not pray I would not weep
uɱi'raja
умирая,
dying

a 'slatka zadŗe'mal i 'ʃtobɨ 'sɲilaş
А сладко задремал, и чтобы снилось
But sweetly dream and so that dreamt
'mɲe
мне …
(to) me

'ʃto ja plɨ'vu plɨ'vu i 'ʃto val'na
Что я плыву … плыву и что волна
That I float float and that wave
ɲe'maja
немая
silent

b̦ez 'vutʃna atda'jot ɱe'ɲja dru'goĭ
Безвучно отдаёт меня другой
Noiselessly gives me (to) another
val'ɲe
волне …
wave

10
'pred i'konaĭ
Пред иконой
Before icon

Date of composition: ***1902.***
Date of publication: ***1902.***
Publisher: ***A. Gutheil, Moscow.***
Dedicated to Anna A. Ivanova.
Source: ***Arseny Golenischev-Kutuzov.***

a'nɑ 'pŗed i'konaĭ sta'jala sɣja'toju
Она пред иконой стояла святою;
She before icon stood holy

skŗes'ţiļişja 'ruķi us'tɑ ʃɛɣe'ļiļiş
Скрестилися руки, уста шевелились;
Crossed hands lips moved

iz 'glɑs je'jo 'sļjozɨ ad'nɑ za dru'goju
Из глаз её слёзы одна за другою
From eyes her tears one after another

pa 'b̦ļednɨm ʃʃe'kam ʒɛmʧu'gɑm̧i
По бледным щекам жемчугами
Along pale cheeks (as) pearls
ka'ţiļiş
катились.
flowed

a'nɑ pafta'ŗjala 'f̦sjo 'ʧ̦io-ta
Она повторяла всё чьё-то
She repeated constantly someone's
na'zvɑņjȩ
names,
name

i 'vzor aza'ŗjalsa ma'ļitɣennɨm 'sɣetam
И взор озарялся молитвенным светом;
And gaze lit up (with) prayerful light

i 'bɨla tak 'mnoga ļjub'ɣi i stra'dɑņja
И было так много любви и страданья,
And was so much love and suffering

tɑk 'mɑla na'ḑeʒdɨ v ma'ļeņii 'ɛtam
Так мало надежды в молении этом!
So little hope in prayer this

a'nɑ pŗekla'ņilaş i 'dolga
Она преклонилась и долго
She bowed and (for a) long (time)
ļe'ʒɑla
лежала,
was lying

pŗiļ'nuf gala'voju k z̧em'ļe b̧ezat'ɣetnaĭ
Прильнув головою к земле безответной,
Touching head to earth silent

kɑk 'butta f tam'ļeņii ņe'mom aʒɨ'dɑla
Как будто в томлении немом ожидала,
As if in weariness silent expected

'ʃto 'golas nat 'ņeju rɑz'dɑstsa
Что голос над нею раздастся
That voice over her will be heard
pŗi'ɣetnɨĭ
приветный.
loving

'no 'bɨlo 'fşjo 'ţixa v mal'ʧɑņii 'noʧi
Но было всё тихо в молчании ночи,
But was all quiet in silence (of) night

Она пред иконой стояла святою;
Скрестилися руки, уста шевелились;
Из глаз её слёзы одна за другою
По бледным щекам жемчугами катились.
Она повторяла всё чьё-то названье,
И взор озарялся молитвенным светом;
И было так много любви и страданья,
Так мало надежды в молении этом!
Она преклонилась и долго лежала,
Прильнув головою к земле безответной,
Как будто в томлении немом ожидала,
Что голос над нею раздастся приветный.
Но было всё тихо в молчании ночи,
Лампада мерцала во мраке тревожном,
И скорбно смотрели Спасителя очи
На очи, просящие о невозможном.

lam'pɑda ɱer'tsɑla va 'mrɑķe ţŗe'voʒnam
Лампада мерцала во мраке тревожном,
Icon light shone in darkness troubled

i 'skorbna smat'ŗeļi spɑ''şiţeļja 'oʧi
И скорбно смотрели Спасителя очи
And sorrowfully looked Savior's eyes

nɑ 'oʧi pra'şjaʃʃije 'o ņevaz'moʒnam
На очи, просящие о невозможном.
Onto eyes asking about impossible

She stood before the holy icon,
Hands clasped, lips whispering,
Glistening tears flowing
Down her pale cheeks.
She repeated a name, many times,
Her gaze brightened with prayerful light …
There was much love and suffering,
And so little hope in her prayer.
She bowed down and remained thus,
Touching her head to the silent earth,
As if in her quiet weariness she waited
For a loving voice to be heard.
But the night was silent,
The icon-lamp flame shone in the anxious darkness,
And sorrowfully the eyes of the Savior looked
On the eyes of her asking for the impossible.

11
ja ņe pra'rok
Я не пророк
I not prophet

Date of composition: ***1902.***
Date of publication: ***1902.***
Publisher: ***A. Gutheil, Moscow.***
Source: ***Alexander Kruglov.***

ja ņe pra'rok ja ņe ba'jets
Я не пророк, я не боец,
I not prophet I not fighter

ja ȵe u'ʧiţeļ 'ɱira
Я не учитель мира;
I not teacher (of) world

ja 'bozjeĭ 'ɱilasţju pe'ɣets
Я, Божьей милостью, певец,
I (by) God's mercy singer

ma'jo a'ruʒɨje 'ļira
Моё оружие лира.
My arms (are) lyre

ja 'voļju 'gospada tva'ŗju
Я волю Господа творю;
I will (of) Lord do

saju'zɑ izbe'gaja s 'loʒju
Союза избегая с ложью,
Union avoiding with lie

ja 'şertsu 'pesȵeĭ gava'ŗju
Я сердцу песней говорю,
I (to) heart (with) song speak

bu'ʒu v 'ȵjom 'iskru 'boʒɨju
Бужу в нём искру Божию.
Awaken in it spark (of) God

Я не пророк, я не боец,
Я не учитель мира;
Я, Божьей милостью, певец,
Мое оружие лира.
  Я волю Господа творю;
  Союза избегая с ложью,
  Я сердцу песней говорю,
  Бужу в нём искру Божию.

I am not a prophet, nor a warrior am I,
I am not a teacher of the world;
By God's grace I am a singer.
The instrument I bear is a lyre.
  I perform the will of the Lord,
  I do not keep trust with a lie,
  I speak to hearts through a song,
  Waking in them the spark of God!

12
kak 'mņe 'boļna
Как мне больно
How (to) me painful

Date of composition: ***1902.***
Date of publication: ***1902.***
Publisher: ***A. Gutheil, Moscow.***
Dedicated to Vladimir A. Satin.
Source: ***Glafira Galina.***

kak	'mņe	'boļna	kak	'xotʃetsa	'ʒɨţ
Как	**мне**	**больно,**	**как**	**хочется**	**жить …**
How	(to) me	painful	how	wish	to live

kak	sɣe'ʒɑ	i	du'ʃɨsta	ɣes'na
Как	**свежа**	**и**	**душиста**	**весна!**
How	fresh	and	fragrant	spring

'ņet	ņe	f	'şilɑx	ja	'şertsa	u'ḅiţ
Нет!	**не**	**в**	**силах**	**я**	**сердца**	**убить**
No	not		able	I	heart	to kill

v	'ɛtu	'notʃ	galu'buju	ḅes	'snɑ
В	**эту**	**ночь**	**голубую**	**без**	**сна.**
In	this	night	blue	without	sleep

'xoţ	bɨ	'stɑrasţ	priʃ'lɑ	paska'ŗeĭ
Хоть	**бы**	**старость**	**пришла**	**поскорей,**
Only	if	old age	would come	quicker

'xoţ	bɨ	'iņeĭ	f	kud'ŗjax	zɑbļes'ţel
Хоть	**бы**	**иней**	**в**	**кудрях**	**заблестел,**
Only	if	frost	in	curls	would glisten

Как мне больно, как хочется жить …
Как свежа и душиста весна!
Нет! не в силах я сердца убить
В эту ночь голубую без сна.

Хоть бы старость пришла поскорей,
Хоть бы иней в кудрях заблестел,
Чтоб не пел для меня соловей,
Чтобы лес для меня не шумел,

Чтобы песнь не рвалась из души
Сквозь сирени в широкую даль,
Чтобы не было в этой тиши
Мне чего-то мучительно жаль!

'ʃtop ŋ̡e 'p̡el 'dl̡ja m̡e'ŋ̡ja sala'γeĭ
Чтоб не пел для меня соловей,
So that would not sing for me nightingale

'ʃtobɨ l̡es dl̡ja m̡e'ŋ̡ja ŋ̡e ʃu'm̡el
Чтобы лес для меня не шумел,
So that forest for me would not rustle

'ʃtobɨ 'p̡esŋ̡ ŋ̡e rvɑ'lɑs̡ iz du'ʃɨ
Чтобы песнь не рвалась из души
So that song would not burst from soul

'skvoz̡ s̡i'r̡eŋ̡i f ʃɨ'rokuju 'dɑl̡
Сквозь сирени в широкую даль,
Through lilacs into wide expanse

'ʃtobɨ 'ŋ̡e bɨla v 'ɛtaĭ t̡i'ʃɨ
Чтобы не было в этой тиши
So that would not be in this stillness

'mŋ̡e ʧe'vo-tə mu'ʧit̡el̡na 'ʒɑl̡
Мне чего-то мучительно жаль!
(For) me something painfully sad

How pained I am, how I wish to live …
How fresh and fragrant is spring!
No! My heart can't be still
On this moonlit, sleepless night.

If only old age would come soon,
And frost in my hair would glisten,
And the nightingale for me would not sing,
And the forest to me would not murmur.

And a song would not pour forth from my soul
Through the lilacs toward that expanse,
In this stillness tonight I would not
About something be painfully sad!

V. Songs of Opus 26

1. **Есть много звуков (There are many sounds)**
2. **Все отнял у меня (All was taken from me)**
3. **Мы отдохнем (We shall rest)**
4. **Два прощания (Two farewells)**
5. **Покинем, милая (Let us leave, my sweet)**
6. **Христос Воскрес (Christ is risen)**
7. **К детям (To my children)**
8. **Пощады я молю! (I beg for mercy)**
9. **Я опять одинок (I am again alone)**
10. **У моего окна (At my window)**
11. **Фонтан (The fountain)**
12. **Ночь печальна (Night is sorrowful)**
13. **Вчера мы встретились (Yesterday we met)**
14. **Кольцо (The ring)**
15. **Проходит все (All passes)**

"It is so peaceful here that I started counting anxiously the days left till our departure and every evening at tea, with a sigh, I deduct one more day from our stay here. Thus, when tonight I shall say '42' [days left] there will be so little, so little time left. And it will pass quickly and then Moscow, half a grief, and the theater, lots of grief";[6] wrote Rachmaninoff from Ivanovka in the summer of 1906.

Concerts both at home and abroad and his post as conductor for the Russian operatic repertoire at the Bolshoi Theater in Moscow placed a considerable demand on Rachmaninoff's time as a composer, and it was at Ivanovka that he found the peaceful hours for his creative work. After his marriage to Natasha Satina in 1902, the family spent summers at their country home, where Rachmaninoff enjoyed working on the estate or at composition, often writing at a table outdoors, surrounded by the quiet fields. These were productive years when he wrote two operas, *The Covetous Knight* from a play by Pushkin, and *Francesca da Rimini* from Dante, and started composing his Second Symphony.

The songs of Opus 26 were written for a performance at the *Kruzhok Lyubitelei Russkoi Musyki* (Group for the Performance of Russian music), founded by Arkady and Maria Kerzin in

Moscow. In March 1906, Rachmaninoff asked Mme. Kerzina to send him some poems that he could set to music for this cycle. After selecting several texts (there is no indication which texts were sent by Mme. Kerzina and which were added by the composer), Rachmaninoff wrote the songs in less than a month, dating them "August 14–September 8, 1906, Ivanovka." The songs were performed in February of the following year by four artists from the Bolshoi Theater, and accompanied on the piano by Alexander N. Goldenveiser of the Moscow Conservatory.

Several of the texts in this cycle reflect Rachmaninoff's meditations on the passage of time. The music is restrained and austere and the melodic principle often gives way to a narrative style when Rachmaninoff strives for a correct interpretation of the texts in his musical "translations," sometimes working with the intonations of everyday speech. The recitatives and monologues show his perceptive talent in outlining the psychological and emotional motivation of his characters, where he amplifies Musorgsky's research on vocal intonation and presents new possibilities in music, later evident in compositions for voice by Shostakovich.

The cycle is defined by two pensive adagios—the first song, "There are many sounds," meditates on the poet's or composer's visions and songs silenced by the anxiety of cares and contrasts life, which "storms as a tempest," to the poet's voice, which "whispers as a murmur of waters." The last song concludes that dreams and anxieties and "the sounds of words which once to us resounded" disappear in the passage of time.

Within this philosophic framework, the composer presents songs commenting on many facets of life—on consoling love when life is ending in "All was taken from me" by Tyutchev, Russia's metaphysical poet; and man's intellectual seeking in his poem "The fountain," a metaphor for thoughts reaching upward and destined to fall to earth again. Rachmaninoff uses only the first strophe of the poem to write a sparkling commentary in music.

The recitative "We shall rest" is unusual for the chamber vocal genre of the period, as Rachmaninoff uses a prose text, from the concluding lines of Chekhov's play *Uncle Vanya*. He keeps the nuances and caesuras of the original text and gives

Chekhov's wistful words of hope for a tranquil world a sensitive but somber accompaniment. He may have chosen the text as he was becoming closely acquainted with the work of Chekhov and Stanislavsky and the Moscow Art Theater as well as seeking new modes of expression for the operas he was composing at the time.

A yearning for a better world is expressed in the recitative "Christ is risen," in which Merezhkovsky's melodramatic and strained tone is reinterpreted with a disciplined feeling in music set to an ancient church melody. To these philosophic meditations Rachmaninoff adds personal monologues such as the compassionate "To my children" and "Yesterday we met," the anxious "I beg for mercy" and "The ring," and the somewhat ironic dialogue on love in "Two farewells." The two lyrical songs in this group are the elegy "Let us leave, my sweet" and the miniature "At my window," which gives a subtle and shimmering effect to a simple text, the effect of light and shadow on a flowering tree touched by the spring wind.

In his lyrical impressions of nature Rachmaninoff has much in common with Ivan Bunin, a writer with whom he was personally acquainted—in his economy and clarity of diction and the sparse and often nostalgic quality of his poetic imagery. "I am again alone" to words by Bunin is one of several songs on spring where Rachmaninoff contrasts the beauty of nature with a mood of sadness and loneliness. "Night is sorrowful" is a masterpiece of Russian vocal literature, in which Bunin in eight lines and Rachmaninoff in only twenty-four measures create a personal image of a traveler on a lonely road, at night, in a deep and spacious steppe. The opening intonational "gesture" is similar to the one in the song "How peaceful"; the melody is sorrowful and is accompanied by a flowing, rhythmic movement, interrupted at the words "But to whom and how does one explain what beckons, what fills one's heart?" An expressive melody develops in the piano accompaniment that becomes the unifying element in the song. Rachmaninoff emphasized that "in this song, it is the piano and not the singer, it is the accompanist who should be singing."[7] Although the declamatory vocal element predominates in this cycle, in songs such as "Let us leave, my sweet," "At my window," and "Night is sorrowful" we hear

Rachmaninoff the pianist, who lets his instrument sing with the voice.

In his meditations on time, Rachmaninoff comments in music that all passes, joys and anxieties pass away, and he reflects the words of a distant writer of song, who exclaimed: "In Thy sight a thousand years are as yesterday … and our years die away like a sound!"[8]

1
'jesţ 'mnoga 'zvukaf
Есть много звуков
(There) are many sounds

Date of composition: ***1906.***
Date of publication: ***1906.***
Publisher: ***A. Gutheil, Moscow.***
Dedicated to Maria S. and Arkady M. Kerzin.
Source: ***Alexei Tolstoy.***

'jesţ 'mnoga 'zvukaf f 'şertsa
Есть много звуков в сердца
(There) are many sounds in heart's
gluḅi'ņe
глубине,
depth

ņe'jasnɨx 'dum ņe'petɨx 'pesņeĭ 'mnoga
Неясных дум, непетых песней много;
Vague visions unsung songs many

'no zaglu'ʃɑjet 'ɣetʃna ix va 'mņe
Но заглушает вечно их во мне
But silenced always them in me

Есть много звуков в сердца глубине,
Неясных дум, непетых песней много;
Но заглушает вечно их во мне
Забот немолчных скучная тревога.
Тяжёл её непрошенный напор,
Издавна сердце с жизнию боролось,
Но жизнь шумит, как вихорь ломит бор,
Как ропот струй, так шепчет сердца голос.

za'bot ņe'moltʃnɨx 'skutʃnaja ţŗe'voga
Забот немолчных скучная тревога.
(Of) cares unsilent tedious anxiety

ţja'ʒol je'jo ņe'proʃɛnnɨĭ na'por
Тяжёл её непрошенный напор,
Heavy its unwanted pressure

iz'dɑvna 'şertsɛ s 'ʒɨzņiju ba'rolaş
Издавна сердце с жизнию боролось,
Long heart with life struggled

'no 'ʒɨzņ ʃu'ɱit kak 'ɣixaŗ 'loɱit 'bor
Но жизнь шумит, как вихорь ломит бор,
But life storms as wind breaks forest

kak 'ropat st'ruĭ tak 'ʃɛpţʃet 'şertsa 'golas
Как ропот струй, так шепчет сердца голос.
As murmur (of) waters so whispers heart's voice

There are many sounds deep in my heart,
Vague visions, many songs unsung,
But they are always silenced in me
By the tedious anxiety of unsilent cares.
A burdensome and unwanted pressure—
Long has my heart struggled with life,
But life storms, as the wind of tempest breaks a forest,
As a murmur of waters, so whispers my heart's voice.

2
'fşjo 'otņjal u ɱe'ņja
Всё отнял у меня
All taken from me

Date of composition: ***1906.***
Date of publication: ***1906.***
Publisher: ***A. Gutheil, Moscow.***
Dedicated to Maria S. and Arkady M. Kerzin.
Source: ***Feodor Tyutchev.***

'fşjo 'otņjal u m̧e'ņja kaz'ņjaʃʃiĭ 'b̧ox
Всё отнял у меня казнящий Бог,
All taken from me punishing God

zda'roɣje 'şilu 'voļi 'vozdux 'son
Здоровье, силу воли, воздух, сон.
Health willpower air sleep

ad'nu ţe'b̧ja pŗi 'mņe as'tɑɣil 'on
Одну тебя при мне оставил Он,
Alone you by me left He

'ʃtop ja je'mu je'ʃʃo ma'ļitsa 'mok
Чтоб я Ему ещё молиться мог.
So that I (to) Him still pray could.

Всё отнял у меня казнящий Бог,
Здоровье, силу воли, воздух, сон.
Одну тебя при мне оставил Он,
Чтоб я Ему ещё молиться мог.

All was taken from me by a punishing God,
My health, my willpower, freedom and dreams.
You alone He left to be by my side,
So that I could still pray to Him.

3
mɨ atdax'ņjom
Мы отдохнём
We (shall) rest

Date of composition: *1906*.
Date of publication: *1906*.
Publisher: *A. Gutheil, Moscow*.
Dedicated to Maria S. and Arkady M. Kerzin.
Source: *Anton Chekhov*.

mɨ atdax'ņjom mɨ u'slɨʃɨm 'ɑnģelof mɨ
Мы отдохнём! Мы услышим ангелов, мы
We (shall) rest We (shall) hear angels we

u'ɣiḑim 'fʂjo 'ɲeba v al'mazax mɨ
увидим всё небо в алмазах, мы
(shall) see all sky in diamonds we
u'ɣiḑim kak
увидим как
(shall) see how

'fʂjo 'zlo ʐem'noje 'fʂe 'naʃɨ stra'daɲija
всё зло земное, все наши страдания
all evil earthly all our sufferings
pa'tonut
потонут
(will be) submerged

v ɱila'ʂerḑii ka'toraje na'polɲit
в милосердии, которое наполнит
in mercy which (will) fill
sa'boju ɣeʂ 'ɱir
собою весь мир,
(with) itself all world

i na'ʃa ʒɨzɲ 'staɲet 'ţixaju
и наша жизнь станет тихою,
and our life (will) become tranquil,
'ɲeʒnaju 'slatkaju
нежною, сладкою,
gentle, sweet

kak 'laska ja 'ɣeruju 'ɣeruju mɨ
как ласка. Я верую, верую … Мы
like caress I believe believe we
atdax'ɲjom
отдохнём …
(shall) rest

mɨ atdax'ɲjom
Мы отдохнём.
We (shall) rest

Мы отдохнём! Мы услышим
ангелов, мы
увидим всё небо в алмазах,
мы увидим как
всё зло земное, все наши
страдания потонут
в милосердии, которое
наполнит собою весь мир,
и наша жизнь станет тихою,
нежною, сладкою,
как ласка. Я верую, верую …
Мы отдохнём …
Мы отдохнём.

We shall rest! We shall hear angels, we shall see the whole sky in diamonds, we shall see how all earthly evil, all our sufferings, will be submerged in mercy, which will fill the whole world, and our life will become tranquil, gentle, sweet, like a caress. I believe, I believe it shall be … We shall rest … We shall rest.

4
'dva pra'ʃʃaŋija
Два прощания
Two farewells

Диалог
Dialogue

Date of composition: ***1906.***
Date of publication: ***1906.***
Publisher: ***A. Gutheil, Moscow.***
Dedicated to Maria S. and Arkady M. Kerzin.
Source: ***Alexei Koltsov.***

2ой голос:
2nd voice
tak 'tɨ ma'ja
Так ты, моя
So you my

kra'saγitsa
Красавица,
Lovely one

ḻi'ʃɨlaş vd'ruk
Лишилась вдруг
Lost suddenly

'dvux 'molatşef
Двух молодцев,
Two young men

2ой голос:
Так ты, моя
Красавица,
Лишилась вдруг
Двух молодцев,
Скажи же мне,
Как с первым ты
Рассталася,
Прощалася?

ska'ʒɨ ʒɛ 'mņe
Скажи же мне,
Tell — me

kak s 'p̦ervɨm tɨ
Как с первым ты
How with first (one) you

ras'stɑlaşja
Расстался,
Parted

pra'ʃʃɑlaşja
Прощалася?
Said farewell

1ый голос:
1st voice
ras'stɑlaş s 'ņim
Рассталась с ним
Parted with him

ja 'ɣ̦eşila
Я весело,
I merrily

pra'ʃʃɑlaşja
Прощалася,
Said farewell

sm̦i'jalaşja
Смеялася …
Laughed

ɑ 'on ka 'mņe
А он ко мне,
And he to me

1ый голос:
Рассталась с ним
Я весело,
Прощалася,
Смеялася …
А он ко мне,
Бедняжечка,
Припал на грудь
Головушкой;
И долго так
Лежал, молчал;
Смочил платок
Горючими …
"Ну, Бог с тобой!"
Промолвил мне;
Схватил коня,
Поехал в путь,
В чужих краях
Коротать век.

2ой голос:
И ты над ним
Смеялася?
Его слезам
Не верила?
Скажи ж теперь,
Мудрёная,
Как ты с другим
Прощалася?

b̡i'dn̡jaʒɛʧka
Бедняжечка,
Poor (one)

p̡r̡i'pɑl na 'gruḑ
Припал на грудь
Laid on breast

ga'lovuʃkaĭ
Головушкой;
(With) head

i 'dolga 'tɑk
И долго так
And long so

l̡i'ʒɑl mal'ʧɑl
Лежал, молчал;
Laid was silent

sma'ʧil pla'tok
Смочил платок
Wet handkerchief

ga'r̡juʧim̡i
Горючими …
(With) bitter (tears)

nu 'box s ta'boĭ
"Ну, Бог с тобой!"
Well God with you

pra'molv̡il 'mn̡e
Промолвил мне;
Uttered (to) me

1ый голос:
Другой не то …
Не плакал он,
А и теперь
Всё плачу я
Ах, обнял он
Так холодно,
Так сухо речь
Повёл со мной.
"Я еду, вишь,
Не надолго;
Ещё с тобой увидимся,
И в волюшку
Наплачемся."
По сердцу ли
Такой привет?
Махнул рукой,
Не кланяясь,
В моё лицо
Не смотрючи,
Пустил коня
И был таков!

2ой голос:
Кто ж памятней
Останется
Душе твоей
Красавица?

1ый голос:
Мне первого,
Конечно, жаль;
Люблю же я
Последняго!

sxva'ţil ka'ņja
Схватил коня,
Mounted steed

pa'jexal f 'puţ
Поехал в путь,
Went on journey

f ʧu'ʒɨx kra'jax
В чужих краях
In alien lands

ka'rotaţ 'ɣek
Коротать век.
Live out life

2ой голос:
2nd voice
i 'tɨ nat 'ņim
И ты над ним
And you at him

sm̧i'jalaşja
Смеялася?
Laughed

je'vo sļi'zɑm
Его слезам
His tears

ņi 'ɣeŗila
Не верила?
Not believe

ska'ʒɨ͡ ʃ ţi'p̧eŗ
Скажи ж теперь,
Tell — now

2nd voice:
How is it, my
lovely one,
that you lost suddenly
two young men?
Tell me now,
how with the first one you
parted,
said farewell?

1st voice:
I parted with him
merrily,
said farewell
and laughed …
And he,
the poor one,
onto my breast laid
his head;
and long so
stayed, without a word;
he wet his handkerchief
with bitter tears …
"Well, God be with you!"
he uttered,
mounted his steed,
went on his way,
in alien lands
to live alone.

2nd voice:
And you did
laugh at him?
His tears
did not believe?
tell me now,
O, clever one,
how did you to the other one
say farewell?

mu'dŗjonaja
Мудрёная,
Clever (one)

kak 'tɨ s dru'gim
Как ты с другим
How you with other (one)

pra'ʃʃalaşja
Прощалася?
Said farewell

1ый голос:
1st voice
dru'goĭ ŋi 'to
Другой не то…
Other (one) not so

ŋi 'plɑkɑl 'on
Не плакал он,
(Did) not weep he

ɑ i ţi'peŗ
А и теперь
But even now

'fşjo 'plɑʧu 'ja
Всё плачу я
Still weep I

'ɑx 'obŋjal 'on
Ах, обнял он
Oh embraced he

'tak 'xoladna
Так холодно,
So coldly

1st voice:
The other one was different …
He did not weep,
But even now
I am still weeping.
Oh, he embraced me
so coldly,
so distantly he spoke
to me:
"I will be gone, you see,
but not for long,
we'll see each other yet
and freely then
we'll weep."
How can one's heart
hear this farewell?
He waved his hand,
not bowing,
into my eyes
not looking,
he raced his steed
and sped away!

2nd voice:
Whom will you
remember
in your heart,
my lovely one?

1st voice:
The first one,
I feel sorry for;
But love I will
the latter!

ˈtak ˈsuxa ˈɽetʃ
Так сухо речь
So drily speech

paˈɣjol sa ˈmnoĭ
Повёл со мной.
Started with me

ja ˈjedu ˈɣiʃ
"Я еду, вишь,
I (am) going see

ɲi ˈnɑdalga
Не надолго;
Not for long

iˈʃʃo s taˈboĭ uˈɣiɖimʂja
Ещё с тобой увидимся,
Still with you (we shall) meet

i v͡ˈvoʆjuʃku
И в волюшку
And a lot

nɑˈplaʈimʂja
Наплачемся."
(We shall) weep

pa ˈʂertsu ʆi
По сердцу ли
To heart —

taˈkoĭ pɽiˈɣet
Такой привет?
Such greeting

mɑx'nul ru'koĭ
Махнул рукой,
Waved (with) hand

ɲi 'klɑɲjajaʂ
Не кланяясь,
Not bowing

v ma'jo ʎi'tso
В моё лицо
Into my face

ɲi 'smotʀjutʃi
Не смотрючи,
Not looking

pus'ʈil ka'ɲja
Пустил коня
Raced steed

i 'bɨl ta'kof
И был таков!
And was such

2ой голос:
2nd voice
'kto ʃ 'pɑɱjatɲeĭ
Кто ж памятней
Who — more memorable

as'tɑɲitsa
Останется
(Will) remain

du'ʃɛ tva'jeĭ
Душе твоей
(To) soul your

kra'sɑɣitsa
Красавица?
Lovely one

1ый голос:
1st voice
'mn̡e 'p̡ervava
Мне первого,
(To) me first (one)

ka'n̡eʃna 'ʒɑl̡
Конечно, жаль;
Of course pitied

l̡ub'l̡u ʒɛ 'ja
Люблю же я
Love — I

pɑ's̡l̡edn̡java
Последняго!
Latter (one)

5
pa'k̡in̡em 'm̡ilaja
Покинем, милая
(Let us) leave sweet

Date of composition: ***1906.***
Date of publication: ***1906.***
Publisher: ***A. Gutheil, Moscow.***
Dedicated to Maria S. and Arkady M. Kerzin.
Source: ***Arseny Golenischev-Kutuzov.***

pa'ķiņem 'm̧ilaja ʃu'm̧jaʃʃiĭ 'kruk
Покинем, милая, шумящий круг
(Let us) leave sweet noisome circle
sta'ļitsɨ
столицы...
(of) capital

pa'rɑ v ra'ḑimɨĭ 'krɑĭ pa'rɑ v ļes'nuju
Пора в родимый край, пора в лесную
Time to native land time to forest
'gluʃ
глушь!
depth

tɨ 'slɨʃɨʃ 'nɑs za'ɣ̧jot na 'voļju
Ты слышишь? Нас зовёт на волю
You hear We (are) called to freedom
iz ţem'ņitsɨ
из темницы
from prison

ɣ̧es'nɨ pa'b̧ednɨĭ ʃum i 'peņje
Весны победный шум и пенье
(Of) spring victorious sound and song
'pţits
птиц ...
(of) birds

k 'ʧe'mu ʒ 'nam usm̧i'ŗjaţ du'ʃɨ
К чему ж нам усмирять души
Why — we still (of) soul
val'ʃɛbnɨje pa'rɨvɨ
волшебные порывы?
enchanted yearnings

Покинем, милая, шумящий
круг столицы...
Пора в родимый край, пора в
лесную глушь!
Ты слышишь? Нас зовёт на
волю из темницы
Весны победный шум и пенье
птиц ...
К чему ж нам усмирять души
волшебные порывы?
Иль разлюбила ты
желтеющие нивы,
И рощи свежие, и хмурые
леса,
Где, помнишь, мы вдвоём
задумчиво блуждали
В вечерний час когда темнеют
небеса,
И молча бродит взор в
тумане спящей дали?

Let us leave, my sweet, the
noisome life in the city.
It is time to leave for home and
forest glades!
Listen! We are called to flee our
prison,
Called by the sounds of spring and
songs of birds ...
Why should we still our souls'
enchanted yearnings?
Do you no longer love the
ripening fields,
Green groves, dark forests,
Where, remember, we roamed
pensively
In the evening hour, when skies
darken,
And silently our gaze wandered in
the mist of sleeping distance ...

il̡ razl̡ju'b̡ila ti ʒɛl't̡ejuʃʃije 'n̡ivɨ
Иль разлюбила ты желтеющие нивы,
Or ceased to love you yellowing fields

i 'roʃʃi 'sv̡eʒɨje i 'xmurɨje l̡e'sɑ
И рощи свежие, и хмурые леса,
And groves fresh and dark forests

'gd̡e 'pomn̡iʃ mɨ vdva'jom za'dumtʃiva
Где, помнишь, мы вдвоём задумчиво
Where remember we two pensively
bluʒ'dɑl̡i
блуждали
roamed

v͡ v̡e'tʃern̡iĭ 'tʃɑs kag'dɑ t̡em'n̡ejut n̡eb̡e'sa
В вечерний час когда темнеют небеса,
In evening hour when darken skies

i 'moltʃa 'brod̡it 'vzor f tu'mɑn̡e
И молча бродит взор в тумане
And silently wanders gaze in mist
'sp̡jaʃʃeĭ 'dɑl̡i
спящей дали?
(of) sleeping distance

6

xr̡is'tos vas'kr̡es

Христос воскрес

Christ (is) risen

Date of composition: *1906.*
Date of publication: *1906.*
Publisher: *A. Gutheil, Moscow.*
Dedicated to Maria S. and Arkady M. Kerzin.
Source: *Dmitri Merezhkovsky.*

xr̡is'tos vas'kr̡es pɑ'jut
"Христос воскрес" поют
Christ (is) risen (they) sing
va 'xrɑm̡e
во храме;
in temple/church

'no 'ɡrusna 'mn̡e du'ʃɑ mal'ʧit
Но грустно мне … душа молчит.
But sad I am soul silent

'm̡ir 'polan 'kroɣju i sl̡e'zɑm̡i
Мир полон кровью и слезами,
World full (of) blood and (with) tears

i 'ɛtat ɡ̡imn 'pr̡et ɑltɑ'r̡jam̡i
И этот гимн пред алтарями
And this hymn before altars

tak askar'b̡it̡el̡na zvu'ʧit
Так оскорбительно звучит.
So offensively sounds

kag'da͡ b 'on 'bɨl m̡eʒ 'nɑs i 'ɣid̡el
Когда б Он был меж нас и видел
If He were among us and saw

ʧe'vo das't̡ik nɑʃ 'slɑvnɨĭ 'ɣek
Чего достиг наш славный век,
What achieved our glorious age

kak 'brɑta 'brɑt vazn̡enɑ'ɣid̡el
Как брата брат возненавидел,
How (his) brother brother came to hate

kak apa'zor̡en ʧela'ɣek
Как опозорен человек,
How disgraced man

"Христос воскрес" поют во храме;
Но грустно мне … душа молчит.
Мир полон кровью и слезами,
И этот гимн пред алтарями
Так оскорбительно звучит.
Когда б Он был меж нас и видел
Чего достиг наш славный век,
Как брата брат возненавидел,
Как опозорен человек,
И если б здесь, в блестящем храме
"Христос воскрес" Он услыхал
Какими б горькими слезами
Перед толпой Он зарыдал!

"Christ is risen" they sing in church;
But I am sad … my soul is silent.
The world is full of spilt blood and tears,
And this hymn before the altars
Sounds so offensive.
If only He were among us and saw
What our glorious age has achieved,
How brother came to hate his brother,
How disgraced is man.
And if, here in this resplendent temple,
"Christ is risen" He were to hear,
With such bitter tears
He would begin to sob before the crowd!

i 'jesʎi͡ p 'zɖeʂ v bʎes'ʈjaʃʃem 'xraɱe
И если б здесь, в блестящем храме
And if here in resplendent temple

xɽis'tos vas'kɽes 'on uslɨ'xɑl
"Христос воскрес" Он услыхал
Christ (is) risen He heard

kɑ'ƙiɱi͡ p 'gɑɽƙiɱi sʎe'zɑɱi
Какими б горькими слезами
(With) what bitter tears

ɲe'ɽet tal'poĭ 'on zarɨ'dɑl
Перед толпой Он зарыдал!
Before crowd He would sob

7
k 'ɖeʈjam
К детям
To children

Date of composition: ***1906.***
Date of publication: ***1906.***
Publisher: ***A. Gutheil, Moscow.***
Dedicated to Maria S. and Arkady M. Kerzin.
Source: ***Alexei Khomyakov.***

bɨ'vɑla v glu'boƙiĭ pa'lunatʃnɨĭ 'tʃɑs
Бывало, в глубокий полуночный час,
Used to in deep midnight hour

ma'ļjutķi pŗi'du ļjuba'vɑtsa na
Малютки, приду любоваться на
Little ones (I would) come to admire at
'vɑs
вас;
you

bɨ'vɑla ļjub'ļju 'vɑs kŗes'tom
Бывало, люблю вас крестом
Used to love you (with) cross
znam̧e'nɑţ
знаменать,
make the sign of

ma'ļitsa dɑ 'buḑet na 'vɑs blaga'dɑţ
Молиться, да будет на вас благодать,
Pray that will be on you grace

ļju'boy̧ vşeḑer'ʒɨţeļja 'boga
Любовь Вседержителя Бога.
Love (of) Almighty God

sţe'ŗeʧ um̧i'ļenna 'vɑʃ 'ḑetsķiĭ pa'koĭ
Стеречь умиленно ваш детский покой,
To watch tenderly your child's rest

pa'dumaţ a 'tom kak vɨ 'ʧistɨ
Подумать о том как вы чисты
To think about that how you (are) pure
du'ʃoĭ
душой,
(with) soul

na'ḑejatsa 'dolģix i 'sʧɑsļivɨx 'dņeĭ
Надеяться долгих и счастливых дней,
To hope (for) long and happy days

Бывало, в глубокий полуночный час,
Малютки, приду любоваться на вас;
Бывало, люблю вас крестом знаменать,
Молиться, да будет на вас благодать,
Любовь Вседержителя Бога.
Стеречь умиленно ваш детский покой,
Подумать о том как вы чисты душой,
Надеяться долгих и счастливых дней,
Для вас, беззаботных и милых детей,
Как сладко, как радостно было!

Теперь прихожу я: везде темнота,
Нет в комнате жизни, кроватка пуста,
В лампаде погас пред иконою свет …
Мне грустно, малюток моих уже нет!
И сердце так больно сожмётся!
О, дети! В глубокий полуночный час,
Молитесь о том, кто молился о вас,
О том, кто любил вас крестом знаменать;
Молитесь, да будет и с ним благодать,
Любовь Вседержителя Бога.

dļja 'vɑs bezza'botnɨx i 'm̧ilɨx de'ţeĭ
Для вас, беззаботных и милых детей,
For you carefree and dear children

kak 'slɑtka kak 'rɑdasna 'bɨla
Как сладко, как радостно было!
How sweet how joyful it was

ţe'p̧eŗ p̧ŗixa'ʒu 'ja v̧ez'ḑe ţemna'tɑ
Теперь прихожу я: везде темнота,
Now come I everywhere darkness

'ņet f 'komnaţe 'ʒɨzņi kra'vɑtka pus'tɑ
Нет в комнате жизни, кроватка пуста,
No in room life small bed empty

v lɑm'pɑḑe pa'gɑs 'p̧ŗet i'konaju
В лампаде погас пред иконою
In icon lamp died down before icon
'sv̧et
свет …
light

mņe 'grusna mɑ'ļjutak ma'ix u'ʒɛ
Мне грустно, малюток моих уже
I am sad little ones my anymore
'ņet
нет!
not (here)

i 'şertsɛ 'tak 'boļna saʒ'm̧jotsa
И сердце так больно сожмётся!
And heart so painfully contracts

o 'ḑeţi v glu'boķiĭ pa'lunaʧnɨĭ 'ʧɑs
О, дети! В глубокий полуночный час,
O children In deep midnight hour

Long ago, in the still midnight hour
I would come to gaze upon you, my children;
Long ago, I would bless you with the sign of the cross,
And pray that with you would abide
The grace and the love of Almighty God.
I watched tenderly over your innocent rest
And thought how pure you are in your soul,
Hoping for a long, happy life
For you, my carefree, dear children.
How sweet, how joyful it was!

Now, when I come: it is dark everywhere,
There is no life in this room, the small bed is empty,
The light before the icon died down …
I am sad, my little ones are gone!
And my heart is distressed!
O, children! in the still midnight hour
Pray for him who prayed for you,
For him, who blessed you with the sign of the cross,
Pray that he too will receive grace
And the love of Almighty God.

ma'ļiţeş	a	'tom	'kto	ma'ļilsa	a	'vas
Молитесь	**о**	**том,**	**кто**	**молился**	**о**	**вас,**
Pray	about	one	who	prayed	for	you

a	'tom	'kto	ļju'b̧il	vas	kŗes'tom
О	**том,**	**кто**	**любил**	**вас**	**крестом**
About	one	who	loved	you (with)	cross
znaņe'naţ					
знаменать;					
make the sign of					

ma'ļiţeş	da	'buḑet	i	s	'ņim
Молитесь,	**да**	**будет**	**и**	**с**	**ним**
Pray	that	will be	too	with	him
blaga'daţ					
благодать,					
grace					

ļju'boɣ	vşeḑer'ʒiţeļja	'boga
Любовь	**Вседержителя**	**Бога.**
Love (of)	Almighty	God

8
pa'ʃʃadɨ ja ma'ļju
Пощады я молю!
(For) mercy I beg

Date of composition: ***1906.***
Date of publication: ***1906.***
Publisher: ***A. Gutheil, Moscow.***
Dedicated to Maria S. and Arkady M. Kerzin.
Source: ***Dmitri Merezhkovsky.***

pa'ʃʃɑdɨ ja ma'ļju ņe 'mutʃ m̧e'ņja
Пощады я молю! не мучь меня,
(For) mercy I beg (do) not torment me
yes'nɑ
весна,
spring

ņe patxa'ḑi ka 'mņe s
Не подходи ко мне с
(Do) not approach to me with
ba'ļezņennaju 'lɑskaĭ
болезненною лаской,
pained caress

i 'şertsɑ ņe bu'ḑi at 'm̧ertyennava
И сердца не буди от мертвенного
And heart (do) not wake from deathly
'snɑ
сна,
sleep

sva'jeĭ mlɑ'ḑentʃeskaĭ 'no 'trogaţeļnaĭ
Своей младенческой, но трогательной
(With) your childlike but moving
'skɑzkaĭ
сказкой.
fairy tale

tɨ 'yiḑiʃ kak ja 'slɑp 'o s'ʒɑļşja
Ты видишь, как я слаб, о, сжалься
You see how I (am) weak O take pity
'nɑda 'mnoĭ
надо мной!
at me

Пощады я молю! не мучь меня, весна,
Не подходи ко мне с болезненною лаской,
И сердца не буди от мертвенного сна,
Своей младенческой, но трогательной сказкой.
Ты видишь, как я слаб, о, сжалься надо мной!
Меня томит и жжёт твой ветер благовонный,
Я дорого купил забвенье и покой,
Оставь же их душе, страданьем утомлённой …

I beg for mercy! Do not torment me, spring,
Do not approach me with your pained caress,
And do not wake my heart from deathly slumber
With your childlike, but moving tale.
You see how weak I am, O, take pity!
I am parched and burnt by your fragrant wind,
I dearly bought oblivion and peace,
Leave them to my soul, by suffering wearied …

m̧e'ņja ta'm̧it i 'ʒʒot 'tvoĭ 'ɣeţer
Меня томит и жжёт твой ветер
Me parches and burns your wind
blɑga'vonnɨĭ
благовонный,
fragrant

ja 'doraga ku'p̧il zab'ɣeņje i pa'koĭ
Я дорого купил забвенье и покой,
I dearly bought oblivion and peace

as'tɑţ ʒɛ 'ix du'ʃɛ strɑ'dɑņjem
Оставь же их душе, страданьем
Leave — them (to) soul (by) suffering
u'tam'ļjonnaĭ
утомлённой …
wearied

9

ja a'p̧jaţ aḑi'nok
Я опять одинок
I (am) again alone

Date of composition: ***1906.***
Date of publication: ***1906.***
Publisher: ***A. Gutheil, Moscow.***
Dedicated to Maria S. and Arkady M. Kerzin.
Source: ***Ivan Bunin*** **(translation by Roland John Wiley).**

kak sɣet'lɑ kak na'ŗjadna ɣes'nɑ
Как светла, как нарядна весна!
How bright how dressy (is) spring

pag̡ja'd̡i 'mn̡e v gla'zɑ kak bɨ'vɑla
Погляди мне в глаза, как бывало,
Look me into eyes as used to

i ska'ʒɨ atʃe'vo tɨ grust'nɑ
И скажи: отчего ты грустна,
And tell why you (are) sad

atʃe'vo tɨ tak 'lɑskava 'stɑla
Отчего ты так ласкова стала?
Why you so caring became

'no mol'tʃiʃ 'tɨ sla'bɑ kak tsv̡e'tok
Но молчишь ты, слаба, как цветок …
But silent you (are) weak like flower

'o mal'tʃi mn̡e n̡e 'nɑda pr̡iz'nɑn̡ja
О, молчи! Мне не надо признанья …
O be silent (to) me not needed confession

ja uz'nɑl 'ɛtu 'lɑsku pra'ʃʃɑn̡ja
Я узнал эту ласку прощанья …
I recognized this caress (of) farewell

ja a'p̡jat̡ ad̡i'nok
Я опять одинок!
I (am) again alone

Как светла, как нарядна весна!
Погляди мне в глаза, как бывало,
И скажи: отчего ты грустна,
Отчего ты так ласкова стала?
Но молчишь ты, слаба, как цветок …
О, молчи! Мне не надо признанья …
Я узнал эту ласку прощанья …
Я опять одинок!

How bright, how elegant is spring!
Look into my eyes, as often before,
And tell me: why are you sorrowful,
Why have you become so caring?
But you are silent—weak like a flower …
Be silent, then! I need no confession …
I recognize this tenderness of farewell …
I am again alone!

10
u maje'vo ak'nɑ
У моего окна
At my window

Date of composition: ***1906.***
Date of publication: ***1906.***
Publisher: ***A. Gutheil, Moscow.***
Dedicated to Maria S. and Arkady M. Kerzin.
Source: ***Glafira Galina.***

u maje'vo ak'nɑ ʧe'ŗjomuxa
У моего окна черёмуха
At my window bird
tsye'ţjot
цветёт,
cherry blossoms

tsye'ţjot zɑ'dumʧiva pat 'ŗizaĭ
Цветёт задумчиво под ризой
Blossoms pensively under raiment
şeŗe'bŗistaĭ
серебристой …
silvery

i 'yetkaĭ 'syeʒɛĭ i du'ʃɨstaĭ
И веткой свежей и душистой,
And (with) branch fresh and fragrant

skla'ņilaş i za'yjot
Склонилась и зовёт …
Inclines and beckons

je'jo tŗe'ŗeʃʃuʃʃix vaz'duʃnɨx ļeŗest'kof
Её трепещущих воздушных лепестков
(Of) its quivering ethereal petals

У моего окна черёмуха цветёт,
Цветёт задумчиво под ризой серебристой …
И веткой свежей и душистой,
Склонилась и зовёт …
Её трепещущих воздушных лепестков
Я радостно ловлю весёлое дыханье,
Их сладкий аромат туманит мне сознанье,
И песни о любви они поют без слов …

ja 'radasna lav'ļju ye'şjolaje dɨ'xaŋje
Я радостно ловлю весёлое дыханье,
I joyfully catch cheerful breath

ix 'slatkiĭ ara'mat tu'maŋit mŋe
Их сладкий аромат туманит мне
Their sweet aroma obscures (to) me
saz'naŋje
сознанье,
consciousness

i 'ȿesŋi 'o ļjub'ɣi a'ŋi pa'jut ƀes
И песни о любви они поют без
And songs of love they sing without
'slof
слов ...
words

At my window a bird cherry blossoms,
Blossoms pensively in its silvery raiment ...
And with its fresh and fragrant branch
It inclines and beckons ...
Of its quivering, ethereal petals
I joyfully take in the cheerful breath,
Their sweet fragrance obscures my consciousness,
And they sing love songs without words ...

11
fan'tan
Фонтан
Fountain

Date of composition: ***1906.***
Date of publication: ***1906.***
Publisher: ***A. Gutheil, Moscow.***
Dedicated to Maria S. and Arkady M. Kerzin.
Source: ***Feodor Tyutchev*** **(translation by Roland John Wiley).**

smat'ŗi kak 'oblakam ʒɨ'vɨm
Смотри, как облаком живым,
See like cloud living

fan'tan şi'jajuʃʃiĭ klu'ƀitsa
Фонтан сияющий клубится,
Fountain shining swirls

kak plaɱe'ŋejet kak dra'ƀitsa
Как пламенеет, как дробится
How blazes how disperses

je'vo nɑ 'sontsɛ 'vlɑʒnɨĭ dɨm
Его на солнце влажный дым.
Its in sun moist spray

lu'ʧom pad'ŋjafʃiş k 'ŋebu
Лучом поднявшись к небу,
(As) ray having rose to heaven

'on kas'nulsa vɨsa'tɨ za'ɣetnaĭ
Он коснулся высоты заветной
It touched height longed for

i 'snova 'pɨļju agŋe'tsɣetnaĭ
И снова пылью огнецветной
And again (as) dust fiery-colored

ŋis'pɑsţ na 'ʐemļju asuʒ'ḑjon
Ниспасть на землю осуждён …
To fall on earth is destined

Смотри, как облаком живым,
Фонтан сияющий клубится,
Как пламенеет, как дробится
Его на солнце влажный дым.
Лучом поднявшись к небу,
Он коснулся высоты заветной
И снова пылью огнецветной
Ниспасть на землю
осуждён …

See, like a living cloud
The shining fountain swirls,
How its moist spray
Blazes and disperses in the
sunlight.
A shaft of it, having risen toward
heaven,
Touched the longed-for heights
But it is destined to fall again
In fiery dust, to earth …

12
'noʧ ꝑe'ʧɑļna
Ночь печальна
Night (is) sorrowful

Date of composition: ***1906.***
Date of publication: ***1906.***
Publisher: ***A. Gutheil, Moscow.***
Dedicated to Maria S. and Arkady M. Kerzin.
Source: ***Ivan Bunin*** **(translation by Roland John Wiley and Natalia Challis).**

'notʃ ᶈe'tʃɑᶅna kak ᶆetʃ'tɨ ma'i
Ночь печальна как мечты мои …
Night (is) sorrowful, like dreams my

daᶅe'ko v glu'xoĭ sƫe'ᶈi ʃɨ'rokaĭ
Далеко, в глухой степи широкой,
Far in remote steppe wide

aga'ᶇjok ᶆer'tsɑjet aᶁi'noᶄiĭ
Огонёк мерцает одинокий …
Small light glows solitary

v 'ᶊertsɛ 'mnoga 'grusƫi i ᶅjub'ɣi
В сердце много грусти и любви.
In heart much sadness and love

'no ka'mu i 'kak ras'skɑʒɛʃ 'tɨ
Но кому и как расскажешь ты,
But (to) whom and how will tell you

'ʃto za'ɣjot ƫe'bja 'tʃem 'ᶊertsɛ 'polna
Что зовёт тебя, чем сердце полно?
What beckons you (with) what heart (is) full

puƫ da'ᶅjok glu'xɑja 'sƫeᶈ bez'molvna
Путь далёк, глухая степь безмолвна,
Path (is) long remote steppe (is) silent

'notʃ ᶈe'tʃɑᶅna kak ma'i ᶆetʃ'tɨ
Ночь печальна, как мои мечты.
Night (is) sorrowful like my dreams

Ночь печальна как мечты мои …
Далеко, в глухой степи широкой,
Огонёк мерцает одинокий …
В сердце много грусти и любви.
Но кому и как расскажешь ты,
Что зовёт тебя, чем сердце полно?
Путь далёк, глухая степь безмолвна,
Ночь печальна, как мои мечты.

Night is sorrowful, as my dreams are …
Far away, in the deep and spacious steppe
Glows a solitary light …
In my heart there is much sadness and much love.
But to whom and how does one explain
What beckons, what fills one's heart?
The path is long, the silent steppe remote,
Night is sorrowful, as my dreams are …

13

fʧe'rɑ mɨ fst'ŗeţiļiş

Вчера мы встретились

Yesterday we met

Date of composition: ***1906.***
Date of publication: ***1906.***
Publisher: ***A. Gutheil, Moscow.***
Dedicated to Maria S. and Arkady M. Kerzin.
Source: ***Yakov Polonsky.***

fʧe'rɑ	mɨ	fst'ŗeţiļiş	a'nɑ
Вчера	**мы**	**встретились:**	**она**
Yesterday	we	met	she

astana'ɣilaş
остановилась,
stopped

ja	'tɑkʒɛ	mɨ	v	gla'zɑ	druk	'drugu
Я	**также …**	**Мы**	**в**	**глаза**	**друг**	**другу**
I	also	We	into	eyes	to each	other

pasmat'ŗeļi
посмотрели …
looked

'o	'boʒɛ	kak	a'nɑ	s	ţex	'por
О,	**Боже!**	**как**	**она**	**с**	**тех**	**пор**
O	God	how	she	since	then	has

p̧eŗem̧e'ņilaş
переменилась,
changed

Вчера мы встретились: она остановилась,
Я также … Мы в глаза друг другу посмотрели …
О, Боже! как она с тех пор переменилась,
В глазах потух огонь, и щёки побледнели …
И долго на неё глядел я, молча, строго …
Мне руку протянув, бедняжка улыбнулась;
Я говорить хотел, она же, ради Бога,
Велела мне молчать, и тут же отвернулась,
И брови сдвинула, и выдернула руку,
И молвила: "Прощайте, до-свиданья!"
А я хотел сказать: на вечную разлуку
Прощай, погибшее, но милое созданье!

v glaˈzax paˈtux aˈgoņ i ˈʃʃoki
В глазах потух огонь, и щёки
In eyes died light and cheeks
pabļed'ņeļi
побледнели …
became pale

i ˈdolga na ņiˈjo gļjaˈḑel ja ˈmolʧa
И долго на неё глядел я, молча,
And long at her looked I silently
ˈstroga
строго …
severely

mņe ˈruku praţjaˈnuf ḅeˈdņjaʃka
Мне руку протянув, бедняжка
(To) me hand giving poor one
ulɨbˈnulaş
улыбнулась;
smiled

ja gavaˈŗiţ xaˈţel aˈnɑ ʒɛ ˈrɑḑi ˈboga
Я говорить хотел, она же, ради Бога,
I to speak wanted she — for sake of God

ɣeˈļela ˈmņe malˈʧɑţ i ˈtut ʒɛ
Велела мне молчать, и тут же
Implored me to be silent and at once
atɣerˈnulɑş
отвернулась,
turned away

i ˈbroɣi sdˈɣinuf i ˈvɨḑernula
И брови сдвинула, и выдернула
And eyebrows frowning and pulled out
ˈruku
руку,
hand

Yesterday we met: she stopped
And so did I … We looked into each other's eyes …
My God! How she has changed since then,
Her eyes have lost their light, her cheeks were pale …
And long I looked at her, silently, severely …
She gave me her hand, sadly smiled,
I wished to speak, but she implored me
To be silent, turned away
And frowned, took her hand from mine
And said: "Farewell, goodbye!"
But I wished to say: "We part forever,
Farewell, lost but dear soul!"

i 'moly̦ila pra'ʃʃɑĭţe da sy̦i'dɑņja
И молвила: "Прощайте, до-свиданья!"
And said Farewell good-bye

ɑ ja xa'ţel ska'zaţ na 'y̦eʧnuju raz'luku
А я хотел сказать: на вечную разлуку
And I wanted to say for eternal parting

pra'ʃʃɑĭ pa'g̦ipʃɛje 'no 'm̦ilaje saz'dɑņje
Прощай, погибшее, но милое созданье!
Farewell lost but dear creature

14
kaļ'tso
Кольцо
Ring

Date of composition: *1906.*
Date of publication: *1906.*
Publisher: *A. Gutheil, Moscow.*
Dedicated to Maria S. and Arkady M. Kerzin.
Source: *Alexei Koltsov.*

'ja za'ţepļju sy̦e'ʧu
Я затеплю свечу
I will light candle

'vosku 'jarova
Воску ярова,
(Of) wax pure

raspa'jaju kaļ'tso
Распаяю кольцо
Will undo ring

'druga 'm̡ilava
Друга милова …
(Of) friend dear

zaga'ŗiş razga'ŗiş
Загорись, разгорись,
Burn burn fiercely

raka'voĭ a'goņ
Роковой огонь!
Fateful fire

raspa'jaĭ rasta'p̡i
Распаяй, растопи
Undo melt

'ʧista 'zolata
Чисто золото!
Pure gold

'b̡ez ņe'vo 'dļja m̡i'ņja
Без него для меня
Without him for me

tɨ ņe 'nadabna
Ты не надобно;
You (are) not needed

'bez ņe'vo na ru'ķe
Без него на руке
Without it on hand

'kam̡eņ 'na şer'tsɛ
Камень на сердце.
Stone on heart

Я затеплю свечу
Воску ярова,
Распаяю кольцо
Друга милова …
Загорись, разгорись,
Роковой огонь!
Распаяй, растопи
Чисто золото!
Без него для меня
Ты не надобно;
Без него на руке
Камень на сердце.
Что взгляну, то вздохну,
Затоскуюся.
И зальются глаза
Горьким горем слёз.
Возвратится ли он?
Или весточкой
Оживит меня,
Безутешную?
Нет надежды в душе …
Ты рассыпься же
Золотой слезой,
Память милова!
Невредимо, черно
На огне кольцо
И звенит по столу
Память вечную …

'ʃto vzgļja'nu 'to vzdax'nu
Что взгляну, то вздохну,
When (I) look then (I) sigh

zatas'kujuşja
Затоскуюся.
Grieve

i za'ļjutsa gla'zɑ
И зальются глаза
And filled eyes

'goŗķim 'goŗem 'sļjoz
Горьким горем слёз.
(With) bitter grief (of) tears

vazvra'ţitsa ļi 'on
Возвратится ли он?
Will return — he

'iļi 'yestatʃkaĭ
Или весточкой
Or (with) a word (from him)

aʒɨ'yit m̦e'ņja
Оживит меня,
Will liven me

bezu'ţeʃnuju
Безутешную?
Inconsolable

ņet nɑ'ḑeʒdɨ v du'ʃɛ
Нет надежды в душе …
No hope in soul

I will light a candle
of pure wax,
will undo the ring
of my beloved …
Burn, burn fiercely,
fateful fire!
Undo and melt
this pure gold!
Without my beloved
I do not need you.
Without the ring on my hand
my heart is heavy.
When I look at the ring, I sigh
and grieve,
bitter tears
fill my eyes.
Will he return?
Or with a word will he
gladden me,
so inconsolable?
There is no hope in my soul …
Then dissolve
like a golden tear,
the memory of my beloved!
Intact and blackened
by the fire is my ring
and falling on the table in knells
eternal memory …

ti ras'sɨp̡ʂja ʒɛ
Ты рассыпься же
You scatter then

zala'toĭ sl̡e'zoĭ
Золотой слезой,
(In) golden tear

'pam̡jat̡ 'm̡ilava
Память милова!
Memory (of) beloved

n̡evr̡e'd̡ima tʃer'no
Невредимо, черно
Intact black

na ag'n̡e kal̡'tso
На огне кольцо
In fire ring

i zɣe'n̡it pa sta'lu
И звенит по столу
And rings on table

'pam̡jat̡ 'ɣetʃnuju
Память вечную …
Memory eternal

15
pra'xoḑit 'fşjo
Проходит всё
Passes all

Date of composition: ***1906.***
Date of publication: ***1906.***
Publisher: ***A. Gutheil, Moscow.***
Dedicated to Maria S. and Arkady M. Kerzin.
Source: ***Daniil Rathaus.***

pra'xoḑit 'fşjo i 'ņet k ņe'mu vaz'vrɑta
Проходит всё, и нет к нему возврата.
Passes all and no to it return

ʒɨzņ 'mʧitşa 'vdaļ mgna'ɣeņija
Жизнь мчится вдаль, мгновения
Life rushes (into) distance, (than) instant
bɨst'ŗeĭ
быстрей.
faster

'gḑe 'zvuķi 'slof zvu'ʧɑʃʃix
Где звуки слов, звучащих
Where (are) sounds (of) words, sounding
'nɑm kag'dɑ ta
нам когда-то?
(to) us once

'gḑe 'sɣet za'ŗi 'nɑs aza'ŗjafʃɨx
Где свет зари нас озарявших
Where (is) light (of) dawn us brightened
'dņeĭ
дней?
days

Проходит всё, и нет к нему возврата.
Жизнь мчится вдаль, мгновения быстрей.
Где звуки слов, звучащих нам когда-то?
Где свет зари нас озарявших дней?
Расцвёл цветок, а завтра он увянет.
Горит огонь, чтоб вскоре отгореть …
Идёт волна, над ней другая встанет …
Я не могу весёлых песен петь!

rɑs'tsy̧jol	tsy̧e'tok	ɑ	'zɑftra	'on	u'y̧jaņet
Расцвёл	**цветок,**	**а**	**завтра**	**он**	**увянет.**
Blossoms	flower	and	tomorrow	it	will fade

ga'ŗit	a'goņ	'ʃtop	fs'koŗe	atga'ŗeţ
Горит	**огонь,**	**чтоб**	**вскоре**	**отгореть …**
Burns	fire	to	soon	burn out

i'ḑjot	val'nɑ	nat	'ņeĭ	dru'gɑja	'fstɑņet
Идёт	**волна,**	**над**	**ней**	**другая**	**встанет …**
Comes	wave	over	it	another	will rise

ja	ņe	ma'gu	y̧e'şjolɨx	'p̧eşen	'p̧eţ
Я	**не**	**могу**	**весёлых**	**песен**	**петь!**
I	not	can	joyful	songs	sing

All passes, and to the past there is no return.
Life rushes on, faster than an instant.
Where are the sounds of words which once to us resounded?
Where is the light of dawn which brightened us?
A flower blossoms, tomorrow it will fade,
A fire burns, soon to die out …
A wave appears, another wave will rise above it …
And joyful songs I cannot sing!

VI. Songs of Opus 34

1. **Муза (The Muse)**
2. **В душе у каждого из нас (In the soul of each of us)**
3. **Буря (The storm)**
4. **Ветер перелётный (A passing breeze)**
5. **Арион (Arion)**
6. **Воскрешение Лазаря (The raising of Lazarus)**
7. **Не может быть! (It cannot be!)**
8. **Музыка (Music)**
9. **Ты знал его (You knew him)**
10. **Сей день я помню (I remember this day)**
11. **Оброчник (The herald)**
12. **Какое счастье (What happiness)**
13. **Диссонанс (Dissonance)**
14. **Вокализ (Vocalise)**

Although the early years of the twentieth century were a time of increasing modernism in the Russian arts, Rachmaninoff followed his distinct aesthetic vision in the magnificent cycles of vocal compositions written during this time—the Liturgy of Saint John Chrysostom, the Vespers and the Songs of Opus 34, in which he brought together the melodic elements of ancient Russian chants and the classical tradition of the nineteenth century.

Rachmaninoff composed the songs of Opus 34 in 1912, in just sixteen days at Ivanovka. The texts, some suggested by the poet Marietta Shaginyan, reflect the spiritual and intellectual aspirations of a poet-singer. Rachmaninoff does not reconceive the texts in music as he does in his earlier song cycles; he lets the poet speak in a declamatory vocal line and adds his musical inflections, elegiac and refined, austere in form and emotion.

It should be noted that Rachmaninoff chose classical nineteenth-century texts for this cycle, and three of these texts are by Alexander Pushkin, who presented in his poem "The Prophet" the artistic and ethical credo followed by the best Russian poets to this day. Pushkin speaks of the vision of the Prophet Isaiah, when a Seraphim touches the prophet-poet's lips with a glowing coal of inspiration "to burn with sounds of words the hearts of men."[9] Pushkin's "The Muse," "The

Storm," and "Arion" develop the theme of poetic inspiration, and each poem is followed by Rachmaninoff with an antiphonal comment of another poem.

The prologue to the cycle is "The Muse," a poem compared by the critic Belinsky to a magnificent classical sculpture that can be seen in the sounds of words.[10] Rachmaninoff gives this singularly beautiful text a harmonious image in music. The poetic lines are divided in the vocal part by brief caesuras, which do not break the melodic line but give the declamation suppleness and versatility. The classical imagery of the text is preserved in the simplicity of the musical texture, and a melodic figure in the piano accompaniment, reminiscent of the "flute of seven pipes" in the poem, is rich in implied and actual modulations. At the concluding lines "The reed was animated by divine breath/And my heart filled with sacred enchantment," the poetic and musical diapason grows, filled with the joy and ecstasy of inspiration, then returns to the original key of E minor (the key of the Muse in Rachmaninoff's songs?). The second song, "In the soul of each of us," written with great restraint in vocal style and accompaniment, reflects that a wellspring of creative joy and sorrow exists in the soul of each of us.

In the songs "The storm" and "A passing breeze" Rachmaninoff contrasts an image of poetic inspiration amid the clash of elemental forces of nature with that of a passing breeze gently touching a dark and sullen sea. The metaphor of the sea as "the sea of life surging with vain tempests"[11] is a recurring one in Russian liturgical poetry and was often used in vocal lyrics of the early nineteenth century. "The Storm" begins in the tonality of E minor and progresses in powerful chromatic passages in the piano accompaniment to create the image of wind and waves surging at the feet of the Muse. Inspiration as the quiet voice of a breeze is rendered by Rachmaninoff in a soaring melodic line on the words "A passing breeze flowed in a ripple," as the darkness of the sea is lit by the dawn, also a recurring image for creativity in his songs.

"Arion" and "The raising of Lazarus" conclude Rachmaninoff's reflections on inspiration. The stormy sea is triumphant in "Arion"; all perish, and only the poet lives to sing hymns as before. The musical realization in this song is similar to the old *znamenny* chants and is repeated in "The raising of Lazarus," in which the poet asks to overcome the storms of the sea of life and to be given the prophetic gift of praise to God and His creation in song.

"It cannot be" was written by Apollon Maykov on the death of his young daughter. Rachmaninoff set Maykov's words to music as he mourned the death of the actress Vera Komissarzhevskaya, who personified "the voice of eternal spring on the Russian stage,"[12] in the words of the poet Alexander Blok.

Dedicated to Tchaikovsky the melodist, "Music" is the prologue to the second set of songs in this cycle, which reflect on the "ethereal world of sounds" and their creators. "Melody is music," wrote Rachmaninoff, "the elemental foundation of music, inasmuch as a perfect melody presupposes and calls to life a harmonic activity."[13] As in a number of his lyrical songs, Rachmaninoff's melodic intonation in this song is not easily discerned but gradually captivates the listener and enchants him by its inexhaustible source for melodic development.

The songs "You knew him" and "The herald" project the composer's own artistic aspirations and create an image not unlike one given him by a friend: "In Rachmaninoff there was not a shadow of false emotion nor a hint of pose or theatricality. He had an ideally wise simplicity, a manliness and chastity of expression. He possessed restraint, peace, concentration, a seeming coldness, and at the same time all his being was filled with the music he performed. He made us participate in his joys, sorrow, laughter, in his tenderness. He led us where he wanted to lead us, and we followed him without murmur and joyfully."[14]

The lyrical miniature "This day I remember" is contrasted with the harmonious unity of "The Muse." Its pastoral mood is enhanced by a reed pipe figure in the piano accompaniment, and the song develops the vocal and piano parts on two planes, now joining, now crossing over, now leaving each other. The poet compares his Muse to the dawn of creativity, when the world is seen by him in a new light.

"What happiness" echoes the love lyrics of the composer's youth, as he shares the beauty of the world with a beloved in a moment of rapture and inspiration. When such love becomes only a reminiscence as in "Dissonance," Rachmaninoff delineates the psychological nuances and contrasts of mood in a dramatic and lyrical lament, with a complex vocal line and a virtuoso piano accompaniment.

The last song of the cycle, "Vocalise," was written in 1915, and here words give precedence to the world of pure sounds. "Vocalise" is remarkable for its freely moving melody, which has as its basis a brief *popevka* (an initial motif) sung in variations in the style of the Russian *znamenny* chant, with its free meter and rhythm and a classical clarity of form, similar to the endless melodies of Bach.

In the songs of Opus 34 there is no immediacy of emotion as evident in Rachmaninoff's earlier works, and the thematic material is concentrated in the piano accompaniment, a departure from the romance genre of the nineteenth century. The cycle is similar in musical concept to the hymn-songs of the Liturgy and the Vespers, written during the same period as Opus 34, where "the emotional reaction is not brought about by a mood created by the music; rather the mood first is created by reaction to concrete ideas expressed in the text, and only then it is reflected by the character of the music, which is inseparably linked to the text."[15] Upon completing the cycle, Rachmaninoff wrote to Marietta Shaginyan: "All in all, I am satisfied with the songs and I rejoice that they were written easily, without much suffering. May God grant that my future work will continue as well."[16]

1
'muza
Муза
Muse

Date of composition: ***1912.***
Date of publication: ***1913–1916.***
Publisher: ***A. Gutheil, Moscow.***
Dedicated to R. E. (Marietta Shaginyan).
Source: ***Alexander Pushkin*** **(translation by Roland John Wiley).**

v mlɑ'ḑentʃestye ma'jom a'nɑ m̧e'ņja
В младенчестве моём она меня
In childhood my she me
ļju'b̧ila
любила
loved

i şem̧i'stvoļnuju tsɛv'ņitsu 'mņe
И семиствольную цевницу мне
And seven-piped flute (to) me
vru'tʃila
вручила;
handed

a'nɑ vņi'mɑla 'mņe s u'lɨpkaĭ i
Она внимала мне с улыбкой, и
She listened (to) me with smile and
sļex'kɑ
слегка
lightly

pa 'zvonķim 'skvɑʒɨnam pus'tova
По звонким скважинам пустого
On resonant holes (of) hollow
trastņi'kɑ
тростника
reed

u'ʒɛ nɑ'igrɨval ja 'slɑbɨm̧i p̧er'stɑm̧i
Уже наигрывал я слабыми перстами,
Already played I (with) weak fingers

i 'ģimnɨ 'vɑʒnɨe vnu'ʃonnɨe ba'gɑm̧i
И гимны важные, внушённые богами,
Both hymns solemn inspired (by) gods

В младенчестве моём она меня любила
И семиствольную цевницу мне вручила;
Она внимала мне с улыбкой, и слегка
По звонким скважинам пустого тростника
Уже наигрывал я слабыми перстами,
И гимны важные, внушённые богами,
И песни мирные фригийских пастухов.
С утра до вечера в немой тени дубров
Прилежно я внимал урокам девы тайной;
И радуя меня наградою случайной,
Откинув локоны от милого чела,
Сама из рук моих свирель она брала.
Тростник был оживлён божественным дыханьем
И сердце наполнял святым очарованьем.

i 'p̡esn̡i 'm̡irnɨe fr̡i'g̡iĭsk̡ix pastu'xof
И песни мирные фригийских пастухов.
And songs peaceful (of) Phrygian shepherds

c ut'rɑ da 'ɣetʃera v n̡e'moĭ t̡e'n̡i
С утра до вечера в немой тени
From morn to evening in mute shade
dub'rof
дубров
(of) groves

pr̡i'l̡eʒna ja vn̡i'mɑl u'rokam 'd̡evɨ
Прилежно я внимал урокам девы
Diligently I heeded (to) lessons (of) maiden
'tɑĭnaĭ
тайной;
secret

i 'rɑduja m̡e'n̡ja na'grɑdaju
И радуя меня наградою
And rejoicing me (with) reward
slu'tʃɑĭnaĭ
случайной,
unexpected

at'k̡inuf 'lokanɨ at 'm̡ilava tʃe'lɑ
Откинув локоны от милого чела,
Brushing back curls from sweet brow

sa'mɑ iz 'ruk ma'ix svi'r̡el̡ a'nɑ
Сама из рук моих свирель она
Herself from hands mine flute/reed pipe she
bra'lɑ
брала.
took

In my childhood she loved me
And handed me the flute of seven pipes;
Smiling, she listened to me,
And gently touching the soundholes of the hollow reed
With my weak fingers, I played already then
Both solemn hymns inspired by the gods
And songs of peaceful Phrygian shepherds.
From morn to evening in the groves' mute shade,
I heeded diligently the secret maiden's words;
And rejoicing me with unexpected favor,
Having brushed back the curls from her sweet brow,
She herself took the panpipes from my hands.
The reed was animated by divine breath
And my heart filled with sacred enchantment.

trast'ɲik bɨl aʒɨv'ʎon ba'ʒɛstvennɨm
Тростник был оживлён божественным
Reed was animated (by) divine
dɨ'xaɲjem
дыханьем
breath

i 'ʂertsɛ napal'ɲjal svja'tɨm
И сердце наполнял святым
And heart was filled (with) sacred
atʃara'vaɲjem
очарованьем.
enchantment

2
v du'ʃɛ u 'kaʒdava iz 'nas
В душе у каждого из нас
In soul of each of us

Date of composition: ***1912.***
Date of publication: ***1913–1916.***
Publisher: ***A. Gutheil, Moscow.***
Dedicated to Feodor I. Chaliapin.
Source: ***Apollon Korinfsky.***

v du'ʃɛ u 'kaʒdava iz 'nas
В душе у каждого из нас
In soul of each of us

ʒur'tʃit rad'ɲik sva'jei̯ pe'tʃaʎi
Журчит родник своей печали;
Murmurs well-spring (of) our own sorrow

iz	'ᶀᶅiʒᶇix	'stran	iz	'daᶅnaĭ	'daᶅi
Из	**ближних**	**стран,**	**из**	**дальной**	**дали**
From	nearby	lands	from	distant	distance

je'jo	ᶈᶉi'ᶅivɨ	praᶀe'gaᶅi
Её	**приливы**	**пробегали**
Its	flows	surged

v	za'ɣetnɨĭ	ᶆik	v	bla'ʒɛnnɨĭ	'ʧas
В	**заветный**	**миг,**	**в**	**блаженный**	**час**
At	secret	moment	in	blessed	hour

v	du'ʃɛ	u	'kaʒdava	iz	'nas
В	**душе**	**у**	**каждого**	**из**	**нас.**
In	soul	of	each	of	us

ag'ᶇjom	stras'ƫeĭ	apaᶅe'na
Огнём	**страстей**	**опалена**
(By) fire	(of) passions	burnt

du'ʃa	ᶇe	'ɣeᶉit	upa'jeᶇju
Душа	**не**	**верит**	**упоенью**
Soul	does not	believe	rapture

ᶇi	ᶆima'ᶅjotnamu	vᶅe'ʧeᶇju
Ни	**мимолётному**	**влеченью**
Neither	(to) fleeting	enchantment

ᶇi	ᶀeska'ᶇeʧnamu	zab'ɣeᶇju
Ни	**бесконечному**	**забвенью**
Nor	(to) endless	oblivion

ᶇe	paka'ᶉjajetsa	a'na
Не	**покоряется**	**она,**
Does not	surrender	she

В душе у каждого из нас
Журчит родник своей печали;
Из ближних стран, из дальной дали
Её приливы пробегали
В заветный миг, в блаженный час
В душе у каждого из нас.
Огнём страстей опалена
Душа не верит упоенью
Ни мимолётному влеченью
Ни бесконечному забвенью
Не покоряется она,
Огнём страстей опалена …
Моя любовь- печаль моя,
В ней солнца свет, в ней мрак неволи,
В ней жизнь, в ней крик предсмертный боли
В ней глубина паденья воли,
В ней путь к вершинам бытия,
Моя печаль- любовь моя! …

agˈŋjom strasˈţeĭ apaļeˈnɑ
Огнём страстей опалена ...
(By) fire (of) passions burnt

maˈja ļjuˈboʃ peˈʧɑļ maˈja
Моя любовь- печаль моя,
My love (is) sorrow my

v ˈŋeĭ ˈsontsa ˈsyet v ˈŋeĭ ˈmrɑk
В ней солнца свет, в ней мрак
In it sun's light in it gloom
ŋeˈvoļi
неволи,
(of) bondage

v ˈŋeĭ ˈʒɨzŋ v ŋeĭ ˈkʈik pʈetˈsʍertnɨĭ
В ней жизнь, в ней крик предсмертный
In it life in it cry before death
ˈboļi
боли
(of) pain

v ˈŋeĭ gluɓiˈnɑ paˈḑeŋja ˈvoļi
В ней глубина паденья воли,
In it depth (of) fall (of) will

v ˈŋeĭ ˈpuţ k yerˈʃɨnam bɨţiˈja
В ней путь к вершинам бытия,
In it path to heights (of) being

maˈja peˈʧɑļ ļjuˈboʃ maˈja
Моя печаль- любовь моя! ...
My sorrow (is) love my

In the soul of each of us
Murmurs the wellspring of our sorrow;
From nearby lands, from distant places
Its waters surge
At that secret moment, that blessed hour
In the soul of each of us.
Burnt by the flame of passions,
The soul does not believe the rapture;
To enchantment fleeting
Nor immense oblivion
It does not surrender,
Burnt by the flame of passions.
My love is my sorrow,
In it there is the light of sun, the gloom of bondage,
In it flows life, and sounds the cry of death,
In it lies the depth to which the will can fall,
In it leads a path to the heights of being,
My sorrow is my love! ...

3
'buŗja
Буря
Storm

Date of composition: ***1912.***
Date of publication: ***1913–1916.***
Publisher: ***A. Gutheil, Moscow.***
Dedicated to Leonid V. Sobinov.
Source: ***Alexander Pushkin.***

ja 'ɣiḑel 'ḑevu na ska'ļe
Я видел деву на скале,
I saw maiden on cliff

v a'ḑeʒḑe 'ţelaĭ 'nad val'naɱi
В одежде белой над волнами,
In raiment white above waves

kag'da bu'ʃuja v 'burnaĭ mg'ļe
Когда бушуя в бурной мгле,
When surging in stormy haze

ig'rala 'moŗe s ţeŗe'gaɱi
Играло море с берегами.
Played sea with shores

kag'da 'lutʃ 'molņiĭ aza'ŗjal
Когда луч молний озарял
When ray (of) lightning illumined

je'jo fşe'tʃasna 'bļeskam 'alɨm
Её всечасно блеском алым,
Her continually (with) brilliance scarlet

Я видел деву на скале,
В одежде белой над волнами,
Когда бушуя в бурной мгле,
Играло море с берегами.
Когда луч молний озарял
Её всечасно блеском алым,
И ветер бился и летал,
С её летучим покрывалом!
Прекрасно море в бурной мгле,
И небо в блестках, без лазури;
Но верь мне: дева на скале
Прекрасней волн, небес и бури.

i ˈyeţer ˈb̦ilsa i ļeˈtal
И ветер бился и летал,
And wind struggled and flew

s jeˈjo ļeˈtuʧim pakrɨˈvalam
С её летучим покрывалом!
With her flying veil

pŗeˈkrasna ˈmoŗe v ˈburnaĭ mgˈļe
Прекрасно море в бурной мгле,
Beautiful (is) sea in stormy haze

i ˈņeba v ˈbļeskax ˈb̦ez laˈzuŗi
И небо в блесках, без лазури;
And sky in flashes without azure

ˈno ˈyeŗ ˈmņe ˈḑeva na skaˈļe
Но верь мне: дева на скале
But believe me maiden on cliff

pŗeˈkrasņeĭ ˈvoln ņeˈb̦es i ˈbuŗi
Прекрасней волн, небес и бури.
(Is more) beautiful (than) waves, heavens and storm

I saw a maiden on a cliff,
In white raiment, above the waves,
When, surging in the stormy haze,
The sea played with the shores;
When lightning's glow illumined her
Continually with scarlet brilliance,
And the wind soared and struggled
With her flying veil!
Beautiful is the sea, in stormy haze,
The sky in lightning streaks, sky without azure,
But do believe me: the maid on the cliff
Is more beautiful than waves, than heavens, than the storm.

4

ɣe'ţer p̧eŗe'ļjotnɨĭ
Ветер перелётный
Breeze passing

Date of composition: ***1912.***
Date of publication: ***1913–1916.***
Publisher: ***A. Gutheil, Moscow.***
Dedicated to Leonid V. Sobinov.
Source: ***Konstantin Balmont.***

'ɣeţer	p̧eŗe'ļjotnɨĭ	abla'skɑl	m̧e'nja
Ветер	**перелётный**	**обласкал**	**меня**
Breeze	passing	caressed	me

i	ʃɛp'nul	pe'ʧɑļna	'noʧ	şiļ'n̡eje
И	**шепнул**	**печально:**	**“Ночь**	**сильнее**
And	whispered	sorrowfully	Night	(is) stronger
'dn̡ja				
дня.”				
(than) day				

i	za'kɑt	pa'm̧erknul	'tuʧi	paʧer'n̡eļi
И	**закат**	**померкнул.**	**Тучи**	**почернели.**
And	sunset	dimmed	Clouds	darkened

'drognuļi	smu'ţiļiş	'pɑsmurnɨe	'jeļi
Дрогнули,	**смутились**	**пасмурные**	**ели**
Shuddered	disturbed	somber	firs

i	'nɑt	'ţjomnɨm	'moŗem	'gd̡e	kru'ţilsa
И	**над**	**тёмным**	**морем,**	**где**	**крутился**
And	over	dark	sea	where	swirled
'vɑl					
вал,					
wave					

Ветер перелётный обласкал меня
И шепнул печально: “Ночь сильнее дня.”
И закат померкнул. Тучи почернели.
Дрогнули, смутились пасмурные ели
И над тёмным морем, где крутился вал,
Ветер перелётный зыбью пробежал.
Ночь царила в мире.
А меж тем далёко
За морем зажглося огненное око.
Новый распустился в небесах цветок,
Светом возрождённым заблистал восток.
Ветер изменился и пахнул мне в очи,
И шепнул с усмешкой:
“День сильнее ночи!”

'ɣ̧eţer p̧eŗe'ļjotnɨĭ 'zɨb̧ju prab̧e'ʒɑl
Ветер перелётный зыбью пробежал.
Breeze passing (in) ripple flowed

'notʃ tsɑ'ŗila v 'm̧iŗe
Ночь царила в мире.
Night reigned in world

ɑ m̧eʃ 'ţem dɑ'ļjoka
А меж тем далёко
But meantime far away

'za maŗem zɑʒ'gloşja 'ogņennaje 'oka
За морем зажглося огненное око.
Beyond sea lit fiery eye

'novɨĭ raspus'ţilsa v ņeb̧e'sɑx tsɣ̧e'tok
Новый распустился в небесах цветок,
New blossomed in heavens flower

'sɣ̧etam vazraʒ'ḑjonnɨm zabļi'stɑl
Светом возрождённым заблистал
(With) light renascent sparkled
vas'tok
восток.
east

'ɣ̧eţer izm̧e'ņilsa i pax'nul mņe v 'otʃi
Ветер изменился и пахнул мне в очи,
Breeze changed and breathed (to) me in eyes

i ʃɛp'nul s us'm̧eʃkaĭ
И шепнул с усмешкой:
And whispered with smile

'ḑeņ şiļ'ņeje 'notʃi
"День сильнее ночи!"
Day (is) stronger (than) night

A passing breeze caressed me
And whispered sorrowfully:
"Night is more powerful than day."
The sunset dimmed. Clouds darkened.
Somber firs shuddered and swayed.
Over the dark sea, where waves wash ashore,
A passing breeze flowed in a ripple.
Night reigned in the world.
But—far away,
Beyond the sea, a fiery eye was lit.
A radiant flower blossomed in the heavens,
The east glowed with a renascent light.
The wind changed, touched my face
And whispered with a smile:
"Day is stronger than the night!"

5
aŗi'on
Арион
Arion

Date of composition: ***1912.***
Date of publication: ***1913–1916.***
Publisher: ***A. Gutheil, Moscow.***
Dedicated to Leonid V. Sobinov.
Source: ***Alexander Pushkin.***

nɑs 'b̧ɨla 'mnoga na ʧel'ņe
Нас было много на челне:
(Of) us were many on bark

i'nɨje 'pɑrus napŗja'gɑļi
Иные парус напрягали,
Some sail manned

dru'ɡ̧ije druʒ'na up̧i'rɑļi
Другие дружно упирали
Others as one plunged

vg'lup̧ 'moʃʃnɨ 'ɣ̧josla f ţiʃɨ'ņe
Вглубь мощны вёсла. В тишине
Into depth powerful oars. In calm

na 'ruļ skla'ņjaş 'nɑʃ 'kormʃʃik 'umnɨi
На руль склонясь, наш кормщик умный
Onto wheel bent our helmsman wise

v mal'ʧɑņji 'prɑɣ̧il 'gruznɨĭ ʧoln
В молчаньи правил грузный чёлн;
In silence guided heavy bark

Нас было много на челне:
Иные парус напрягали,
Другие дружно упирали
Вглубь мощны вёсла. В тишине
На руль склонясь, наш кормщик умный
В молчаньи правил грузный чёлн;
А я беспечной верой полн
Пловцам я пел … Вдруг лоно волн
Измял с налёту вихорь шумный …
Погиб и кормщик и пловец.
На берег выброшен грозою,
Я гимны прежние пою,
И ризу влажную мою
Сушу на солнце под скалою.

ɑ 'ja b̧es'p̧etʃnaĭ 'ɣeraĭ 'poln
А я беспечной верой полн
And I (with) carefree trust full

plaf'tsɑm ja 'p̧el vd'ruk 'lona
Пловцам я пел … Вдруг лоно
(To) seafarers I sang Suddenly bosom
'voln
волн
(of) waves

iz'm̧jal s nɑ'ļjotu 'ɣixaŗ
Измял с налёту вихорь
Was crushed with swoop whirlwind
'ʃumnɨĭ
шумный …
roaring

pa'ģip i 'kormʃʃik i pla'ɣets
Погиб и кормщик и пловец.
Perished both helmsman and seafarer

na 'b̧eŗek 'vɨbraʃɛn gra'zoju
На берег выброшен грозою,
Onto shore thrown (by) storm

ja 'ģimnɨ 'pŗeʒņije pa'ju
Я гимны прежние пою,
I hymns former sing

i 'ŗizu 'vlɑʒnuju ma'ju
И ризу влажную мою
And raiment damp my

su'ʃu na 'sontsɛ pat ska'loju
Сушу на солнце под скалою.
Dry in sun under cliff

There were many of us in the bark:
Some manned the sails,
Others, as one, plunged the powerful oars
Deep in the waters. In calm seas,
Our wise helmsman, bent over the wheel,
Guided the heavily laden bark.
And I, trusting and carefree,
Sang to the seafarers … Suddenly, the waves' bosom
Was crushed by a roaring whirlwind …
The helmsman and the seamen perished.
Onto the shore thrown by the storm,
I sing the hymns I sang before,
And my damp raiment
I dry by the cliff, in the sun.

6
vaskŗe'ʃɛņije 'lɑzaŗja
Воскрешение Лазаря
Raising (of) Lazarus

Date of composition: ***1912.***
Date of publication: ***1913–1916.***
Publisher: ***A. Gutheil, Moscow.***
Dedicated to Feodor I. Chaliapin.
Source: ***Alexei Khomyakov.***

'o	'tsɑŗ	i	'box	'moĭ	'slova	'şilɨ
О	**Царь**	**и**	**Бог**	**мой!**	**Слово**	**силы**
O	King	and	God	my	Word	(of) power

va	'vŗeɱja	'onə	tɨ	ska'zɑl
Во	**время**	**оно**	**Ты**	**сказал,**
In	time	(of) yore	You	spoke

i	sakru'ʃon	'bɨl	'pļen	ma'ģilɨ
И	**сокрушён**	**был**	**плен**	**могилы,**
And	shattered	was	bondage	(of) grave

i	'lɑzaŗ	'oʒɨl	i	vas'stɑl
И	**Лазарь**	**ожил**	**и**	**восстал.**
And	Lazarus	came to life	and	rose

ma'ļju	da	'slova	'şilɨ	'gŗjaņet
Молю	**да**	**слово**	**силы**	**грянет,**
(I) pray	that	word	(of) power	will sound

da	'skɑʒɛʃ	fs'tɑņ	du'ʃɛ	ma'jeĭ
Да	**скажешь**	**"Встань!"**	**душе**	**моей,**
That	(You) will say	"Arise"	(to) soul	my

О Царь и Бог мой! Слово силы
Во время оно Ты сказал,
И сокрушён был плен могилы,
И Лазарь ожил и восстал.
Молю да слово силы грянет,
Да скажешь "Встань!" душе моей,
И мёртвая из гроба встанет,
И выйдет в свет Твоих лучей;
И оживёт, и величавый
Ея хвалы раздастся глас,
Тебе сиянью Отчей славы,
Тебе умершему за нас!

i 'ɱjortvaja iz 'groba fs'taņet
И мёртвая из гроба встанет,
And dead from grave will rise

i 'vɨĭḑet f 'sɣet tva'ix
И выйдет в свет Твоих
And will come forth into light (of) Your
lu'ʧeĭ
лучей;
rays

i aʒɨ'ɣjot i ɣeļi'ʧɑvɨĭ
И оживёт, и величавый
And will live and august

je'ja xva'lɨ raz'dɑstşa 'glɑs
Ея хвалы раздастся глас,
(Of) its praise will resound voice

ţe'b̡e şi'jaņju 'oʧeĭ 'slɑvɨ
Тебе сиянью Отчей славы,
(To) You radiance (of) Father's glory

ţe'b̡e u'ɱerʃɛmu za 'nɑs
Тебе умершему за нас!
(To) You (Who) died for us

O, my King and God! The word of power
You had spoken in the time of yore—
The bondage of the grave was shattered
And Lazarus rose to life.
I pray the word of power will be sounded,
That You will say "Arise" to my soul,
Dead, it will rise from the grave
And will come forth into the radiance of Your light.
My soul will live, and the august voice
Of its praise will resound,
Praise to You, the radiance of our Father's glory,
To You, Who died for us!

7
ņe 'moʒɛt bɨţ
Не может быть!
(It) cannot be

Date of composition: ***1910, revised 1912.***
Date of publication: ***1913–1916.***
Publisher: ***A. Gutheil, Moscow.***
Dedicated to Vera F. Komissarzhevskaya.
Source: ***Apollon Maykov.***

ņe 'moʒɛt 'bɨţ ņe 'moʒɛt 'bɨţ
Не может быть! не может быть!
(It) cannot be (it) cannot be

a'nɑ ʒɨ'vɑ şeĭ'ʧɑs pra'sņjotsa
Она жива … сейчас проснётся …
She (is) alive now will wake

sma'tŗiţe 'xoʧet gava'ŗiţ
Смотрите: хочет говорить,
Look wants to speak

at'krojet 'oʧi ulɨb'ņjotsa
Откроет очи, улыбнётся,
Will open eyes will smile

m̦e'ņja u'ɣiḑefʃɨ paĭ'm̦jot
Меня увидевши, поймёт,
Me seeing will understand

'ʃto ņeu'ţeʃnɨĭ 'plɑʧ 'moĭ 'znɑʧit
Что неутешный плач мой значит,
What inconsolable weeping my means

Не может быть! не может быть!
Она жива … сейчас проснётся …
Смотрите: хочет говорить,
Откроет очи, улыбнётся,
Меня увидевши, поймёт,
Что неутешный плач мой значит,
И вдруг с улыбкою шепнёт:
“Ведь я жива! О чём он плачет
Но нет! лежит … тиха, нема, недвижна …

i vd'ruk s u'lɨpkaju ʃɛp'ņjot
И вдруг с улыбкою шепнёт:
And suddenly with smile will whisper

ɣeḑ 'ja ʒɨ'vɑ a 'ʧom 'on 'plɑʧet
"Ведь я жива! О чём он плачет
But I (am) alive Why he weeps

'no 'ņet ļe'ʒɨt ţi'xɑ ņe'mɑ ņe'dɣiʒnɑ
Но нет! лежит … тиха, нема, недвижна …
But no lies quiet mute not moving

It cannot be! It cannot be!
She is alive … now she will wake …
Look: she is about to speak,
Her eyes will open, she will smile,
And seeing me, she will understand
My grief, which no one can console,
And then, with a smile, she will whisper:
"I am alive! Why does he weep?"
But no! she lies … quiet, silent, still …

8
'muzɨka
Музыка
Music

Date of composition: ***1912.***
Date of publication: ***1913–1916.***
Publisher: ***A. Gutheil, Moscow.***
Dedicated to P. Tch.
Source: ***Yakov Polonsky*** **(translation by Roland John Wiley).**

i plɨ'vut i ras'tut 'ɛţi 'ʧudnɨje
И плывут, и растут эти чудные
And hover and grow these marvelous
'zvuķi
звуки!
sounds

zaxva'ţila m̧e'ņja ix val'nɑ
Захватила меня их волна …
Swept me their wave

padŋja'lɑş padŋja'lɑ i ŋe'ɣedamaĭ
Поднялась, подняла и неведомой
Rose lifted and (with) mysterious
'muķi
муки
torment

i bla'ʒɛnstva pal'nɑ
И блаженства полна …
And (with) bliss filled

i ba'ʒɛstɣennɨĭ 'ļik na mgna'ɣeŋje
И божественный лик на мгновенье
And divine image for instant

ŋeula'ɣimaĭ sɣerk'nuf krasa'toĭ
Неуловимой сверкнув красотой,
(With) elusive flashing beauty

fs'plɨl kɑk ʒɨ'voje ɣi'ɖeŋje
Всплыл, как живое виденье,
Rose like living vision

nɑt 'ɛtaĭ vaz'duʃnaĭ kŗi'stɑļnaĭ val'noĭ
Над этой воздушной, кристальной волной,
Above this ethereal crystal wave

i atra'ʐilşa i pakaʧ'nulsa
И отразился, и покачнулся,
And was reflected and slightly moved

ŋe 'to ulɨb'nulşa
Не то улыбнулся …
Perhaps (it) smiled

ŋe 'to prasļe'ʐilşa
Не то прослезился …
Perhaps (it) shed a tear

И плывут, и растут эти
чудные звуки!
Захватила меня их волна …
Поднялась, подняла и
неведомой муки
И блаженства полна …
И божественный лик на
мгновенье
Неуловимой сверкнув
красотой,
Всплыл, как живое виденье,
Над этой воздушной,
кристальной волной,
И отразился, и покачнулся,
Не то улыбнулся …
Не то прослезился …

How it hovers and grows, this
wave of marvelous sounds!
It swept me away …
It rose, and filled with mysterious
torment and with bliss,
It lifted me up …
And for an instant a divine image,
A flash of elusive beauty
Glowed, like a living vision
Above this wave, ethereal and
clear,
And was reflected, and slightly
moved,
Perhaps it smiled …
Perhaps it shed a tear …

9
tɨ 'znɑl je'vo
Ты знал его
You knew him

Date of composition: ***1912.***
Date of publication: ***1913–1916.***
Publisher: ***A. Gutheil, Moscow.***
Dedicated to Feodor I. Chaliapin.
Source: ***Feodor Tyutchev.***

tɨ 'znɑl je'vo f kru'gu baḽ'ʃova 'sʏetɑ
Ты знал его в кругу большого света,
You knew him in circle (of) high society

'to svajen'rɑvna 'ʏeşel 'to u'gr̦jum
То своенравно весел, то угрюм,
Now willfully lighthearted, now morose

rɑs'şejan 'ḑik 'iḽ 'polan 'taĭnɨx
Рассеян, дик, иль полон тайных
Lost in thought, wild, or full (of) secret
'dum
дум,
thoughts

ta'kof po'ɛt i tɨ pr̦ez'r̦el po'ɛta
Таков поэт и ты презрел поэта!
Such (is) poet and you disdained poet

na m̦e'şjats vz'gḽjɑn̦ 'ʏeş ḑen̦ kak
На месяц взглянь: весь день, как
At crescent moon look all day as
'oblak 'toʃʃiĭ
облак тощий,
cloud thin

Ты знал его в кругу большого света,
То своенравно весел, то угрюм,
Рассеян, дик, иль полон тайных дум,
Таков поэт и ты презрел поэта!
На месяц взглянь: весь день, как облак тощий,
Он в небесах едва не изнемог;
Настала ночь, и светозарный бог,
Сияет он над усыплённой рощей!

on v ɲeɓe'sɑx jed'vɑ ɲe izɲe'mok
Он в небесах едва не изнемог;
It in heavens barely languishes

nɑ'stɑla 'notʃ i sʏeta'zɑrnɨĭ bok
Настала ночь, и светозарный бог,
Came night and lightbearing god

ʂi'jajet 'on nat usɨ'pʎjonnaĭ 'roʃʃeĭ
Сияет он над усыплённой рощей!
Shines it over lulled to sleep grove

You knew him in society's circles,
Now willfully lighthearted, now morose,
Or lost in thought, unsociable, bearing a secret muse,
Such is a poet, and you disdained a poet!
Glance at the crescent moon: all day, like a veiled cloud,
It languishes in heaven.
But night comes, and a lightbearing god
It shines above the grove, which has been lulled to sleep.

10

'ʂeĭ 'ɖeɲ ja 'pomɲju
Сей день я помню
This day I remember

Date of composition: ***1912.***
Date of publication: ***1913–1916.***
Publisher: ***A. Gutheil, Moscow.***
Dedicated to Leonid V. Sobinov.
Source: ***Feodor Tyutchev.***

'sʂĭ 'ɖeɲ ja 'pomɲju 'dʎja ɱe'ɲja
Сей день я помню, для меня
This day I remember for me

bɨl 'utram 'ʒizɲennava 'dɲja
Был утром жизненного дня.
(It) was morning (of) life's day

sta'jala 'moltʃa 'pʂeda 'mnoju
Стояла молча предо мною,
(She) stood silently before me

Сей день я помню, для меня
Был утром жизненного дня.
Стояла молча предо мною,
Вздымалась грудь ея.
Алели щёки как заря,
Всё жарче рдея и горя …
И вдруг, как солнце золотое,
Любви признанье молодое,
Исторглось из груди ея,
И новый мир увидел я!

vzdɨ'mαlaş 'grudٰ je'ja
Вздымалась грудь ея.
Was rising breast her

a'ļeļi 'ʃʃoķi kak za'ŗja
Алели щёки как заря,
Glowed cheeks like dawn

'fşjo 'ʒαrʧe 'rḑeja i gα'ŗja
Всё жарче рдея и горя…
All hotter blushing and burning

i vd'ruk kak 'sontsɛ zala'toje
И вдруг, как солнце золотое,
And suddenly like golden sun

ļjub'ɣi pŗi'znαņje mala'doje
Любви признанье молодое,
Love's confession young

is'torglaş iz gru'ḑi je'ja
Исторглось из груди ея,
Was forced from breast her

i 'novɨĭ 'm̧ir u'ɣiḑel ja
И новый мир увидел я!
And new world saw I

I remember this day,
It was the morning of my life.
Silently, she stood before me,
Her breast rising,
Her cheeks aglow like the dawn,
Blushing and afire …
Suddenly, as the golden sun,
Love's young confession
Came from her breast,
And a new world appeared before me!

11
a'broʧņik
Оброчник
Herald

Date of composition: ***1912.***
Date of publication: ***1913–1916.***
Publisher: ***A. Gutheil, Moscow.***
Dedicated to Feodor I. Chaliapin.
Source: ***Afanasy Fet.***

xa'rugɣ	sɣja'ʃʃennuju	paḑ'jaf	sva'jeĭ
Хоругвь	**священную**	**подьяв**	**своей**
Banner	holy	having lifted	(with) my

ḑes'noĭ
десной,
right hand

i'du	i	'tronulaş	za	'mnoĭ	tal'pɑ
Иду.	**И**	**тронулась**	**за**	**мной**	**толпа**
(I) walk.	And	started	behind	me	crowd

ʒɨ'vaja
живая,
living

i	paţja'nuļiş	'fşe	pa	'proşeķe	ļes'noĭ
И	**потянулись**	**все**	**по**	**просеке**	**лесной,**
And	stretched	all	along	clearing	woods'

i	ja	bla'ʒɛn	i	'gort	sɣja'tɨņju
И	**я**	**блажен**	**и**	**горд,**	**святыню**
And	I (am)	blessed	and	proud	holy things

vaşpe'vaja
воспевая.
singing

Хоругвь священную подьяв своей десной,
Иду. И тронулась за мной толпа живая,
И потянулись все по просеке лесной,
И я блажен и горд, святыню воспевая.
Пою и помыслам неведом детский страх:
Пускай на пенье мне ответят воем звери,
С святыней над челом, и песней на устах,
С трудом, но я дойду до вожделенной двери.

pa'ju i 'pomɨslam ņe'γedam
Пою и помыслам неведом
(I) sing and (to) thoughts (is) unknown
'ḑetsķiĭ 'strɑx
детский страх:
child's fear

pus'kɑĭ na 'peņje mņe at'γeţjat
Пускай на пенье мне ответят
Let to singing (to) me answer
'vojem 'zγeŗi
воем звери,
(with) howling animals

s‿sγja'tɨņeĭ 'nɑt ʧe'lom i 'p̧esņeĭ na
С святыней над челом, и песней на
With holy thing over brow and song on
us'tɑx
устах,
lips

s tru'dom 'no ja daĭ'du da
С трудом, но я дойду до
With difficulty but I will reach towards
vaʒḑe'ļennaĭ 'dγeŗi
вожделенной двери.
longed for door.

Lifting the holy banner in my arm
I walk. The multitude started moving after me,
In slow procession, along the clearing in the woods.
I am blessed and proud, hymning the holy things.
I sing, and to my thoughts a child's fear is unknown:
If my hymn will be answered by a howl of animals,
With holy banner over my head, and with a song on my lips,
I will reach, though arduously, the longed-for portal.

12
ka'koje 'sʧɑsţje
Какое счастье
What happiness

Date of composition: ***1912.***
Date of publication: ***1913–1916.***
Publisher: ***A. Gutheil, Moscow.***
Dedicated to Leonid V. Sobinov.
Source: ***Afanasy Fet.***

ka'koje 'sʧɑsţje i 'noʧ i
Какое счастье: и ночь, и
What happiness (it is) both night and
mɨ ad'ņi
мы одни!
we (are) alone

ŗe'kɑ kak 'z̧erkala i 'fşja bļes'ţit
Река как зеркало и вся блестит
River like mirror and all glistening
zɣez'dɑm̧i
звездами,
(with) stars

ɑ tam tɨ 'golavu za'ķiņ ka da
А там ты голову закинь-ка, да
And there you head toss and
vzgļja'ņi
взгляни:
look

ka'kɑja glub̧i'nɑ i ʧista'tɑ nad 'nɑm̧i
Какая глубина и чистота над нами!
What depth and purity above us

Какое счастье: и ночь, и мы одни!
Река как зеркало и вся блестит звездами,
А там ты голову закинь-ка, да взгляни:
Какая глубина и чистота над нами!
О, называй меня безумным!
Назови чем хочешь: в этот миг я разумом слабею
И в сердце чувствую такой прилив любви,
Что не могу молчать, не стану, не умею!
Я болен, я влюблён, но мучась и любя,
О, слушай! о пойми! я страсти не скрываю,
И я хочу сказать, что я люблю тебя,
Тебя, одну тебя люблю я и желаю!

'o nazɨ'vɑĭ m̧e'ņja b̧ez'umnɨm
О, называй меня безумным!
O call me mad

naza'v̧i ʧem 'xoʧeʃ v 'ɛtat m̧ik ja
Назови чем хочешь: в этот миг я
Call what (you) will at this moment I
'rɑzumam sla'b̧eju
разумом слабею
(in) reason grow weak

i f 'sertsɛ 'ʧustvuju ta'koĭ p̧ŗi'ļif
И в сердце чувствую такой прилив
And in heart feel such flood
ļub'v̧i
любви,
(of) love

'ʃto ņe ma'gu mal'ʧɑţ ņe 'stɑnu ņe
Что не могу молчать, не стану, не
That cannot be silent will not (am) not
u'm̧eju
умею!
able

ja 'boļen ja vļub'ļon 'no 'muʧɑş i
Я болен, я влюблён, но мучась и
I ache I (am) in love but tormented and
ļu'b̧ja
любя,
loving

'o 'sluʃɑĭ o pɑĭ'm̧i ja 'strɑşţi ņe
О, слушай! о пойми! я страсти не
O listen O understand I passion (do) not
skrɨ'vɑju
скрываю,
conceal

What happiness: it is night, and we are alone!
The river is like a mirror, all glistening from starlight,
And there, do toss your head, have a look:
What distance and purity above us!
O, call me mad!
Call me what you will: at this moment my reason grows weak
And in my heart I feel such a flood of love
That I cannot keep silence, I will not be silent!
I ache, I am in love, but tormented and loving,
O listen! O understand! I am not concealing my passion,
And I want to say that I love you,
You, you alone I love and desire!

i ja xa'ʧu ska'zɑt̡ 'ʃto ja l̡jub'l̡ju t̡e'b̡ja
И я хочу сказать, что я люблю тебя,
And I want to say that I love you

t̡e'b̡ja ad'nu t̡e'b̡ja l̡jub'l̡ju ja i ʒɛ'lɑju
Тебя, одну тебя люблю я и желаю!
You alone you love I and desire

13
d̡isso'nɑns
Диссонанс
Dissonance

Date of composition: ***1912.***
Date of publication: ***1913–1916.***
Publisher: ***A. Gutheil, Moscow.***
Dedicated to Felia Litvin.
Source: ***Yakov Polonsky.***

'pus̡t̡ pa 'vol̡e su'd̡ep ja rɑs'stɑlɑs̡ s
Пусть по воле судеб я рассталась с
Let by will (of) fates I parted with
ta'boĭ
тобой,
you

'pus̡t̡ dru'goĭ obla'dɑjet ma'jeĭ krasa'toĭ
Пусть другой обладает моей красотой!
Let another possess my beauty

iz ab'jat̡iĭ je'vo iz natʃ'noĭ duxa'tɨ
Из объятий его, из ночной духоты
From embrace his from night's closeness

una'ʃus̡ ja dɑ'l̡joka na 'krɨl̡jax
Уношусь я далёко на крыльях
Carried (am) I far on wings
m̡etʃ'tɨ
мечты.
(of) dream

'v̡iʒu 'snova 'nɑʃ 'stɑrɨĭ za'puʃʃennɨĭ
Вижу снова наш старый, запущенный
(I) see again our old overgrown
'sɑt
сад:
garden

atra'ʒonnɨĭ f pru'd̡e patu'xɑjet za'kɑt
Отражённый в пруде потухает закат;
Reflected in pond dims sunset

'pɑxn̡et 'l̡ipavɨm 'tsv̡etam f pra'xlɑd̡e
Пахнет липовым цветом в прохладе
Smells (of) linden blossom in cool
pa'l̡eĭ
полей,
(of) fields

za pru'dom gd̡e ta v 'roʃʃe ur'tʃit
За прудом, где-то в роще, урчит
Beyond pond somewhere in grove trills
sala'v̡eĭ
соловей …
nightingale

ja s̡t̡ek'l̡jannuju 'dv̡er̡ atva'r̡ila dra'ʒu
Я стеклянную дверь отворила, дрожу,
I glass door opened tremble

Пусть по воле судеб я
расстались с тобой,
Пусть другой обладает моей
красотой!
Из объятий его, из ночной
духоты
Уношусь я далёко на крыльях
мечты.
Вижу снова наш старый,
запущенный сад:
Отражённый в пруде
потухает закат;
Пахнет липовым цветом в
прохладе полей,
За прудом, где-то в роще,
урчит соловей …
Я стеклянную дверь отворила,
дрожу,
Я из мрака в таинственный
сумрак гляжу …
Чу! там хрустнула ветка, не
ты ли шагнул?!
Встрепенулася птичка, не ты
ли спугнул?!
Я прислушиваюсь, я
мучительно жду,
Я на шелест шагов твоих
тихо иду,
Холодит мои члены то
страсть, то испуг …
Это ты меня за руку взял,
милый друг
Это ты осторожно так
обнял меня!
Это твой поцелуй, поцелуй
без огня.
С болью в трепетном сердце,
с волненьем в крови,
Ты не смеешь отдаться
безумствам любви,
И внимая речам благородным
твоим,

ja iz 'mrɑka f ta'jinstɣennɨĭ 'sumrak
Я из мрака в таинственный сумрак
I from dark into mysterious twilight
gļe'ʒu
гляжу …
look

'ʧu 'tam 'xrusnula 'ɣetka ņe tɨ ļi
Чу! там хрустнула ветка, не ты ли
Hark there snapped branch (is it) not you
ʃɑg'nul
шагнул?!
(who) stepped

fstŗeņe'nulaşja 'pţiʧka ņe tɨ ļi
Встрепенулася птичка, не ты ли
Shook wings bird (is it) not you
spug'nul
спугнул?!
(who) startled (it)

ja pŗi'sluʃɨvajuş ja mu'ʧiţeļna 'ʒdu
Я прислушиваюсь, я мучительно жду,
I listen I anxiously wait

ja na 'ʃɛļest ʃa'gof tva'ix 'ţixa i'du
Я на шелест шагов твоих тихо иду,
I to rustle (of) steps your slowly walk

xala'ḑit ma'i 'ʧļenɨ 'to 'strɑsţ 'to
Холодит мои члены то страсть, то
Chills my limbs either passion or
is'puk
испуг …
fear

Я не смею дать волю
влеченьям своим,
И дрожу, и шепчу тебе:
Милый ты мой!
Пусть владеет он жалкой
моей красотой!
Из объятий его, из ночной
духоты
Я опять улетаю на крыльях
мечты
В этот сад, в эту темь, вот
на эту скамью,
Где впервые подслушал ты
душу мою …
Я душою сливаюсь с твоею
душой,
Пусть владеет он жалкой
моей красотой!

'ɛta tɨ ᶆe'ᶇja 'zɑ 'ruku 'vᶎjal 'ᶆilɨĭ 'druk
Это ты меня за руку взял, милый друг
It is you me by hand took dear friend

'ɛta tɨ asta'roʒna tak 'obᶇjal ᶆe'ᶇja
Это ты осторожно так обнял меня!
It is you carefully so embraced me

'ɛta 'tvoĭ patsɛ'luĭ patsɛ'luĭ ᶀez ag'ᶇja
Это твой поцелуй, поцелуй без огня.
It is your kiss kiss without fire

s 'boᶅju f 'ƫreᶈetnam 'ᶊertsɛ s
С болью в трепетном сердце, с
With pain in anxious heart with
val'ᶇeᶇjem f kra'ᶌi
волненьем в крови,
agitation in blood

tɨ ᶇe 'sᶆejeʃ at'dɑtᶊa ᶀez'umstvam
Ты не смеешь отдаться безумствам
You not dare surrender (to) madness
ᶅjub'ᶌi
любви,
(of) love

i vᶇi'mɑja ᶉe'ʧɑm blɑga'rodnɨm tva'im
И внимая речам благородным твоим,
And hearing words noble your

ja ᶇe 'sᶆeju 'dɑƫ 'voᶅju vᶅe'ʧeᶇjam
Я не смею дать волю влеченьям
I not dare give rein (to) attraction
sva'im
своим,
my

By the will of fate, I am parted from you,
And another possesses my beauty!
From his embrace, from the closeness of night
I am carried far on the wings of my dream.
Again do I see our old, overgrown garden,
The sunset's reflection dims in the pond,
There's a fragrance of lindens in the cool of the fields
And beyond, in the grove, a nightingale sings.
I open the glass door, I shiver,
From a darkened house I gaze into the mysterious twilight …
Hark! a branch snapped, was it under your feet?
A bird shook its wings, was it you who startled it?
I listen and anxiously wait,
Then walk slowly toward the sound of your footsteps,
My limbs are cold from passion or fear …
You take me by the hand, dear friend,
And embrace me so quietly!
Your kiss is a kiss without fire.
Pained, anxious, impassioned,
You dare not surrender to the maelstrom of love,
And hearing your noble words,
I dare not show my desire,
I tremble and whisper: Oh, my beloved!
Another possesses my wretched beauty!
From his embrace, from the closeness of night,

i dra'ʒu i ʃɛp'ʧu ʈe'ƥe 'ɱiliĭ
И дрожу, и шепчу тебе: Милый
And tremble and whisper (to) you Dear
tɨ 'moĭ
ты мой!
you (are) my

'pusʈ vlɑ'ɖejet 'on 'ʒɑlkaĭ ma'jeĭ
Пусть владеет он жалкой моей
Let (it be) possesses he wretched my
krasa'toĭ
красотой!
beauty

iz aƥ'jaʈiĭ je'vo iz natʃ'noĭ duxa'tɨ
Из объятий его, из ночной духоты
From embrace his from night's closeness

ja a'ƥjaʈ uʎe'tɑju na 'krɨʎjax ɱetʃ'tɨ
Я опять улетаю на крыльях мечты
I again fly away on wings (of) dream

v 'ɛtat 'sɑt v 'ɛtu 'ʈeɱ 'vot na 'ɛtu
В этот сад, в эту темь, вот на эту
To this garden to this darkness here to this
ska'ɱju
скамью,
bench

'gɖe fƥer'vɨje pat'sluʃɑl tɨ 'duʃu
Где впервые подслушал ты душу
Where for the first time overheard you soul
ma'ju
мою …
my

I again fly away on the wings of my dream
To that garden, its darkness, to this bench,
Where you first listened to my soul …
I become one with your soul,
My wretched beauty belongs to another!

ja	du'ʃoju	sļi'vɑjuş	s	tva'jeju
Я	**душою**	**сливаюсь**	**с**	**твоею**
I (with)	soul	merge	with	your

du'ʃoĭ
душой,
soul

'pusţ	vla'ḑejet	'on	'ʒɑlkaĭ	ma'jeĭ
Пусть	**владеет**	**он**	**жалкой**	**моей**
Let (it be)	possesses	he	wretched	my

krasa'toĭ
красотой!
beauty

14
voka'ļiz
Вокализ
Vocalise

Date of composition: ***1915.***
Date of publication: ***1913–1916.***
Publisher: ***A. Gutheil, Moscow.***
Dedicated to Antonina V. Nezhdanova.

Melody without words.

VII. Songs of Opus 38

1. Ночью в саду у меня (At night in my garden)
2. К ней (To her)
3. Маргаритки (Daisies)
4. Крысолов (The pied piper)
5. Сон (Sleep)
6. А у ("A-oo")

"... always love—love as a never weakening source of inspiration. It inspires as no other source does. Love becomes the stimulus for the flowering of intellectual energy," suggested Rachmaninoff in his reminiscences.[17]

Love in its emotional urgency of youth inspired the composer's first songs, and love interpreted by a mature artist is the unifying element in his last cycle of songs. As in Opus 34, he departed from the romance genre and named the cycle "Six poems for voice and piano," emphasizing the importance of both musical voices—the melodic declamation with cantilena episodes and the interpretative virtuoso music for the piano. The songs were dedicated to the young singer Nina Koshitz, considered a most sensitive interpreter of Rachmaninoff's songs.

Two songs on the sadness and elusiveness of love frame the cycle. The first song, "At night in my garden," is a stylized lament by Alexander Blok, in which Rachmaninoff uses all means of expression to interpret the sorrow of a weeping woman, symbolized by the weeping willow tree. The gentle movement for voice and the delicate piano figurations evoke the grieving over a lost love as in Desdemona's Willow Song in Verdi's *Otello*.

Rachmaninoff overcomes the artificiality of syntax and metaphor in the three poems by his contemporaries. He renders Bely's invocation to his beloved in a capricious rhythm with soaring flights for voice, and captures the capriciousness of sensual love in the "Pied Piper" in the now provocative, now foreboding quality of its music, with a rhythm characteristic of Russian folk incantations and love spells. The languorous world of the poem "Sleep" is interpreted with an enchanting melody for voice and a delicate pianistic texture.

The song "Daisies" has the composer's familiar intonational gesture as an invitation to share in nature's wonder, with a vocal line of considerable beauty and a transparent, flowing melody in the piano that suffuse the song with a feeling of spaciousness and the joy of springtime. "A-oo", in Russian a call to someone in the distance, sings of the elusiveness of romantic love, of which only an echo remains amid the beauty of nature and springtime, when "a flower lights the candle of another flower," an image of the Feast of the Resurrection in Russia when all share in the joy by extending a candle to light the candle of another. This radiant love shared by all is reflected upon in the postlude for the piano, which echoes the words of the song amid the distant ringing of the bells.

In his songs, written over a quarter of a century, Rachmaninoff reflected on the emotional and ethical states he experienced and observed, and he presents both the performer and the listener with images in music as his meditations on the beauty of art and life.

1
'notʃju f sa'du u m̡e'n̡ja
Ночью в саду у меня
At night in garden my

Date of composition: ***1916.***
Date of publication: ***1916.***
Publisher: ***Russian Music Publishers, Moscow.***
Dedicated to Nina P. Koshitz.
Source: ***Alexander Blok.***

'notʃju f sa'du u m̡e'n̡ja
Ночью в саду у меня
At night in garden my

'plɑtʃet pla'kutʃaja 'iva
Плачет плакучая ива,
Weeps weeping willow

i ḅezu'ţeʃna a'nɑ
И безутешна она
And inconsolable she

'ivuʃka 'grustnaja 'iva
Ивушка, грустная ива.
(Dear) willow, sad willow

'rɑnņeje 'utra bļes'ņjot
Раннее утро блеснёт,
Early morning will sparkle

'neʒnaja 'ḑevuʃka 'zoŗka
Нежная девушка Зорька.
Tender maiden Dawn

'ivuʃķe 'plɑʧuʃʃeĭ 'goŗka
Ивушке, плачущей горько,
(To dear) willow weeping bitterly

'sļjozɨ ku'dŗjaņi sa'ţŗjot
Слёзы кудрями сотрёт.
Tears (with) tresses will wipe.

Ночью в саду у меня
Плачет плакучая ива,
И безутешна она
Ивушка, грустная ива.
Раннее утро блеснёт,
Нежная девушка Зорька.
Ивушке, плачущей горько,
Слёзы кудрями сотрёт.

At night in my garden,
A weeping willow laments,
She can't be consoled,
My willow, sad willow tree.
Early morning will sparkle
And Dawn, tender maiden,
My willow's tears, bitter tears,
Will wipe with her tresses.

2
k 'ņeĭ
К ней
To her

Date of composition: ***1916.***
Date of publication: ***1916.***
Publisher: ***Russian Music Publishers, Moscow.***
Dedicated to Nina P. Koshitz.
Source: ***Andrei Bely.***

'trɑvɨ	a'ḑetɨ	'p̧erlam̧i
Травы	**одеты**	**перлами.**
Grasses	dressed	(with) pearls

'gḑe ta	p̧ŗi'ɣetɨ	'grustnɨje	'slɨʃu
Где-то	**приветы**	**грустные**	**слышу,**
Somewhere	greeting calls	sad	(I) hear

p̧ŗi'ɣetɨ	'm̧ilɨje
приветы	**милые …**
greeting calls	sweet

'm̧ilaja	'gḑe	tɨ	'm̧ilaja
Милая	**где**	**ты,**	**милая!**
Sweet	where (are)	you	sweet

'ɣetʃera	'sɣetɨ	'jasnɨje	'ɣetʃera
Вечера	**светы**	**ясные,**	**вечера**
(Of) evening	lights	clear	(of) evening

'sɣetɨ	'krɑsnɨje
светы	**красные!**
lights	radiant

'ruķi	vaz'ḑetɨ	'ʒdu	ţe'b̧ja	'm̧ilaja
Руки	**воздеты:**	**жду**	**тебя,**	**милая,**
Arms	uplifted	(I) await	you	sweet

'gḑe	tɨ	'm̧ilaja
где	**ты,**	**милая?**
where (are)	you	sweet

'ruķi	vaz'ḑetɨ	'ʒdu	ţe'b̧ja	f	st'rujax
Руки	**воздеты:**	**жду**	**тебя,**	**в**	**струях**
Arms	uplifted	(I) await	you	in	streams

'ļetɨ	'smɨtuju
Леты	**смытую**
(of) Lethe	washed away

Травы одеты перлами.
Где-то приветы грустные слышу, приветы милые …
Милая где ты, милая!
Вечера светы ясные, вечера светы красные!
Руки воздеты: жду тебя, милая, где ты, милая?
Руки воздеты: жду тебя, в струях Леты смытую
Бледными Леты струями …
Милая где ты, милая!

Grasses are adorned with pearls.
Somewhere, I hear calls, sad calls, sweet calls …
Sweet one where are you, my sweet!
Clear lights of the evening, radiant lights of the evening!
My arms are uplifted: I await you, sweet one, where are you, my sweet?
My arms are uplifted: I await you, in the streams of Lethe forgotten
By the pale streams of Lethe …
Sweet one, where are you, sweet one!

'b̧ļednɨm̧i 'ļetɨ 'strujam̧i
Бледными Леты струями ...
(By) pale (of) Lethe streams

'm̧ilaja 'gḑe tɨ 'm̧ilaja
Милая где ты, милая!
Sweet where (are) you sweet

3
marga'ŗitķi
Маргаритки
Daisies

Date of composition: ***No date.***
Date of publication: ***1916.***
Publisher: ***Russian Music Publishers, Moscow.***
Dedicated to Nina P. Koshitz.
Source: ***Igor Severyanin.***

'o pasma'ţŗi kak 'mnoga marga'ŗitak
О, посмотри, как много маргариток
O look how many daisies

i 'tam i 'tut
И там, и тут.
Both here and there

a'ņi tsv̧e'tut ix 'mnoga ix
Они цветут, их много, их
They blossom (of) them many (of) them
iz'bɨtak
избыток.
plenty

a'ņi tsye'tut
Они цветут.
They blossom

ix ļep̧est'ķi 'ţjox'grannɨje kak 'krɨļja
Их лепестки трёхгранные, как крылья,
Their petals three-edged like wings

kak 'b̧elɨĭ 'ʃolk
Как белый шёлк.
Like white silk

v ņix 'ļeta 'moʃʃ
В них лета мощь!
In them summer's might

v ņix 'radaşţ iza'b̧iļja
В них радость изобилья,
In them joy (of) abundance

v ņix 'syetlɨĭ 'polk
В них светлый полк.
In them radiant multitude

ga'toʄ z̧im'ļja tsye'tam iz 'ros
Готовь, земля цветам из рос
Prepare earth (to) flowers from dews
ńa'p̧itak
напиток,
draught

'daĭ 'sok şţeb'ļju
Дай сок стеблю …
Give sap (to) stalk

О, посмотри, как много
маргариток
И там, и тут.
Они цветут, их много, их
избыток.
Они цветут.
Их лепестки трёхгранные, как
крылья,
Как белый шёлк.
В них лета мощь!
В них радость изобилья,
В них светлый полк.
Готовь, земля цветам из рос
напиток,
Дай сок стеблю …
О, девушки, О, звёзды
маргариток, я вас люблю!

O, look, how many daisies
Both here and there.
They blossom, they blossom in
abundance.
Their three-edged petals are like
wings,
Like whitened silk.
The summer's essence fills them!
Joy of abundance
In their radiant multitude.
Earth, prepare a draught of dews
for these flowers,
Give life to their stalk …
O, maidens, O, stars of daisies, I
love you!

'o 'ḑevuʃķi 'o 'zɣjozdɨ marga'ŗitak ja 'vɑs
О, девушки, О, звёзды маргариток, я вас
O maidens O stars (of) daisies I love
ļjub'ļju
люблю!
you

4
krɨsa'lof
Крысолов
Pied piper

Date of composition: ***1916.***
Date of publication: ***1916.***
Publisher: ***Russian Music Publishers, Moscow.***
Dedicated to Nina P. Koshitz.
Source: ***Valery Bryusov.***

ja na 'dudaʧķe ig'rɑju
Я на дудочке играю,
I on pipe play

trɑ-ļja-ļja-ļja-ļja-ļja-ļja
Тра-ля-ля-ля-ля-ля-ля,
Tra-la-la-la-la-la-la

ja na 'dudaʧķe ig'rɑju
Я на дудочке играю,
I on pipe play

'ʧi ta 'duʃɨ ɣeşe'ļja
Чьи-то души веселя.
Some souls making merry

ja i'du 'vdoļ 'ţixaĭ 'ŗetʃķi
Я иду вдоль тихой речки,
I walk along quiet river

trɑ-ļja-ļja-ļja-ļja-ļja-ļja
Тра-ля-ля-ля-ля-ля-ля,
Tra-la-la-la-la-la-la

'dŗemļjut 'ţix̧ije a'ɣetʃķi
Дремлют тихие овечки,
Doze gentle lambs

'krotka 'zɨbļjutsa pa'ļja
Кротко зыблются поля.
Softly wave fields

'sp̧iţe 'ovtsɨ i ba'rɑʃķi
Спите овцы и барашки,
Sleep sheep and lambs

trɑ-ļja-ļja-ļja-ļja-ļja-ļja
Тра-ля-ля-ля-ля-ля-ля,
Tra-la-la-la-la-la-la

za lu'gɑm̧i 'krɑsnaĭ 'kɑʃķi
За лугами красной кашки
Beyond meadows (of) red clover

'stroĭna 'fstɑļi tapa'ļja
Стройно встали тополя.
Gracefully stand poplars

'mɑlɨĭ 'dom̧ik tam ta'itsa
Малый домик там таится,
Small house there is hidden

Я на дудочке играю,
Тра-ля-ля-ля-ля-ля-ля,
Я на дудочке играю,
Чьи-то души веселя.
Я иду вдоль тихой речки,
Тра-ля-ля-ля-ля-ля-ля,
Дремлют тихие овечки,
Кротко зыблются поля.
Спите овцы и барашки,
Тра-ля-ля-ля-ля-ля-ля,
За лугами красной кашки
Стройно встали тополя.
Малый домик там таится,
Тра-ля-ля-ля-ля-ля-ля,
Милой девушке приснится,
Что ей душу отдал я.
И на нежный зов свирели,
Тра-ля-ля-ля-ля-ля-ля,
Выйдет словно к светлой
цели,
Через сад, через поля.
И в лесу под дубом тёмным,
Тра-ля-ля-ля-ля-ля-ля,
Будет ждать в бреду
истомном,
В час когда уснёт земля.
Встречу гостью дорогую,
Тра-ля-ля-ля-ля-ля-ля,
Вплоть до утра зацелую,
Сердце лаской утоля.
И, сменившись с ней
колечком,
Тра-ля-ля-ля-ля-ля-ля,
Отпущу её к овечкам,
В сад, где стройны тополя.
Тра-ля-ля-ля!

trɑ-l̡ja-l̡ja-l̡ja-l̡ja-l̡ja-l̡ja
Тра-ля-ля-ля-ля-ля-ля,
Tra-la-la-la-la-la-la

'm̡ilaĭ 'd̡evuʃk̡e pr̡i'sn̡itsa
Милой девушке приснится,
Sweet maiden will dream

'ʃto 'jeĭ 'duʃu 'otdɑl ja
Что ей душу отдал я.
That (to) her (my) soul gave I

i na 'n̡eʒnɨĭ 'zof sv̡i'r̡el̡i
И на нежный зов свирели,
And to tender call (of) reed pipe

trɑ-l̡ja-l̡ja-l̡ja-l̡ja-l̡ja-l̡ja
Тра-ля-ля-ля-ля-ля-ля,
Tra-la-la-la-la-la-la

'vɨĭd̡et 'slovna k 'sv̡etlaĭ 'tsɛl̡i
Выйдет словно к светлой цели,
Will come as to bright goal

'ʧer̡es 'sɑt 'ʧer̡es pa'l̡ja
Через сад, через поля.
Through garden through fields

i v l̡e'su pat 'dubam 't̡jomnɨm
И в лесу под дубом тёмным,
And in forest under oak dark

trɑ-l̡ja-l̡ja-l̡ja-l̡ja-l̡ja-l̡ja
Тра-ля-ля-ля-ля-ля-ля,
Tra-la-la-la-la-la-la

I am playing my pipe,
Tra-la-la-la-la-la-la,
I am playing my pipe,
Making some souls merry.
I am walking along a quiet river,
Tra-la-la-la-la-la-la,
Gentle lambs doze,
Fields softly wave.
Sleep, sheep and lambs,
Tra-la-la-la-la-la-la,
Beyond meadows of red clover
Slender poplars rise.
There a small house is hidden,
Tra-la-la-la-la-la-la,
A sweet maiden will dream
That my soul I gave to her.
To the tender call of reed pipe,
Tra-la-la-la-la-la-la,
She will come as to a bright star,
Through the garden, through the fields.
Under a dark oak, in the forest,
Tra-la-la-la-la-la-la,
She will wait in a languorous dream,
At the hour when earth falls asleep.
I will meet the cherished guest,
Tra-la-la-la-la-la-la,
Till the morning I will kiss her,
My heart quenched with caresses.
And, exchanging rings with her,
Tra-la-la-la-la-la-la,
I will let her go, to the lambs,
Into the garden, where poplars rise.
Tra-la-la-la!

'buḑet 'ʒdaţ v bŗe'du is'tomnam
Будет ждать в бреду истомном,
Will wait in dream languorous

f 'ʧas kag'da us'ņjot z̧em'ļja
В час когда уснёт земля.
At hour when falls asleep earth

fst'ŗeʧu 'gosţju dara'guju
Встречу гостью дорогую,
Will meet guest cherished

tra-ļja-ļja-ļja-ļja-ļja-ļja
Тра-ля-ля-ля-ля-ля-ля,
Tra-la-la-la-la-la-la

fp'loţ da 'utra zatsɛ'luju
Вплоть до утра зацелую,
Right up to morning will kiss

'şertsɛ 'laskaĭ uta'ļja
Сердце лаской утоля.
Heart (with) caress quenching

i sm̧e'ņifʃiş s ņeĭ ka'ļeʧkam
И, сменившись с ней колечком,
And exchanging with her small ring

tra-ļja-ļja-ļja-ļja-ļja-ļja
Тра-ля-ля-ля-ля-ля-ля,
Tra-la-la-la-la-la-la

atpu'ʃʃu je'jo k a'v̧eʧkam
Отпущу её к овечкам,
Will let go her to lambs

f 'sɑt 'gɖe 'stroĭnɨ tapa'ʎja
В сад, где стройны тополя.
Into garden where (are) graceful poplars.

trɑ-ʎja-ʎja-ʎja
Тра-ля-ля-ля!
Tra-la-la-la

5
'son
Сон
Sleep

Date of composition: ***1916.***
Date of publication: ***1916.***
Publisher: ***Russian Music Publishers, Moscow.***
Dedicated to Nina P. Koshitz.
Source: ***Feodor Sologub.***

v 'ɱiɽe 'ɲet ɲiʧe'vo
В мире нет ничего
In world there is nothing

vaʒɖe'ʎenɲeje 'snɑ
Вожделеннее сна,
More desired (than) sleep

'ʧɑrɨ 'jesʈ u ɲe'vo
Чары есть у него,
Enchantments has it

u ɲe'vo ʈiʃɨ'nɑ
У него тишина,
It has peace

В мире нет ничего
Вожделеннее сна,
Чары есть у него,
У него тишина,
У него на устах
Ни печаль и ни смех,
И в бездонных очах
Много тайных утех.
У него широки,
Широки два крыла,
И легки, так легки,
Как полночная мгла.
Не понять как несёт,
И куда и на чём
Он крылом не взмахнёт
И не двинет плечом.

u ņe'vo na us'tɑx
У него на устах
It has on lips

ņi p̧e'tʃɑļ i ņi 'sm̧ex
Ни печаль и ни смех,
Neither sorrow and nor laughter

i v b̧ez'donnɨx a'tʃɑx
И в бездонных очах
And in fathomless eyes

'mnoga 'tɑĭnɨx u'ţex
Много тайных утех.
Many secret pleasures

u ņe'vo ʃɨra'ķi
У него широки,
It has wide

ʃɨraķi 'dvɑ krɨ'lɑ
Широки два крыла,
Wide two wings

i ļix'ķi tak ļix'ķi
И легки, так легки,
And light so light

kak pal'notʃnaja mg'lɑ
Как полночная мгла.
As midnight haze

ņe pa'ņjaţ kak ņe'şjot
Не понять как несёт,
(One) cannot understand how (it) carries

In this world there is nothing
More desired than sleep,
Sleep has enchantments
And peace.
On its lips
Neither sorrow nor laughter,
In its fathomless eyes
Secret pleasures abound.
It has wings,
Wide wings,
They are light, so light,
As the midnight mist.
How does it carry us,
Whence and on what?
Its wings do not open
And its body is still.

i ku'dɑ i na 'ʧom
И куда и на чём
And where and on what

'on krɨ'lom n̦e vzmax'n̦jot
Он крылом не взмахнёт
It (with) wing does not flap

i n̦e 'dyinet pl̦e'ʧom
И не двинет плечом.
And does not move shoulder.

6
ɑ u
А у
A-oo

Date of composition: ***1916.***
Date of publication: ***1916.***
Publisher: ***Russian Music Publishers, Moscow.***
Dedicated to Nina P. Koshitz.
Source: ***Konstantin Balmont.***

'tvoĭ 'n̦eʒnɨĭ 'sm̦ex bɨl 'skɑskaju
Твой нежный смех был сказкою
Your gentle laughter was fairy tale
iz'm̦enʧivaju
изменчивою,
changeable

'on 'zvɑl kak f 'son za'ɣjot sɣi'ŗeɭnɨĭ
Он звал как в сон зовёт свирельный
It called as to sleep calls reed-pipe's
'zvon
звон.
sound

i 'vot ɣen'kom sţi'xom ţe'ḅja
И вот венком, стихом тебя
And now (with) wreath (with) verse you
u'ɣenʧivaju
увенчиваю,
(I) crown

uĭ'ḑjom ḅe'ʒɨm vdva'jom na 'gornɨĭ
Уйдём, бежим вдвоём на горный
Let us go flee together to mountain
'sklon
склон.
side

'no 'gḑe ʒɛ 'tɨ
Но где же ты?
But where (are) — you

'ļiʃ 'zvon ɣer'ʃɨn paz'vɑņivajet
Лишь звон вершин позванивает.
Only sound (of) tops resounds

tsɣet'ku tsɣe'tok 'sŗeḑ 'dņja za'ʒok sɣe'ʧu
Цветку цветок средь дня зажёг свечу.
(To) flower flower midst day lit candle

Твой нежный смех был
сказкою изменчивою,
Он звал как в сон зовёт
свирельный звон.
И вот венком, стихом тебя
увенчиваю,
Уйдём, бежим вдвоём на
горный склон.
Но где же ты?
Лишь звон вершин
позванивает.
Цветку цветок средь дня
зажёг свечу.
И чей-то смех всё вглубь меня
заманивает.
Пою, ищу, "А-у!" "А-у!"
кричу.

Your gentle laughter was a fleeting
fairy tale,
It enticed, as sounds of reed pipe
entice into a dream,
And so with a wreath, with verses
I adorn you,
Let us go, let us flee together to
the mountainside.
But where have you gone?
Only the sounds of mountain tops
resound …
In midst of day, a flower lights the
candle of another flower,
And someone's laughter entices me
forever deeper,
I sing, I search, "a-oo, a-oo" I cry.

i	'ʧeĭ ta	'sm̧ex	'fşjo	vg'lup̧	m̧e'ņja
И	**чей-то**	**смех**	**всё**	**вглубь**	**меня**
And	someone's	laughter	ever	further	me

za'maņivajet
заманивает.
entices

pa'ju	i'ʃʃu	ɑ-u	ɑ-u	kŗi'ʧu
Пою,	**ищу,**	**"А-у!"**	**"А-у!"**	**кричу.**
(I) sing	(I) search	A-oo	A-oo	(I) cry

VIII. Songs without an Opus Number

(Songs not published by Rachmaninoff; manuscripts at the State Central Museum of Musical Culture, Moscow.)

1. **У врат обители святой (At the gates of the holy cloister)**
2. **Я тебе ничего не скажу (Nothing shall I say to you)**
3. **Опять встрепенулось ты, сердце (Again you are bestirred, my heart)**
4. **Апрель! Вешний праздничный день (April! A festive day in the spring)**
5. **Смеркалось (Dusk was falling)**
6. **Ты помнишь ли вечер (Do you remember the evening)**
7. **Песня разочарованного (Song of the disenchanted)**
8. **Увял цветок (The flower died)**
9. **Икалось ли тебе (Were you hiccoughing, Natasha)**
10. **Ночь (Night)**
11. **Письмо К. С. Станиславскому (Letter to K. S. Stanislavsky)**
12. **Из Евангелия от Иоанна (From the Gospel of Saint John)**

In 1892 Rachmaninoff wrote to his friend the singer Michael Slonov that he did not have any songs published and that he doubted if any would be in the near future, as those that he had written were not worthy of publication. Only two of his early songs, "O, no, I beg you, do not leave" and "In the silence of the secret night," were included in the first song cycle Opus 4, the latter song considerably reworked by the composer.

"By the gates of the holy cloister" is the earliest of Rachmaninoff's songs, written in 1890 to the words of one of Russia's greatest poets, Michael Lermontov. The short poem, which speaks of one who begs for sustenance and receives a stone instead, is presented in a dramatic musical form, introduced and concluded by piano accompaniment. The declamatory, expressive melody is similar in style to the operatic sketches composed during the same period: a monologue "A night without sleep" from Lermontov's play *Mas-*

querade and two monologues from Pushkin's play *Boris Godunov*.

Tchaikovsky's influence on the young composer is apparent in the song "Nothing I shall say to you," setting of a text by Afanasy Fet, a poet to whom Rachmaninoff returned for texts for his later songs, and whose verse Tchaikovsky considered as "overflowing into music." In this song love is expressed in few words, humbly and silently, and Rachmaninoff reveals a quiet understanding and gentleness in his musical reconception, a trait that remained with him in his mature work.

The remaining six songs written during the period 1890–1893, which the composer did not include in his song cycles, illustrate the formation of his style in the vocal genre as he was completing his studies at the Moscow Conservatory. The songs offer images Rachmaninoff developed and commented upon in his work: the color and movement of spring, the spacious landscapes, the meditative mood of eventide. The song "Night" is a sensitive interpretation of artistic inspiration when images and memories find consonance in the sounds and stillness of night.

In 1899 Rachmaninoff wrote music to a text by Prince Peter Viazemsky, which he paraphrased in jest and dedicated to his future wife, Natasha Satina. The song was written at a time when he was depressed by the failure of his First Symphony and ceased composing; hence the dedication of the song, "No, my muse is not yet dead, sweet Natasha." He admonished her to read the music carefully, as he accompanied the phrase "loving Natasha" with the motif of Lensky's words "I love you" from Tchaikovsky's *Eugene Onegin*.

In 1908 Rachmaninoff wrote a musical letter to K. S. Stanislavsky and the members of the Moscow Art Theater, who brought excellence and a new understanding of theatre arts to the Russian stage. The letter was performed by Chaliapin at the festivities marking the tenth anniversary of the founding of the Theater and a successful production of Maeterlinck's *The Blue Bird*. It was sent from Dresden, where Rachmaninoff was working on several compositions, including the music for an opera based on Maeterlinck's *Monna Vanna* (he wrote the first act and a few sketches for the second act, but did not complete the opera). Rachmaninoff knew

Chekhov and admired his work for the theatre, which influenced him to compose for texts in prose, such as his song "We shall rest" in Opus 26, to the words in Chekhov's play *Uncle Vanya*. The First World War and the ensuing changes in Russia interrupted his work, and the last music to a text in prose was written in 1915 to words from The Gospel of Saint John in Slavonic translation: "Greater than this love no one can have, than one should lay down one's soul for one's friends."

1

u 'vrɑt a'ḅiţeḽi sɣja'toĭ
У врат обители святой
At gates (of) cloister holy

Date of composition: ***1890.***
Dedicated to Michael Slonov.
Source: ***Michael Lermontov.***

u 'vrɑt a'ḅiţeḽi sɣja'toĭ
У врат обители святой
At gates (of) cloister holy

sta'jal pra'şjaʃʃiĭ pada'jaṉja
Стоял просящий подаянья,
Stood begging alms

ḅes'şiḽnɨĭ 'ḅḽednɨĭ i xu'doĭ
Бессильный, бледный и худой
Weak pale and haggard

at 'glɑda 'ʒɑʒdɨ i stra'dɑṉja
От глада, жажды и страданья.
From hunger thirst and suffering

У врат обители святой
Стоял просящий подаянья,
Бессильный, бледный и худой
От глада, жажды и страданья.
Куска лишь хлеба он просил,
И взор являл живую муку.
И кто-то камень положил
В его протянутую руку.
Так я молил твоей любви,
С слезами горькими, с тоскою;
Так чувства лучшие мои
Навек обмануты тобою.

kus'kɑ ļiʃ 'xļeba 'on pra'şil
Куска лишь хлеба он просил,
Piece only (of) bread he asked

i 'vzor jav'ļjal ʒɨ'vuju 'muku
И взор являл живую муку.
And gaze showed living torment

i 'kto ta 'kɑm̧eņ pala'ʒɨl
И кто-то камень положил
And someone stone put

v je'vo pra'ţjanutuju 'ruku
В его протянутую руку.
Into his outstretched hand

'tɑk 'ja ma'ļil tva'jeĭ ļjub'y̧i
Так я молил твоей любви,
Thus I begged (for) your love

s‿sļe'zɑm̧i 'goŗķim̧i s tas'koju
С слезами горькими, с тоскою;
With tears bitter with anguish

tɑk 'ʧustva 'luʧʃɨje ma'i
Так чувства лучшие мои
Thus feelings best my

na'y̧ek ab'mɑnutɨ ta'boju
Навек обмануты тобою.
Forever betrayed by you

At the gates of the holy cloister
He stood begging alms,
Weak, pale and haggard
From hunger, thirst and suffering.
A piece of bread was all he asked,
His gaze betrayed a living torment.
And someone put a stone
Into his outstretched hand.
It was thus that I begged for your love,
With bitter tears, with anguish,
Thus my best feelings
Are forever betrayed by you.

2
ja ţe'ḅe ņiʧe'vo ņe ska'ʒu
Я тебе ничего не скажу
I (to) you nothing not say

Date of composition: ***1890*.**
Source: ***Afanasy Fet*** **(translation by Roland John Wiley).**

ja ţe'ḅe ņiʧe'vo ņe ska'ʒu
Я тебе ничего не скажу
I (to) you nothing not say

i ţe'ḅja ņe fstŗe'voʒu ņi'ʧuţ
И тебя не встревожу ничуть,
And you not disturb in the least

i a 'tom 'ʧo ja 'molʧa tʏer'ʒu
И о том, что я молча твержу,
And of that which I silently repeat

ņe ŗe'ʃuş ņi za 'ʃto naməek'nuţ
Не решусь ни за что намекнуть.
Not dare never to hint

'ʧɛlɨĭ 'ḑeņ 'sp̦jat naʧ'nɨje tsʏe'tɨ
Целый день спят ночные цветы
Whole day sleep night flowers

'no ļiʃ 'sontsɛ za 'tuʧi
Но, лишь солнце за тучи
But as soon as sun behind grey clouds
zaĭ'ḑjot
зайдёт,
goes

Я тебе ничего не скажу
И тебя не встревожу ничуть,
И о том, что я молча твержу,
Не решусь ни за что
намекнуть.
Целый день спят ночные
цветы
Но, лишь солнце за тучи
зайдёт,
Раскрываются тихо листы
И я слышу, как сердце цветёт.
И в больную, усталую грудь
Веет влагой ночной … Я
дрожу …
Я тебя не встревожу ничуть,
Я тебе ничего не скажу,
Я тебе ничего не скажу,
Я тебя не встревожу ничуть,
Я тебе ничего не скажу.

raskrɨ'vɑjutsa 'ţixa ļis'tɨ
Раскрываются тихо листы
Open quietly leaves

i ja 'slɨʃu 'kɑk 'şertsɛ tsɣe'ţjot
И я слышу, как сердце цветёт.
And I hear how heart flowers

i v baļ'nuju 'ustɑluju 'gruḑ
И в больную, усталую грудь
And into pained tired breast

'ɣejet 'vlɑgaĭ naʧ'noĭ 'ja dra'ʒu
Веет влагой ночной … Я дрожу …
Wafts moisture (of) night I tremble

ja ţe'b̧ja ņe vstŗe'voʒu ņi'ʧuţ
Я тебя не встревожу ничуть,
I you not disturb in the least

ja ţe'b̧e ņiʧe'vo ņe ska'ʒu
Я тебе ничего не скажу,
I (to) you nothing not say

ja ţe'b̧e ņiʧe'vo ņe ska'ʒu
Я тебе ничего не скажу,
I (to) you nothing not say

ja ţe'b̧ja ņe vstŗe'voʒu ņi'ʧuţ
Я тебя не встревожу ничуть,
I you not disturb in the least

ja ţe'b̧e ņiʧe'vo ņe ska'ʒu
Я тебе ничего не скажу.
I (to) you nothing not say

Nothing shall I say to you
Nor in the least disturb,
Nor leave the merest hint
Of what I silently repeat.
The flow'rs of night sleep through the day
But should gray clouds conceal the sun,
Their petals quietly unfold,
And I hear how the heart blossoms.
And into my sore, exhausted breast
Wafts the freshness of the night …
I tremble …
Never shall I least disturb you,
Nothing shall I say to you,
Nothing shall I say to you,
Never shall I least disturb you,
Nothing shall I say to you.

3

a'p̦jaţ vstŗep̦e'nulaş 'tɨ 'şertsɛ
Опять встрепенулось ты, сердце
Again are bestirred you heart

Date of composition: ***1890.***
Source: ***Nikolai Grekov.***

a'p̦jaţ vstŗep̦e'nulaş 'tɨ 'şertsɛ
Опять встрепенулось ты, сердце,
Again are bestirred you heart

i 'snova v du'ʃɛ ma'jeĭ 'fspɨxnuļi
И снова в душе моей вспыхнули
And again in soul my are kindled
'gŗjozɨ
грёзы,
dreams

i 'rɣjotsa iz 'gruḑi ķi'putʃeje 'slova
И рвётся из груди кипучее слово,
And bursts from breast ebullient word

i 'ļjutsa ga'ŗjatʃije 'sļjozɨ
И льются горячие слёзы …
And flow passionate tears

i 'sņjatsa a'p̦jaţ 'jeĭ 'fşjo 'zvuķi 'dɑ
И снятся опять ей всё звуки да
And dreams again it all sounds and
'zvuķi
звуки,
sounds

Опять встрепенулось ты, сердце,
И снова в душе моей вспыхнули грёзы,
И рвётся из груди кипучее слово,
И льются горячие слёзы …
И снятся опять ей всё звуки да звуки,
Все, музыки полные, речи,
Да чёрные очи, да белые руки,
Да кудри, да белые плечи.
И снова душа отозваться готова на всё,
В чём есть терньи и розы.
И рвётся из груди кипучее слово,
И льются горячие слёзы.

'fʂe 'muzɨķi 'polnɨje 'ɽetʃi
Все, музыки полные, речи,
All (of) music full words

da 'tʃjornɨje 'otʃi da 'b̦elɨje 'ruķi
Да чёрные очи, да белые руки,
And dark eyes and white arms

da 'kuɖɽi da 'b̦elɨje 'pɭetʃi
Да кудри, да белые плечи.
And curls and white shoulders

i 'snova du'ʃɑ ata'zvɑtʂa gɑ'tova na 'fʂjo
И снова душа отозваться готова на всё,
And again soul to respond is prepared to everything

f 'tʃjom 'jesʈ 'ʈerɳja i 'rozɨ
В чём есть тернья и розы.
In which (there) are thorns and roses

i 'rʏjotsa iz 'gruɖi ķi'putʃeje 'slova
И рвётся из груди кипучее слово,
And bursts from breast ebullient word

i 'ɭjutsa gɑ'ɽjatʃije 'sɭjozɨ
И льются горячие слёзы.
And flow passionate tears

Again you are bestirred, my heart,
And again in my soul dreams are kindled,
Ebullient words burst from my breast
And passionate tears flow again …
And my soul dreams of sounds and sounds,
Of words full of music,
Dark eyes, gentle arms,
And tresses and sensuous shoulders.
And again my soul responds to all
Which has both roses and thorns,
Ebullient words burst from my breast
And passionate tears flow again.

4
ɑp'ŗeļ 'ɣeʃņiĭ 'prɑzņiʧnɨĭ 'ḑeņ
Апрель! Вешний праздничный день
April Spring festive day

Date of composition: ***1891.***
Source: ***E. Pailleron. Translated from the French by I. Tushnova.***

ɑp'ŗeļ 'ɣeʃņiĭ 'prɑzņiʧnɨĭ 'ḑeņ
Апрель! Вешний праздничный день,
April Spring festive day

'dɑ 'veʃņiĭ 'deņ lu'gɑ v ra'şe
Да, вешний день! … Луга в росе.
Yes spring day Meadows in dew.

tɨ p̧riʃ'lɑ v 'b̧eləm 'plɑţje sva'jom
Ты пришла в белом платье своём
You came in white dress your

i dva pat'sņezņika f ka'şe
И два подснежника в косе,
And two snowdrops in braid

'dɑ dva tsɣet'kɑ dva tsɣet'kɑ f 'ţjomnaĭ ka'şe
Да, два цветка, два цветка в тёмной косе.
Yes two flowers two flowers in dark braid

Апрель! Вешний праздничный день,
Да, вешний день! … Луга в росе.
Ты пришла в белом платье своём
И два подснежника в косе,
Да, два цветка, два цветка в тёмной косе.
И без слов мы сели на мох, бархатный мох;
В блеске лучей весь мир зеленел,
Каждый листок влагой блестел,
В лёгкой тени, где-то у ног,
Журчал ручей …
А в кустах звенел голосок
Птички лесной.
Руки твои в своих
Я так бережно сжал
В то ясное утро, весной, светлой весной …
Помнишь, помнишь?

i 'ḇes 'slof mɨ 'şeḻi na 'mox
И без слов мы сели на мох,
And without words we sat on moss
'ƀarxatnɨĭ 'mox
бархатный мох;
velvet moss

v 'ƀḻesķe lu'ʧeĭ 'ɣeş 'ṃir ʐiḻe'ņel
В блеске лучей весь мир зеленел,
In brilliance (of) rays all world was green

'kaʒdɨĭ ḻis'tok 'vlagaĭ bḻes'ţel
Каждый листок влагой блестел,
Each leaf (with) moisture shined

v 'ḻjoxkəĭ ţe'ņi 'gḑe ta u 'nok
В лёгкой тени, где-то у ног,
In light shade somewhere by feet

ʒur'ʧal ru'ʧeĭ
Журчал ручей …
Murmured stream

a f kus'tax zɣe'ņel gala'sok
А в кустах звенел голосок
And in bushes rang out voice

'pţiʧķi ḻes'noĭ
Птички лесной.
(Of) bird forest

'ruķi tva'i f sva'ix
Руки твои в своих
Hands yours in mine

'ja tak 'beţeʒna 's ʒal
Я так бережно сжал
I so carefully pressed

April! A festive day in the spring,
Yes, a day in the spring! … Dew on the meadows.
You came, dressed in white,
Two snowdrops in your tresses,
Yes, two flowers, two flowers in your dark tresses.
Silently we sat on the moss, velvet-like moss.
In the brilliant sun the whole world was verdant,
Each leaf brilliant and moist,
In the shade, somewhere below,
Whispered a brook …
A forest bird's voice
Rang out in the thicket.
I gently held
Your hands in mine
On that clear morning, in the spring, radiant spring …
Remember, remember?

v 'to 'jasnəje 'utra ɣes'noĭ 'sɣetləĭ
В то ясное утро, весной, светлой
On that clear morning (in) spring, bright
ɣes'noĭ
весной ...
spring

'pomņiʃ 'pomņiʃ
Помнишь, помнишь?
Remember remember

5
sm̧er'kɑlaş
Смеркалось
Dusk was falling

Date of composition: ***1891.***
Source: ***Alexei Tolstoy.***

'ʒɑrķiĭ 'ḑeņ bļed'ņel ņeula'ɣima
Жаркий день бледнел неуловимо,
Hot day grew pale imperceptibly

nat 'oẓirəm tu'mɑn ţja'nulsa pala'soĭ
Над озером туман тянулся полосой,
Over lake mist floated (as) band

i 'krot'ķiĭ 'obras 'tvoĭ zna'komɨĭ i
И кроткий образ твой, знакомый и
And gentle image your familiar and
ļju'ḑimɨĭ
любимый,
beloved

v ye'ʧ̡erŋiĭ 'ţiχiĭ 'ʧɑs na'şilsa 'pŗeda
В вечерний тихий час носился предо
At evening quiet hour floated before
'mnoĭ
мной.
me

u'lɨpka 'tɑʒɛ bɨ'lɑ ka'toruju ḽjub'ḽju ja
Улыбка таже была, которую люблю я,
Smile same was which love I

i 'ɱjaxkaja ka'sɑ kak 'pŗeʒḑe
И мягкая коса, как прежде,
And soft braid as before
raspḽe'lɑş
расплелась,
untwined

i 'otʃi 'grustnɨje pa'pŗeʒŋemu tas'kuja
И очи грустные, попрежнему тоскуя,
And eyes sad as before yearning

gḽja'ḑeḽi na ɱe'ŋja v ye'ʧerŋiĭ 'ţiχiĭ 'ʧɑs
Глядели на меня в вечерний тихий час.
Looked at me at evening quiet hour

'ʒɑrķiĭ 'ḑeŋ bḽed'ŋel ŋeula'yima
Жаркий день бледнел неуловимо,
Hot day grew pale imperceptibly

nat 'oẓirəm tu'mɑn ţja'nulsa pala'soĭ
Над озером туман тянулся полосой,
Over lake mist stretched (as) band

Жаркий день бледнел неуловимо,
Над озером туман тянулся полосой,
И кроткий образ твой, знакомый и любимый,
В вечерний тихий час носился предо мной.
Улыбка таже была, которую люблю я,
И мягкая коса, как прежде, расплелась,
И очи грустные, попрежнему тоскуя,
Глядели на меня в вечерний тихий час.
Жаркий день бледнел неуловимо,
Над озером туман тянулся полосой,
И кроткий образ твой, знакомый и любимый,
В вечерний тихий час носился предо мной,
В вечерний тихий час.

i 'krotķii 'obras 'tvoĭ zna'komiĭ i
И кроткий образ твой, знакомый и
And gentle image your familiar and
ļju'ḅimiĭ
любимый,
beloved

v ɣe'ʧerņii 'ţiχii 'ʧɑs na'şilsa 'pŗeda
В вечерний тихий час носился предо
At evening quiet hour floated before
'mnoĭ
мной,
me

v ɣe'ʧerņiĭ 'ţiχiĭ 'ʧɑs
В вечерний тихий час.
At evening quiet hour

Slowly, the hot day grew pale,
A mist floated across the lake,
And your gentle image, familiar and beloved,
Appeared before me in that quiet evening hour.
I remembered your smile, which I love,
Your soft braid, untwined as before,
And your sad eyes, as always yearning,
Glanced at me in that quiet evening hour.
Slowly, the hot day grew pale,
A mist floated across the lake,
And your gentle image, familiar and beloved,
Appeared before me in that quiet evening hour,
In that quiet evening hour.

6
tɨ 'pomņiʃ ļi 'ɣeʧer
Ты помнишь ли вечер
You remember—evening

Date of composition: ***1891.***
Source: ***Alexei Tolstoy.***

tɨ 'pomņiʃ ļi 'ɣeʧer kak 'moŗe
Ты помнишь ли вечер, как море
You remember — evening how sea
ʃu'ɱela
шумело,
sounded

v ʃɨ'povn̡ik̡e 'p̡el sala'ɣeĭ
В шиповнике пел соловей …
In rose bush sang nightingale

du'ʃistɨje 'ɣetk̡i a'katsɨi 'b̡eləĭ
Душистые ветки акации белой
Fragrant stems (of) acacia white

ka'ʧal̡is̡ nat 'ʃl̡japəĭ tva'jeĭ
Качались над шляпой твоей …
Swayed over hat your

m̡eʃ 'kamn̡eĭ ab'rosʃɨx gus'tɨm
Меж камней, обросших густым
Amidst cliffs overgrown (with) thick
ɣina'gradəm
виноградом,
grapes

da'roga bɨ'la tak uz'ka
Дорога была так узка;
Road was so narrow

v mal'ʧan̡ii nat 'mor̡em mɨ 'jexal̡i
В молчании над морем мы ехали
In silence over sea we rode
'r̡jadəm
рядом,
side by side

k ru'k̡e pr̡il̡e'gala ru'ka
К руке прилегала рука!
To arm was close arm

Ты помнишь ли вечер, как
море шумело,
В шиповнике пел соловей …
Душистые ветки акации белой
Качались над шляпой
твоей …
Меж камней, обросших
густым виноградом,
Дорога была так узка;
В молчании над морем мы
ехали рядом,
К руке прилегала рука!
В молчаньи над морем ехали
мы рядом,
К руке прилегала рука.
Ты помнишь ли рёв
дождевого потока
И пену, и брызги кругом?
И нам наше горе казалось
далёко,
И как мы забыли о нём!

Do you remember the evening,
when the sea sighed,
Amidst roses the nightingale
sang …
Branches of white fragrant acacia
Swayed over your head …
The road was so narrow
Amidst cliffs, overgrown with
grape leaves …
In silence, by the sea, we rode
Our arms touching …
In silence, by the sea, rode we
Our arms touching …
Do you remember the roar of the
waterfall,
The froth and the spray all around
us?
Our grief seemed to be so far
away,
And was, briefly, forgotten.

v mal'ʧan̡ii nat 'mor̡em 'jexal̡i mɨ
В молчаньи над морем ехали мы
In silence over sea rode we
'r̡jadəm
рядом,
side by side

k ru'k̡e p̡r̡il̡e'gala ru'ka
К руке прилегала рука.
To arm was close arm

tɨ 'pomn̡iʃ l̡i 'r̡jof daʒd̡e'vova pa'toka
Ты помнишь ли рёв дождевого потока
You remember — roar (of) rain stream

i 'p̡enu i 'brɨzg̡i kru'gom
И пену, и брызги кругом?
And froth and spray around

i 'nam 'naʃɛ 'gor̡e ka'zalas̡ da'l̡joka
И нам наше горе казалось далёко,
And (to) us our grief seemed far away

i 'kak mɨ za'bɨl̡i a 'n̡jom
И как мы забыли о нём!
And how we forgot about it

7
'pesņja razaʧa'rovanava
Песня разочарованного
Song (of) disenchanted

Date of composition: ***1893.***
Source: ***Daniil Rathaus.***

um'ŗi	tɣer'ḑit	'mņe	'deņ
“Умри!”-	**Твердит**	**мне**	**день,**
Die	repeats	(to) me	day

ta'm̧iţeļnɨĭ	i	'skuʧnɨĭ
томительный	**и**	**скучный.**
wearying	and	boring

um'ŗi	'mņe	'ʃɛpʧet	'noʧ
“Умри!”-	**Мне**	**шепчет**	**ночь**
Die	(to) me	whispers	night

tɑ'instɣennaju	'mgloĭ
таинственною	**мглой.**
(in) mysterious	darkness

i	v	'ʒɨzņi	'ţjagastnəĭ	s	tas'koju
И	**в**	**жизни**	**тягостной,**	**с**	**тоскою**
And	in	life	burdensome	with	anguish

ņeraz'luʧnɨĭ
неразлучный,
inseparable

b̧es	'tsɛļi	ja	bra'ʒu	us'tɑlaju	sta'poĭ
Без	**цели**	**я**	**брожу**	**усталою**	**стопой.**
Without	aim	I	wander	(in) tired	step

“Умри!”- Твердит мне день,
томительный и скучный.
“Умри!”- Мне шепчет ночь
таинственною мглой.
И в жизни тягостной, с
тоскою неразлучный,
Без цели я брожу усталою
стопой.
“Умри!”- твердил мне ум,
когда в душе унылой
Почуял я намёк на светлый
сон любви …
Но ты, мой нежный друг, мой
ангел светлокрылый,
Ты взором ласковым мне всё
твердишь “Живи!”
О, как я жить хочу! Как
страстно жажду света,
Возврата пылких грёз,
несбыточной мечты! …
Скажи, как возвратить
умчавшееся лето?
Скажи, как оживить увядшие
цветы?
Скажи!

um'ŗi tɣer'ḑil 'mŋe 'um kag'da v
"Умри!"- твердил мне ум, когда в
Die repeated (to) me mind when in
du'ʃɛ u'nɨləĭ
душе унылой
soul despondent

pa'ʧujal ja na'ɱjok na 'sɣetlɨĭ 'son
Почуял я намёк на светлый сон
Sensed I hint to bright dream
ʝjub'ɣi
любви ...
(of) love

'no 'tɨ 'moĭ 'ŋeʒnɨĭ 'druk 'moĭ 'angel
Но ты, мой нежный друг, мой ангел
But you my gentle friend my angel
sɣetla'krɨlɨĭ
светлокрылый,
radiant-winged

tɨ 'vzorəm 'laskavɨm 'mŋe 'fʂjo
Ты взором ласковым мне всё
You (with) gaze tender (to) me always
tɣer'ḑiʃ ʒɨ'ɣi
твердишь "Живи!"
repeat Live

o kak ja 'ʒɨţ xa'ʧu kak 'strasna
О, как я жить хочу! Как страстно
O how I to live want How passionately
'ʒaʒdu 'sɣeta
жажду света,
thirst (for) radiance

"Die!" the wearying and boring day repeats to me.
"Die!" the night whispers in its mysterious darkness.
And through this burdensome life, inseparable from anguish,
Aimlessly and wearily I wander.
"Die!" my mind repeats to me, when in my despondent soul
I sense a hint of love's bright dream ...
But you, my gentle friend, by radiant-winged angel,
With your tender glance you repeat to me "Live!"
Oh how I want to live! How I yearn for radiance,
For the return of fervent reveries, for the dream unrealized ...
Tell me, how does one bring back a summer flown away?
Tell me, how can withered flowers be revived?
Tell me!

vazv'rɑta 'pɨlķix 'gŗjos ņes'bɨtatʃnəĭ
Возврата пылких грёз, несбыточной
Return (of) fervent reveries (of) unrealized
m̧etʃ'tɨ
мечты! …
dream

ska'ʒɨ kak vazvra'ţiţ um'tʃɑfʃɛjeşja
Скажи, как возвратить умчавшееся
Tell how to bring back flown away
'ļeta
лето?
summer

ska'ʒɨ kak aʒɨ'ɣiţ u'ɣjatʃɨje tsɣe'tɨ
Скажи, как оживить увядшие цветы?
Tell how to revive withered flowers

ska'ʒɨ
Скажи!
Tell

8
u'ɣjal tsɣe'tok
Увял цветок
Has withered flower

Date of composition: ***1893.***
Source: ***Daniil Rathaus.***

u'ɣjal tsɣe'tok lɑ'zurnɨm 'utrəm
Увял цветок! Лазурным утром
Has withered flower (In) azure morning
'mɑja
мая
(of) May

naʃ'lɑ gra'zɑ sla'm̧ilsa sţeb̧e'ļjok
Нашла гроза, сломился стебелёк …
Came storm broke small stem

i 'slovna 'sļjozɨ ļep̧est'ķi ra'ņjaja
И, словно слёзы, лепестки роняя,
And like tears petals dropping

u'ɣjal tsɣe'tok
Увял цветок!
Has withered flower

ţi'bja ļju'b̧il 'on s ņez̧em'noju 'şiləĭ
Тебя любил он с неземною силой,
You loved he with unearthly strength

kak 'toļka 'ʒŗets ļju'b̧iţ ba'ģiņju 'mok
Как только жрец любить богиню мог,
As only priest love goddess could

'no 'tɨ vz̧ja'tɑ b̧ez'ʒɑlasnəĭ ma'ģiləĭ
Но ты взята безжалостной могилой …
But you are taken (by) merciless grave

u'vjal tsɣe'tok
Увял цветок!
Has withered flower

ʧu'ʒoĭ m̧eʧ'tɑm ʧu'ʒoĭ ʒɛ'lɑņjam 'jasnɨm
Чужой мечтам, чужой желаньям ясным,
Alien (to) dreams alien (to) desires clear

'tvoĭ 'b̧ednɨĭ druk du'ʃoju izņe'mok
Твой бедный друг душою изнемог.
Your poor friend (in) soul (is) exhausted

Увял цветок! Лазурным утром мая
Нашла гроза, сломился стебелёк …
И, словно слёзы, лепестки роняя,
Увял цветок!
Тебя любил он с неземною силой,
Как только жрец любить богиню мог,
Но ты взята безжалостной могилой …
Увял цветок!
Чужой мечтам, чужой желаньям ясным,
Твой бедный друг душою изнемог.
Возврата нет к угасшим дням прекрасным …
Увял цветок! Увял цветок!

The flower died! On an azure morning in May
Came a storm, the brittle stem broke …
Its petals falling like tears,
The flower died!
You were loved with an unearthly passion
As only a priest could love a goddess,
But you were taken by a merciless grave …
The flower died!
Alien to dreams, alien to clear desires,
Your sorrowing friend is weary in heart.
There is no return to the days gone by, beautiful days …
The flower died!

vaz'vrata 'ņet k u'gasʃɨm 'dņjam
Возврата нет к угасшим дням
Return (there is) no to gone by days
pŗe'krasnɨm
прекрасным ...
beautiful

u'v̦jal tsv̦e'tok u'v̦jal tsv̦e'tok
Увял цветок! Увял цветок!
Has withered flower Has withered flower

9
i'kalaş ļi ţi'b̦e
Икалось ли тебе
Hiccoughed—you

Date of composition: ***1899.***
Dedicated to Natalia Satina.
Source: ***Peter Viazemsky*** **(translation by J. N. Willis).**

i'kalaş ļi ţi'b̦e na'taʃa
Икалось ли тебе, Наташа,
Hiccoughed — you Natasha

kag'da ʃam'panskoje ja 'p̦il
Когда шампанское я пил
When champagne I drank

raz'ļiʧnɨx 'fkusəf 'svoĭstf i 'v̦idəf
Различных вкусов, свойств и видов,
(Of) different tastes, attributes and kinds

raz'ļiʧnɨx 'vozrastəf i 'şil
Различных возрастов и сил.
(Of) different ages and strength

kag'da v va'roņeʃsķix pad'valax
Когда в воронежских подвалах
When in Voronezh cellars

ja 'ʒadna pam̧i'nal ţi'bja
Я жадно поминал тебя,
I greedily drank to you

ļju'b̧ja na'taʃu poɛ'tɛssu
Любя Наташу, поэтессу,
Loving Natasha poetess

'da i ʃam'panskoje ļju'b̧ja
Да и шампанское любя?
And too champagne loving

'zḑeş 'b̧jot kas'taļsķiĭ 'kļjutʃ
Здесь бьёт кастальский ключ,
Here wells up Kastalsky's key

p̧i'taja ņibasna'slovnaju stru'joĭ
Питая небасловною струёй;
Feeding (with) unfabulous stream

po'ɛz̧ija 'zḑeş 'ɣeʃʃ rutʃ'naja
Поэзия здесь вещь ручная:
Poetry here thing everyday

p̧jaţ 'frankof 'daĭ i 'p̧eĭ i 'poĭ
Пять франков дай и пей, и пой!
Five francs give and drink and sing

Икалось ли тебе, Наташа,
Когда шампанское я пил
Различных вкусов, свойств и видов,
Различных возрастов и сил.
Когда в воронежских подвалах
Я жадно поминал тебя,
Любя Наташу, поэтессу,
Да и шампанское любя?
Здесь бьёт кастальский ключ,
Питая небаснословною струёй;
Поэзия здесь вещь ручная:
Пять франков дай и пей, и пой!

Were you hiccoughing, Natasha,
When I was drinking the champagne
Of different tastes, attributes and classes,
Of different ages and passions.
When in Voronezh cellars
I greedily drank to you,
Loving Natasha, poetess,
Yea and loving champagne too?
Here Kastalsky's key wells up
Sustaining with an unfabulous stream,
Poetry here is an everyday matter:
Pay five francs, then drink and sing!

10
'notʃ
Ночь
Night

Date of composition: ***1900.***
Source: ***Daniil Rathaus*** **(translation by Roland John Wiley).**

'snova 'son na u'stɑlɨje 'otʃi ņeĭ'ḑjot
Снова сон на усталые очи нейдёт.
Again sleep to tired eyes does not come

ja a'ḑin 'no v ņe'moĭ ţiʃɨ'ņe
Я один … Но в немой тишине
I (am) alone But in mute quiet

'kto ta 'ţixa 'mņe 'skorbnɨje 'p̧esņi
Кто-то тихо мне скорбные песни
Someone quietly (to) me mournful songs
pa'jot
поёт,
sings

nakla'ņjajetsa 'ņeʒna ka 'mņe
Наклоняется нежно ко мне.
Inclines gently toward me

zam̧i'rɑjet du'ʃɑ atʃa'rovannɨĭ 'slux
Замирает душа … Очарованный слух
Grows still soul Charmed ear

'loɣit 'zvuķi zna'komɨx ŗe'tʃeĭ
Ловит звуки знакомых речей …
Catches sounds (of) familiar voices

Снова сон на усталые очи
нейдёт.
Я один … Но в немой тишине
Кто-то тихо мне скорбные
песни поёт,
Наклоняется нежно ко мне.
Замирает душа …
Очарованный слух
Ловит звуки знакомых
речей …
То не ты ли, желанный,
неведомый друг,
Грёза детских умчавшихся
дней?
Истомилася грудь от
вседневных тревог,
Гаснет в сердце желаний всех
пыл …
И давно уже мне мой
насмешливый рок
Все дороги к блаженству
закрыл.
Догорает свеча … Ночь
глухая плывёт.
Я один … И в немой тишине
Кто-то тихо мне скорбные
песни поёт,
Наклоняется нежно ко мне.

'to ņe 'tɨ ļi ʒɛ'lannɨĭ ņe'γedamɨĭ 'druk
То не ты ли, желанный, неведомый друг,
Is it not you — wished-for mysterious friend

'gŗjoza 'ḑetsķix um'ʧafʃɨxşja 'dņeĭ
Грёза детских умчавшихся дней?
Reverie (of) childhood flown away days

ista'ɱilaşja 'gruḑ at fşe'dņevnɨx
Истомилася грудь от вседневных
Weary breast from day long
tŗe'vok
тревог,
anxieties

'gasņet f 'şertsɛ ʒɛ'laņiĭ 'fşex pɨl
Гаснет в сердце желаний всех пыл ...
Dies out in heart (of) desires all fervor

i dav'no u'ʒɛ 'mņe 'moĭ na'sɱeʃļivɨĭ
И давно уже мне мой насмешливый
And long since (to) me my derisive
'rok
рок
fate

'fşe da'roģi k bla'ʒɛnstvu za'krɨl
Все дороги к блаженству закрыл.
All roads to bliss closed

daga'rajet sγe'ʧa 'noʧ glu'xaja plɨ'γjot
Догорает свеча ... Ночь глухая плывёт.
Burns down candle Night deaf flows

ja a'ḑin i v ņe'moĭ ţiʃɨņ'e
Я один ... И в немой тишине
I (am) alone And in mute quiet

Sleep won't fall on tired eyes again.
I am alone ... But in the wordless quiet
Someone gently sings me mournful songs,
Inclines toward me affectionately.
My soul grows tranquil ... My charmed ear
Catches the sound of familiar voices ...
Is it not you, wished-for, mysterious friend,
Reveries of childhood flown away?
The breast worn out from day-to-day alarms,
Lets die within the wish for all desires ...
And my derisive fate long since
Has closed all roads to happiness.
The candle flickers ... The dead of night flows by.
I am alone ... And in the wordless quiet
Someone gently sings me mournful songs,
Inclines toward me affectionately.

'kto ta 'ţixa 'mņe 'skorbnɨje 'pesņi
Кто-то тихо мне скорбные песни
Someone quietly (to) me mournful songs
pa'jot
поёт,
sings

nakla'ņjajetsa 'ņeʒna ka 'mņe
Наклоняется нежно ко мне.
Inclines gently toward me

11
pis'mo K. S. Staņi'slavskamu at S. Rax'maņinova
Письмо К. С. Станиславскому от С. Рахманинова
Letter to K. S. Stanislavsky from S. Rachmaninoff

Date of composition: ***1908.***
Source: ***Sergei Rachmaninoff.***

dara'goĭ kanstan'ţin şer'ģejeɣiʧ
Дорогой Константин Сергеевич,
Dear Konstantin Sergeyevich

ja pazdrav'ļjaju vɑs at 'ʧistəĭ du'ʃɨ at
Я поздравляю Вас от чистой души, от
I congratulate You from sincere soul from
fşe'vo
всего
all

'şertsa za 'ɛţi 'ḑeşjaţ 'ļet vɨ 'ʃļi
сердца! За эти десять лет Вы шли
heart For these ten years You went
fp̡i'ŗjot
вперёд,
forward

fp̡i'ŗjot i fp̡i'ŗjot i na 'ɛtəm pu'ţi vɨ
вперёд и вперёд, и на этом пути Вы
forward and forward and on this path You
na'ʃļi
нашли
found

'şiņjuju 'p̡ţitsu a'nɑ 'vɑʃa 'luʧaja
"Синюю птицу"! Она Ваша лучшая
"The Blue Bird" It (is) Your best
pa'b̡eda
победа!
victory

ţi'p̡eŗ 'ja 'oʧeņ saʒa'ļeju 'ʃto 'ja ņi
Теперь я очень сожалею, что я не
Now I (am) very regretful that I (am) not
v mas'kɣe
в Москве,
in Moscow

'ʃto 'ja ņi ma'gu 'vmeşţe sa 'fşem̡i
что я не могу, вместе со всеми,
that I (am) not able together with everyone
vɑs 'ʧestvavaţ
Вас чествовать,
You honor

Дорогой Константин
Сергеевич,

Я поздравляю Вас от чистой души, от всего сердца! За эти десять лет Вы шли вперёд, вперёд и вперёд, и на этом пути Вы нашли "Синюю птицу"! Она Ваша лучшая победа! Теперь я очень сожалею, что я не в Москве, что я не могу, вместе со всеми, Вас чествовать, Вам хлопать, кричать Вам на все лады: "Браво, браво, браво!" И желать Вам многая лета, многая лета, многая, многая лета! Прошу Вас передать всей труппе мой привет, мой душевный привет.

Ваш
Сергей Рахманинов.

Дрезден. Четырнадцатого октября, тысяча девятьсот восьмого года.

Жена моя мне вторит.

'vɑm 'xlopaţ kŗi'ʧɑţ 'vɑm na 'fşe
Вам хлопать, кричать Вам на все
(to) You applaud cry (to) You in all
la'dɨ 'brɑva
лады: "Браво,
tones Bravo

'brɑva 'brɑva i ʒɛ'lɑţ 'vɑm
браво, браво!" И желать Вам
Bravo bravo And (to) wish (to) You
'mnogaja 'ļeta 'mnogaja
многая лета, многая
many years many

'ļeta 'mnogaja 'mnogaja 'ļeta pra'ʃu vɑs
лета, многая, многая лета! Прошу Вас
years many many years (I) ask You
ţiŗi'dɑţ
передать
to give

'fşeĭ 'truppȩ 'moĭ pŗi'ɣet 'moĭ du'ʃɛvnɨĭ
всей труппе мой привет, мой душевный
(to) all company my regards my heartfelt
pŗi'ɣet
привет.
regards

'vɑʃ şergeĭ rax'maņinaf
Ваш Сергей Рахманинов.
Your Sergei Rachmaninoff

Dear Konstantin Sergeyevich,

I congratulate you sincerely, from all my heart! These last ten years you moved forward, forward and forward, and on this path you have found "The Blue Bird"! It is your greatest victory! Now I am very sorry that I am not in Moscow, that I am not able, together with everyone, to honor you, to applaud you, to cry to you in all tones: "Bravo, bravo, bravo!" And to wish you many years, many years, many, many years! I ask you to give to all the company my regards, my heartfelt regards.

Yours
Sergei Rachmaninoff
Dresden, 14th October, 1908.

My wife repeats (my sentiments).

drɛz'dɛn	ʧe'tɨrnatsatavə	akʈjab'ɽja	'tɨʂjaʧa
Дрезден.	**Четырнадцатого**	**октября,**	**тысяча**
Dresden	14th	October	1

ɖiɣjat'sot	vaʂj'movə	'goda
девятьсот	**восьмого**	**года.**
9	08th	year

ʒɛ'nɑ	ma'ja	'mɲe	'ftoɽit
Жена	**моя**	**мне**	**вторит.**
Wife	my	(to) me	repeats/harmonizes

12
iz ye'vangeʈija at io'anna
Из Евангелия от Иоанна
From the Gospel of John

Date of composition: ***1915.***
Source: ***Gospel of John (15:13).***

'boʈʃɨ	ʂe'ja	ʈjub'ye	ɲi'kto	ʒɛ	'imaʈ
Больши	**сея**	**любве**	**никто**	**же**	**имать,**
Greater	(than) this	love	no one	—	to have

'dɑ	'kto	'duʃu	sva'ju	pa'loʒɨt	za
да	**кто**	**душу**	**свою**	**положит**	**за**
that	one	soul	one's	should lay down	for

'druɡi	sva'ja
други	**своя.**
friends	one's

Больши сея любве никто же имать, да кто душу свою положит за други своя.

Greater than this love no one can have, that one should lay down one's soul (life) for one's friends.

The above is a close translation of the Church Slavonic text used by Rachmaninoff. The King James Version differs in wording; the New International Version differs only slightly.

APPENDIX A

Chronology

Sergei Rachmaninoff and his Time

Year	Life	Artistic and Intellectual Events	Political and Scientific Events
1873	Born on March 20 (O.S.)		The Three Emperors' League formed by Austria, Germany, Russia
1880		Dostoevsky completes *The Brothers Karamazov*	
1881		Dostoevsky dies	Alexander II assassinated in St. Petersburg. Alexander III ascends the throne
1882	Rachmaninoff enters St. Petersburg Conservatory	Wagner's *Parsifal* performed at Bayreuth	
1883		Wagner dies	
1885	Starts studies at Moscow Conservatory and with pianist N. S. Zverev		
1886		Franz Liszt dies	
1890		Premiere of Tchaikovsky's *Sleeping Beauty* at the Mayinsky Theater in St. Petersburg Premiere of Tchaikovsky's *Queen of Spades* in St. Petersburg	
1891	Graduates from Moscow Conservatory in piano performance Finishes First Piano Concerto Writes First Symphony	Tchaikovsky in the United States	
1892	Writes opera *Aleko* for graduation in composition from Moscow Conservatory	Tchaikovsky's *The Nutcracker* and *Iolanta* performed in St. Petersburg	
1893	Premiere of *Aleko* at Bolshoi Theatre Completes Songs of Opus 4 Writes Songs of Opus 8	Tchaikovsky's Sixth Symphony performed Tchaikovsky dies Golden Age of Russian Culture ends	
1894			Alexander III dies Nicholas II ascends the throne
1896	Songs of Opus 14	Brahms writes *Four Serious Songs* on the death of Clara Schumann	
1897	Accepts post as conductor of Mamontov's Private Opera in Moscow	Brahms dies	
1898		Diaghilev founds the journal *World of Art* with the artists Benois and Bakst Chekhov's *The Seagull* performed by the Moscow Art Theater	
1899	First concert tour abroad, London *Aleko* performed in St. Petersburg	Centennial of Pushkin's birth celebrated in music and art Early years of the Silver Age of Russian Culture	First Hague Peace Conference held, as proposed by Nicholas II

Year	Life	Artistic and Intellectual Events	Political and Scientific Events
1900	Rachmaninoff meets Chekhov, Bunin, members of the Moscow Art Theatre	Moscow Art Theater produces Chekhov's plays under Stanislavsky: *Uncle Vanya* (1900), *The Three Sisters* (1901), *The Cherry Orchard* (1904)	
1901	Completes Second Piano Concerto	First Nobel Prizes established	Queen Victoria dies
1902	Marries Natalia Satina Writes Songs of Opus 21		
1904	Accepts post as conductor at Bolshoi Theatre		Russo-Japanese War begins
1905	Completes operas *The Covetous Knight, Francesca da Rimini*	Einstein presents theory of relativity	Russian workers revolt
1906	Songs of Opus 26		Theodore Roosevelt wins Nobel Prize for mediation in Russo-Japanese War
1907	Performs in Paris in Russian concerts organized by Diaghilev	Pavlova dances *The Dying Swan*, choreographed by Fokine Rimsky-Korsakov writes *The Golden Cockerel* Rimsky-Korsakov dies	The Triple Entente is created by England, France, Russia
1908	Second Symphony performed	Maeterlinck, *The Blue Bird*	
1909	Works on Third Piano Concerto		
1909–1910	Tours United States		
1910	Writes music to the Liturgy of Saint John Chrysostom	Stravinsky's *Firebird* performed Scriabin, *Prometheus* Tolstoy, Petipa die	
1911		Stravinsky's *Petrushka*, with Benois and Fokine	
1912	Songs of Opus 34	Diaghilev produces *The Afternoon of a Faun*	
1913	Writes *The Bells*	Stravinsky's *Rite of Spring* performed in Paris	
1914			World War I begins
1915	Composes music to the Vespers	D. W. Griffith, *Birth of a Nation*	
1916	Songs of Opus 38		
1917	Leaves Russia with his family		February Revolution in Russia United States enters World War I October Revolution in Russia
1918	Arrives in New York in November Starts concert career in the United States and Europe	Blok writes the poem *The Twelve*	Russian Royal Family killed in July Armistice Day
1919			Civil War in Russia
1920	Concertizes yearly	Sinclair Lewis, *Main Street*	League of Nations formed
1921		Einstein wins Nobel Prize in Physics Prokofieff's *Love for Three Oranges* performed	
1922			U.S.S.R. formed
1924		Gershwin, *Rhapsody in Blue*	
1926	Completes Fourth Piano Concerto	Hemingway, *The Sun Also Rises*	
1927		*The Jazz Singer*, first sound film	Lindbergh flies from New York to Paris

Year	Life	Artistic and Intellectual Events	Political and Scientific Events
1929		Faulkner, *The Sound and the Fury*	The Great Depression begins
1931	Writes *Variations on a Theme by Corelli*		
1932			Franklin D. Roosevelt elected President of the United States
1933		Bunin receives Nobel Prize in Literature	
1934	Composes *Rhapsody on a Theme by Paganini*	*Lady Macbeth of Mtsensk* by Shostakovich performed	
1936	Third Symphony performed in Philadelphia and New York	John Dos Passos, *U.S.A.* trilogy	
1938	Rachmaninoff's friend, the basso Chaliapin, dies in Paris	Prokofieff, *Alexander Nevsky* cantata	
1939			World War II begins in Europe
1940	Works on *Symphonic Dances*		Roosevelt re-relected for the third term
1941	Performs to help in the war effort	Seventh Symphony by Shostakovich performed in Leningrad	Germany invades the Soviet Union 900-day Siege of Leningrad begins Japan attacks the United States at Pearl Harbor
1942	Celebrates 50th anniversary as a performing artist		First self-sustaining nuclear reaction achieved
1943	Final concerts Dies in California on March 28		

List of Rachmaninoff's Compositions for Voice

Date	Opus No.	Type of Work	Title
1890	–	Songs for voice and piano	At the gates of the holy cloister Nothing shall I say to you Again you are bestirred, my heart
1891	–	Songs for voice and piano	April! A festive day in the spring Dusk was falling Do you remember the evening
1890–1891	–	Operatic sketches for voice and piano Monologue from Lermontov's drama *Masquerade* Boris's monologue, Pimen's monologue, from Pushkin's drama *Boris Godunov*	A night without sleep Thou, Father Patriarch One, last testament
1890–1891	–	Cantata for choir a cappella	Deus Meus
1891	–	Harmonization for voice and piano	Song of the boatmen
1892	–	Opera in one act based on Pushkin's poem *The Gypsies*	*Aleko*
1890–1893	Opus 4	Songs for voice and piano	O, no, I beg you, do not leave Morning In the silence of the secret night Sing not, my lovely one Oh, my field It wasn't long ago, my friend

Date	Opus No.	Type of Work	Title
1893	Opus 8	Songs for voice and piano	Water lily My child, your beauty is that of a flower Duma (thoughts, reflection) I fell in love, to my sorrow A dream Prayer
1893	–	Cantata for four voices, a cappella	In prayers, the Ever-Caring Mother of God
1893	–	Songs for voice and piano	Song of the disenchanted The flower died
1894 1896	Opus 14 Opus 14	Songs for voice and piano	I await you Small island How fleeting is delight in love I was with her Summer nights You are so loved by all Do not leave me, friend Oh, do not grieve She is as beautiful as midday In my soul Spring torrents It is time
1895	Opus 15	Six choral songs for women's or children's voices, with piano accompaniment	Glory Night A pine tree The waves are asleep Bondage Angel
1899	–	Song for voice and piano	Were you hiccoughing, Natasha
1899	–	Cantata for choir a cappella to a poem by A. Tolstoy	Saint Panteleimon, who heals
1899	–	Song for chorus a cappella	Ukrainian folk song "Choboty" (Fancy boots)
1900	–	Song for voice and piano	Night
1902	Opus 20	Cantata for baritone, choir and orchestra to a poem by Nekrasov	Spring
1900 1902	Opus 21 Opus 21	Songs for voice and piano	Fate By a fresh grave Twilight They replied Lilacs Fragment from A. Musset How peaceful On the death of a siskin Melody Before the icon I am not a prophet How pained I am
1905	Opus 24	Opera in three scenes based on Pushkin's tragedy by the same name	*The Covetous Knight*
1905	Opus 25	Opera in two scenes, with a prologue and an epilogue, after Dante, libretto by Modeste Tchaikovsky	*Francesca da Rimini*

Date	Opus No.	Type of Work	Title
1906	Opus 26	Songs for voice and piano	There are many sounds
			All was taken from me
			We shall rest
			Two farewells
			Let us leave, my sweet
			Christ is risen
			To my children
			I beg for mercy
			I am again alone
			At my window
			The fountain
			Night is sorrowful
			Yesterday we met
			The ring
			All passes
1907	–	First act and sketches for the second act for an opera based on Maeterlinck's play by the same name	*Monna Vanna*
1908	–	A musical letter	Letter to K. S. Stanislavsky
1910	Opus 31	For choir a cappella	Music to the Liturgy of Saint John Chrysostom
1912	Opus 34	Songs for voice and piano	The muse
			In the soul of each of us
			The storm
			A passing breeze
			Arion
			The raising of Lazarus
1910			It cannot be!
1912			Music
			You knew him
			I remember this day
			The herald
			What happiness
			Dissonance
1915			Vocalise
1915	Opus 34	For voice and orchestra	Vocalise
1913	Opus 35	Poem for orchestra, choir, and soloists to the words of Edgar Allan Poe	The Bells
1915	Opus 37	For choir a cappella	Music to the Vespers
1915	–	Melody for choir a cappella	Heavenly King, a prayer
1915 (published in 1973)	–	Songs for voice and piano	A prayer
			All things wish to sing
1915	–	Phrase for voice and piano	From the Gospel of Saint John
1916	Opus 38	Poems for voice and piano	At night, in my garden
			To her
			Daisies
			The pied piper
			Sleep
			A-oo!
1920 (unpublished?)	–	Song for voice and piano	Luchinushka (My lambent light)
1920 (unpublished?)	–	Song for voice and piano	Apple trees
1926	Opus 41	Songs for choir and orchestra	Three Russian Songs
			Across the river, a fast-flowing river
			Oh, Johnny
			My fair, my rosy cheeked maidens

APPENDIX B

Catalogue of Songs

Opus Number	Date of Composition	Song Title	Poet
Op. 4, No. 1	1892	O, no, I beg you, do not leave	D. Merezhkovsky
Op. 4, No. 2	1891	Morning	M. Yanov
Op. 4, No. 3	1890	In the silence of the secret night	A. Fet
Op. 4, No. 4	1893	Sing not, my lovely one	A. Pushkin
Op. 4, No. 5	1893	Oh, my field	A. Tolstoy
Op. 4, No. 6	1893	It wasn't long ago, my friend	A. Golenischev-Kutuzov
Op. 8, No. 1	1893	Water lily	A. Plescheyev
Op. 8, No. 2	1893	My child, your beauty is that of a flower	A. Plescheyev
Op. 8, No. 3	1893	"Duma" (Thoughts, Reflection)	A. Plescheyev
Op. 8, No. 4	1893	I fell in love, to my sorrow	A. Plescheyev
Op. 8, No. 5	1893	A dream	A. Plescheyev
Op. 8, No. 6	1893	Prayer	A. Plescheyev
Op. 14, No. 1	1894	I await you	M. Davidova
Op. 14, No. 2	1896	Small island	K. Balmont
Op. 14, No. 3	1896	How fleeting is delight in love	A. Fet
Op. 14, No. 4	1896	I was with her	A. Koltsov
Op. 14, No. 5	1896	Summer nights	D. Rathaus
Op. 14, No. 6	1896	You are so loved by all	A. Tolstoy
Op. 14, No. 7	1896	Do not believe me, friend	A. Tolstoy
Op. 14, No. 8	1896	Oh, do not grieve	A. Apukhtin
Op. 14, No. 9	1896	She is as beautiful as midday	N. Minsky
Op. 14, No. 10	1896	In my soul	N. Minsky
Op. 14, No. 11	1896	Spring torrents	F. Tyutchev
Op. 14, No. 12	1896	It is time	S. Nadson
Op. 21, No. 1	1900	Fate	A. Apukhtin
Op. 21, No. 2	1902	By a fresh grave	S. Nadson
Op. 21, No. 3	1902	Twilight	M. Gyuot/I. Tkhorzhevsky
Op. 21, No. 4	1902	They replied	V. Hugo/L. Mey
Op. 21, No. 5	1902	Lilacs	E. Beketova
Op. 21, No. 6	1902	Fragment from A. Musset	A. Apukhtin
Op. 21, No. 7	1902	How peaceful	G. Galina
Op. 21, No. 8	1902	On the death of a siskin	V. Zhukovsky
Op. 21, No. 9	1902	Melody	S. Nadson
Op. 21, No. 10	1902	Before the icon	A. Golenischev-Kutuzov
Op. 21, No. 11	1902	I am not a prophet	A. Kruglov
Op. 21, No. 12	1902	How pained I am	A. Galina
Op. 26, No. 1	1906	There are many sounds	A. Tolstoy
Op. 26, No. 2	1906	All was taken from me	F. Tyutchev
Op. 26, No. 3	1906	We shall rest	A. Chekhov
Op. 26, No. 4	1906	Two farewells	A. Koltsov
Op. 26, No. 5	1906	Let us leave, my sweet	A. Golenischev-Kutuzov
Op. 26, No. 6	1906	Christ is risen	D. Merezhkovsky
Op. 26, No. 7	1906	To my children	A. Khomyakov
Op. 26, No. 8	1906	I beg for mercy	D. Merezhkovsky
Op. 26, No. 9	1906	I am again alone	I. Bunin
Op. 26, No. 10	1906	At my window	G. Galina
Op. 26, No. 11	1906	The fountain	F. Tyutchev
Op. 26, No. 12	1906	Night is sorrowful	I. Bunin
Op. 26, No. 13	1906	Yesterday we met	Ya. Polonsky
Op. 26, No. 14	1906	The ring	A. Koltsov
Op. 26, No. 15	1906	All passes	D. Rathaus
Op. 34, No. 1	1912	The muse	A. Pushkin
Op. 34, No. 2	1912	In the soul of each of us	A. Korinfsky
Op. 34, No. 3	1912	The storm	A. Pushkin
Op. 34, No. 4	1912	A passing breeze	K. Balmont
Op. 34, No. 5	1912	Arion	A. Pushkin
Op. 34, No. 6	1912	The raising of Lazarus	A. Khomyakov

Opus Number	Date of Composition	Song Title	Poet
Op. 34, No. 7	1912 orig. dated 1910, rev. 1912	It cannot be!	A. Maykov
Op. 34, No. 8	1912	Music	Ya. Polonsky
Op. 34, No. 9	1912	You knew him	F. Tyutchev
Op. 34, No. 10	1912	I remember this day	F. Tyutchev
Op. 34, No. 11	1912	The herald	A. Fet
Op. 34, No. 12	1912	What happiness	A. Fet
Op. 34, No. 13	1912	Dissonance	Ya. Polonsky
Op. 34, No. 14	1915	Vocalise	–
Op. 38, No. 1	1916	At night, in my garden	A. Blok
Op. 38, No. 2	1916	To her	A. Bely
Op. 38, No. 3	no date	Daisies	I. Severyanin
Op. 38, No. 4	1916	The pied piper	V. Bryusov
Op. 38, No. 5	1916	Sleep	F. Sologub
Op. 38, No. 6	1916	"A-oo"!	K. Balmont

Titles of songs, which were not published by Rachmaninoff. (Manuscripts at the State Central Museum of Musical Culture, named after M. I. Glinka, Moscow.) Listed under year of composition, no Opus No.

	1890	At the gates of the holy cloister	M. Lermontov
	1890	Nothing shall I say to you	A. Fet
	1890	Again you are bestirred, my heart	N. Grekov
	1891	April! A festive day in the spring	tr. from the French by I. Tushnova
	1891	Dusk was falling	A. Tolstoy
	1891	Do you remember the evening	A. Tolstoy
	1893	Song of the disenchanted	D. Rathaus
	1893	The flower died	D. Rathaus
	1899	Were you hiccoughing, Natasha	P. Viazemsky
	1900	Night	D. Rathaus
	1908	Letter to K. S. Stanislavsky	S. Rachmaninoff
	1915	From the Gospel of Saint John	From the New Testament

Opus Number	Date of Publication	Publisher	Dedication
Op. 4, No. 1	1893	A. Gutheil, Moscow	A. A. Lodyzhenskaya
Op. 4, No. 2	1893	A. Gutheil, Moscow	Yu. S. Sakhnovsky
Op. 4, No. 3	1893	A. Gutheil, Moscow	V. D. Skalon
Op. 4, No. 4	1893	A. Gutheil, Moscow	N. A. Satina
Op. 4, No. 5	1893	A. Gutheil, Moscow	E. N. Lysikova
Op. 4, No. 6	1893	A. Gutheil, Moscow	O. A. Golenischeva-Kutuzova
Op. 8, No. 1	1894	A. Gutheil, Moscow	A. A. Yaroshevsky
Op. 8, No. 2	1894	A. Gutheil, Moscow	M. A. Slonov
Op. 8, No. 3	1894	A. Gutheil, Moscow	L. G. Yakovlev
Op. 8, No. 4	1894	A. Gutheil, Moscow	M. V. Olferieva
Op. 8, No. 5	1894	A. Gutheil, Moscow	N. D. Skalon
Op. 8, No. 6	1894	A. Gutheil, Moscow	M. A. Deisha-Sionitskaya
Op. 14, No. 1	1896	A. Gutheil, Moscow	L. D. Skalon
Op. 14, No. 2	1896	A. Gutheil, Moscow	S. A. Satina
Op. 14, No. 3	1896	A. Gutheil, Moscow	Z. A. Pribytkova
Op. 14, No. 4	1896	A. Gutheil, Moscow	Yu. S. Sakhnovsky
Op. 14, No. 5	1896	A. Gutheil, Moscow	M. I. Gutheil
Op. 14, No. 6	1896	A. Gutheil, Moscow	A. I. Ivanovsky
Op. 14, No. 7	1896	A. Gutheil, Moscow	A. G. Klokacheva
Op. 14, No. 8	1896	A. Gutheil, Moscow	N. A. Alexandrova
Op. 14, No. 9	1896	A. Gutheil, Moscow	E. A. Lavrovskaya
Op. 14, No. 10	1896	A. Gutheil, Moscow	E. A. Lavrovskaya
Op. 14, No. 11	1896	A. Gutheil, Moscow	A. D. Ornatskaya
Op. 14, No. 12	1896	A. Gutheil, Moscow	–

Opus Number	Date of Publication	Publisher	Dedication
Op. 21, No. 1	1900 and 1902	A. Gutheil, Moscow	F. I. Chaliapin
Op. 21, No. 2	1902	A. Gutheil, Moscow	–
Op. 21, No. 3	1902	A. Gutheil, Moscow	N. I. Vrubel
Op. 21, No. 4	1902	A. Gutheil, Moscow	E. Yu. Kreutzer
Op. 21, No. 5	1902	A. Gutheil, Moscow	–
Op. 21, No. 6	1902	A. Gutheil, Moscow	A. A. Liven
Op. 21, No. 7	1902	A. Gutheil, Moscow	N
Op. 21, No. 8	1902	A. Gutheil, Moscow	O. A. Trubnikova
Op. 21, No. 9	1902	A. Gutheil, Moscow	N. N. Lanting
Op. 21, No. 10	1902	A. Gutheil, Moscow	A. A. Ivanova
Op. 21, No. 11	1902	A. Gutheil, Moscow	–
Op. 21, No. 12	1902	A. Gutheil, Moscow	V. A. Satin
Op. 26, No. 1	1906	A. Gutheil, Moscow	M. S. and A. M. Kerzin
Op. 26, No. 2	1906	A. Gutheil, Moscow	M. S. and A. M. Kerzin
Op. 26, No. 1	1906	A. Gutheil, Moscow	M. S. and A. M. Kerzin
Op. 26, No. 4	1906	A. Gutheil, Moscow	M. S. and A. M. Kerzin
Op. 26, No. 5	1906	A. Gutheil, Moscow	M. S. and A. M. Kerzin
Op. 26, No. 6	1906	A. Gutheil, Moscow	M. S. and A. M. Kerzin
Op. 26, No. 7	1906	A. Gutheil, Moscow	M. S. and A. M. Kerzin
Op. 26, No. 8	1906	A. Gutheil, Moscow	M. S. and A. M. Kerzin
Op. 26, No. 9	1906	A. Gutheil, Moscow	M. S. and A. M. Kerzin
Op. 26, No. 10	1906	A. Gutheil, Moscow	M. S. and A. M. Kerzin
Op. 26, No. 11	1906	A. Gutheil, Moscow	M. S. and A. M. Kerzin
Op. 26, No. 12	1906	A. Gutheil, Moscow	M. S. and A. M. Kerzin
Op. 26, No. 13	1906	A. Gutheil, Moscow	M. S. and A. M. Kerzin
Op. 26, No. 14	1906	A. Gutheil, Moscow	M. S. and A. M. Kerzin
Op. 26, No. 15	1906	A. Gutheil, Moscow	M. S. and A. M. Kerzin
Op. 34, No. 1	1913–1916	A. Gutheil, Moscow	Re (Marietta Shaginyan)
Op. 34, No. 2	1913–1916	A. Gutheil, Moscow	F. I. Chaliapin
Op. 34, No. 3	1913–1916	A. Gutheil, Moscow	L. V. Sobinov
Op. 34, No. 4	1913–1916	A. Gutheil, Moscow	L. V. Sobinov
Op. 34, No. 5	1913–1916	A. Gutheil, Moscow	L. V. Sobinov
Op. 34, No. 6	1913–1916	A. Gutheil, Moscow	F. I. Chaliapin
Op. 34, No. 7	1913–1916	A. Gutheil, Moscow	V. F. Komissarzheskaya
Op. 34, No. 8	1913–1916	A. Gutheil, Moscow	P. Tch.
Op. 34, No. 9	1913–1916	A. Gutheil, Moscow	F. I. Chaliapin
Op. 34, No. 10	1913–1916	A. Gutheil, Moscow	L. V. Sobinov
Op. 34, No. 11	1913–1916	A. Gutheil, Moscow	F. I. Chaliapin
Op. 34, No. 12	1913–1916	A. Gutheil, Moscow	L. V. Sobinov
Op. 34, No. 13	1913–1916	A. Gutheil, Moscow	F. Litvin
Op. 34, No. 14	1913–1916	A. Gutheil, Moscow	A. V. Nezhdanova
Op. 38, No. 1	1916	Rossiyskoye muzykal'noye izdatel'stvo (Russian Music Publishers) Moscow	N. P. Koshitz
Op. 38, No. 2	1916	Rossiyskoye muzykal'noye izdatel'stvo (Russian Music Publishers) Moscow	N. P. Koshitz
Op. 38, No. 3	1916	Rossiyskoye muzykal'noye izdatel'stvo (Russian Music Publishers) Moscow	N. P. Koshitz
Op. 38, No. 4	1916	Rossiyskoye muzykal'noye izdatel'stvo (Russian Music Publishers) Moscow	N. P. Koshitz
Op. 38, No. 5	1916	Rossiyskoye muzykal'noye izdatel'stvo (Russian Music Publishers) Moscow	N. P. Koshitz
Op. 38, No. 6	1916	Rossiyskoye muzykal'noye izdatel'stvo (Russian Music Publishers) Moscow	N. P. Koshitz

Titles of songs, which were not published by Rachmaninoff. (Manuscripts at the State Central Museum of Musical Culture, named after M. I. Glinka, Moscow.) Listed under year of composition, no Opus No.

	–	–	M. Slonov
	–	–	–
	–	–	–
	–	–	–
	–	–	–

Date of Publication	Publisher	Dedication
–	–	–
–	–	–
–	–	–
–	–	N. Satina
–	–	–
–	–	–
–	–	–

Notes

Preface

From the Sergei Rachmaninoff archives at the Library of Congress, in Washington, D.C. Archive M.L. 30.55.

"What is Music?"

This question, asked by Walter Koons on December 13, 1932, was answered by Sergei Rachmaninoff about December 30, 1932, in New York. (The English translation made from the Russian original definition was checked by Rachmaninoff.)

"What is Music? How can one define it? Music is a calm moonlight night, a rustling of summer foliage. Music is the distant peal of bells and eveningtide! Music is born only in heart and it appeals only to the heart. It is Love. The sister of Music is Poetry and the mother—Sorrow!

(signed)
Sergei Rachmaninoff"

Rachmaninoff and His Time

1 *Sergei Rakhmaninov, Literaturnoe nasledie* (Literary Heritage), vol. 2, p. 13.
2 Alexander Pushkin, *Sobranie Sochinenii* (Collected Works), p. 490.
3 Ibid., p. 333.
4 Alexander Serov, *Vospominaniya o M. I. Glinke* (Recollections about M. I. Glinka), p. 158.
5 Yuri Keldysh, *Rakhmaninov i ego vremya* (Rachmaninoff and His Time), pp. 27–28.
6 Ibid., p. 38.
7 Boris Asafiev, *Izbrannye trudy* (Selected Works), vol. 2, p. 291.
8 Keldysh, p. 90.
9 Asafiev, p. 294.
10 Olga Sokolova, *Sergei Vasilievich Rakhmaninov*, p. 82.
11 *Sergei Rakhmaninov*, vol. 1, p. 29.

Songs

1 Gregory of Nyssa, Life of Moses, tr. A. Malherbe and E. Ferguson, p. 114.
2 Yuri Keldysh, *Rakhmaninov i ego vremya*, p. 83–84.
3 Ibid., p. 104.
4 Boris Asafiev, *Izbrannye trudy*, vol. 2, p. 295.
5 V. A. Vasina-Grossman, *Russkii klassicheskii romans XIX veka* (Russian Classical Romance of the 19th Century), p. 330.
6 *Sergei Rakhmaninov*, vol. 2, p. 253.
7 Ibid., p. 305.
8 Psalms of David (Russian translation, Psalm 89, verse 9).
9 Alexander Pushkin, *Prorok* (The Prophet).
10 Keldysh, p. 378.
11 Song 6, Heirmos, of the Orthodox Requiem.
12 Keldysh, p. 357.
13 Vasina-Grossman, p. 333.
14 Nina Emelyanova, *Ivanovka v zhizni i tvorchestve Rakhmaninova* (Ivanovka in the Life and Work of Rachmaninoff), p. 155.
15 Johann von Gardner, Russian Church Singing, vol. 1, p. 34.
16 *Sergei Rakhmaninov*, vol. 2, p. 426.
17 Ibid., vol. 1, pp. 94–95.

Bibliography

Alpatov, M. V. *The Art Treasures of Russia.* New York: Harry Abrams, Inc.

Apetyan, Z., ed. *Vospominaniya o Rakhmaninove* (Recollections about Rachmaninoff). Moscow: Muzyka, 1974.

Asafiev, B. V. *Izbrannye trudy* (Selected Works), vol. 2. Moscow: Akademia Nauk (Academy of Sciences), 1954.

Bazhanov, Nikolai. *Rachmaninov.* Moscow: Raduga Publishers, 1983.

Bertensson, Sergei, and Leyda, Jay. *Sergei Rachmaninoff, A Lifetime in Music.* New York: New York University Press, 1956.

Blagoy, D. D. *Istoriya russkoi literatury* (History of Russian Literature). Moscow: Akademia Nauk, 1964.

Bowlt, John E. *Russian Painters and the Stage, 1884–1965.* Texas: University Art Museum, 1977.

Emelyanova, N. *Ivanovka v zhizni i tvorchestve Rakhmaninova* (Ivanovka in the Life and Work of Rachmaninoff). Voronezh: 1984.

Dobuzhinkii, S. A., ed. *Pamyati Rakhmaninova* (To the Memory of Rachmaninoff). New York: S. A. Satina Edition, 1946.

Fitzlyon, Kyril, and Browning, Tatiana. *Before the Revolution, A View of Russia under the Last Tsar.* New York: Overlook Press, 1978.

Gardner, Johann von. *Russian Church Singing.* Crestwood, NY: St. Vladimir's Press, 1980.

Hamilton, George Heard. *The Art and Architecture of Russia.* London: Penguin Books, 1954.

Harkins, William G. *Dictionary of Russian Literature.* Paterson, NJ: Littlefield, Adams & Co., 1959.

Keldysh, Yu. *Rakhmaninov i ego vremya* (Rachmaninoff and His Time). Moscow: Muzyka, 1973.

Lamm, P., ed. Rakhmaninov, S., *Romansy, Polnoe sobranie* (Songs, Complete Collection). Moscow: Muzyka, 1973.

Lossky, N. O. *History of Russian Philosophy.* New York: International Universities Press, 1951.

Massie, Suzanne. *Land of the Firebird, The Beauty of Old Russia.* New York: Simon & Schuster, 1980.

Mirsky, D. S. *A History of Russian Literature.* New York: Vintage Books, 1958.

Novyi Zavet i Psaltir (New Testament and the Psalter). New York: American Bible Society.

Obolensky, Dmitri. *Russian Verse.* London: Penguin Books, 1965.

Pushkin, A. S. *Sobranie Sochinenii* (Collected Works). Moscow: 1984.

Rachmaninoff, S. *Songs, with Piano Accompaniment.* London: Boosey & Hawkes, 1946.

Rakhmaninov, S. *Literaturnoe nasledie* (Literary Heritage). Moscow: Sovetskii Kompozitor, vol. 1, 1978; vol. 2 & 3, 1980.

Riasanovsky, Nicholas V. *A History of Russia.* New York: Oxford University Press, 1963.

Riesemann, Oskar von. *Rachmaninoff's Recollections.* New York: Books for Libraries Press, 1934.

Rudakova, A. *S. V. Rakhmaninov.* Moscow: Muzyka, 1982.

Rytsareva, M. G. *Avtografy S. V. Rakhmaninova* (Rachmaninoff's Autographs). Moscow: Sovetskii Kompozitor, 1980.

Serov, A. N. *Vospominaniya o M. I. Glinke* (Recollections of M. I. Glinka). Moscow: 1950.

Sokolova, O. I. Sergei Vasilievich Rakhmaninov. Moscow: Muzyka, 1983.

Swan, Alfred and Katherine. "Rachmaninoff: Personal Reminiscences." *The Musical Quarterly,* Jan.–Apr. 1944.

Talbot-Rice. Tamara. *Russian Art.* Middlesex: Penguin Books, 1949.

Threlfall, Robert, and Norris, Geoffrey. *A Catalogue of the Compositions of S. Rachmaninoff.* London: Scolar Press.
Vasina-Grossman, V. A. *Russkii klassicheskii romans XIX veka* (Russian Classical Romance of the 19th Century). Moscow: Akademia Nauk, 1956.
Walker, Robert. *Rachmaninoff, His Life and Times.* Kent: Midas Books, 1980.
Ware, Timothy (Father Kallistos Ware). *The Orthodox Church.* Suffolk, England: The Chaucer Press, 1981.
Wiley, Roland John. *Tchaikovsky's Ballets.* Oxford, England: Clarendon Press, 1985.

Index of Titles

Index of First Lines

Index of Names